D0341653

UNIVERSITY OF WINNIPEG
LIBRARY DISCARDED
515 Portage Avenue
Winnipeg, Manitoba R3B 2E9

The Force
So Much Closer Home

Henry Adams and the Adams Family

The publication of this work has
been aided by a grant from the
Andrew W. Mellon Foundation

THE GOTHAM LIBRARY
OF THE NEW YORK UNIVERSITY PRESS

The Gotham Library is a series of original works
and critical studies published in paperback primarily
for student use. The Gotham hardcover edition is
primarily for use by libraries and the general reader.
Devoted to significant works and major authors and
to literary topics of enduring importance, Gotham
Library texts offer the best in literature and criticism.

Comparative Literature and Foreign Language
Literature: Robert J. Clements, Editor
Comparative and English Language Literature:
James W. Tuttleton, Editor

E
175
.5
·A17488
1977

The Force
So Much Closer Home

Henry Adams and the Adams Family

Earl N. Harbert

New York • New York University Press • 1977

Copyright © 1977 by New York University
Library of Congress Catalog Card Number: 76-40744
ISBN: 0-8147-3375-1 (cloth)
        0-8147-3376-X (paperback)

Library of Congress Cataloging in Publication Data

Harbert, Earl N   1934–
  The force so much closer home.

  Includes bibliographical references and index.
  1. Adams, Henry, 1838–1918. 2. Adams family.
3. Historians—United States—Biography. I. Title.
E175.5.A17488   973'.07'2024   76-40744
ISBN 0-8147-3375-1
ISBN 0-8147-3376-X pbk.

Manufactured in the United States of America

Contents

Preface

"The family mind approaches unity more nearly than is given to most works of God."

—Henry Adams (1838–1918)

This volume attempts to identify and discuss only one of the many voices of Henry Adams: the voice of a fourth-generation heir to America's most illustrious family name. Before he became an essayist, historian, biographer, novelist, traveler, or prophet, Henry was first of all a Massachusetts Adams; and in that primary distinction—the complicated fact of his Adams birth—I have found my rationale for the pages that follow. At every point in this study, I have sought to keep in view the remarkable unity of the Adams family, which is especially conspicuous in the abstract conception that Henry Adams labeled "the family mind." At one level of comprehension, defined by his own favorite system of polarities, that abstraction represented a special kind of "Order," a personal shield against the otherwise universal threat of "Chaos." But at another level and in a more important way, Henry knew that only the fact of "family" could explain a basic part of himself. "Family" offered him a special key to self-understanding, a path for exploring the basic causes of his actions and his thoughts, and a unique resource which he made use of in both his writings and his life.

Of course, the Adams heritage included much more than merely an abstract "mind." Despite the flux of four generations, a substantial core of precept, habit, and family personality always remained intact, so that both the human and the intellec-

tual force of a powerful family tradition had to be acknowledged
by every thoughtful heir. Only one such acknowledgement
interests me here, as I attempt to trace the most important lines
of family thought and example, and then to show how one heir,
Henry Adams, responded to the unique and vital heritage
conferred upon him by his birth. Thus, this study is neither a
family biography nor a comprehensive intellectual analysis of
Henry Adams's thought. I have omitted what may be found in
other sources; rich commentary already exists on the lives and
works of other men and women in the Adams line and on other
themes in Henry's thought and writing. Rather, this is a
conscious literary study, conceived with a definite and limited
goal; it treats the world of ideas selectively, for the purpose of
illuminating particular literary texts. In short, I am aware that
my treatment of family influence does not exhaust all the
possibilities, and I have written with the hope that my reader
will enlarge upon what I say and show, to make good use of
these ideas wherever they can be applied.

My original research grew from the belief that close attention to the literature of the Adamses would help me to comprehend the working of that special energy or force to be found
within a single family, as well as to explain what the family has
meant to its members. As a result of this conviction, I have
written a book that should be regarded as an essay in interpretation, based upon a close investigation of the writings of three
generations of Adamses, and directed toward understanding how
these papers and their authors influenced an heir in the fourth
generation. More specifically, my study seeks to achieve two
distinct yet interrelated goals. First, I have tried to bring the chief
parts of the Adams tradition before the reader and to describe
those characteristics, such as responsibility, discipline, professional achievement, that have contributed most significantly to
the intellectual dynamism of the family; second, I have endeavored to show, chiefly by close analysis of selected texts, just what
Henry Adams made of his special heritage during his career as a
writer. I trust that the intimate connection between these two
objectives will explain the organization of this volume, for the
former goal had to be accomplished before the latter could be
achieved.

This study has benefitted from the encouragement and help of many individuals as well as from the support of several institutions. My research has been aided by grants from the American Philosophical Society and the Tulane University Council on Research. Staff members of the Harvard College Library, the Massachusetts Historical Society, and the Howard-Tilton Library of Tulane University have assisted in many ways, and I owe a special debt to Professor Walter B. Rideout, who guided my early efforts. Professor Charles Vandersee and the editors of the Adams Papers, Dr. L. H. Butterfield and Dr. Marc Friedlaender, provided useful suggestions, and Mr. Eric Partridge helped to assure the accuracy of my manuscript. Like other authors, I am grateful to the Director, editors, and staff of the New York University Press for making this volume a reality.

Introduction

American Families and the Adams Family

"The family is the deepest mystery, deeper than love or death."

—"you," Joyce Carol Oates

Among the forces and influences that have shaped American life, the family holds an important place. Our history is filled with family names that have stood for grand achievement in more than a single individual and over more than one generation; so that the Mathers and the Rockefellers, the Lees and the Roosevelts, the Jameses and the Holmeses, the Byrds and the Kennedys, for example, have each come to represent in the public mind some extraordinary cumulative historical value, which far exceeds the total merit of individual family members. In the minds of most Americans there attaches to these great names (and others) that special mystique of "family," an ineffable combination of bright luster and deep mystery, evoked by the merest mention of a prominent surname. Of course, it is paradoxical that, in America, this special appeal of great family names should have always been felt—amidst the almost continuous outpouring of sincere national professions of political and social egalitarianism that have characterized our history for more than 200 years. Yet, for all that democratic history, the magic of family is nonetheless real.

1

Regardless of whether its activities have been centered in business and finance (the DuPonts and Rockefellers), politics (the Roosevelts and Kennedys), or intellectual and artistic endeavors (the Holmeses and Jameses), the great American family has always exacted a special tribute from both historians and the general public—a recognition of its value as something more significant than merely a matter of "blood." Thus, it is not surprising that stories associated with illustrious family names have been told and retold—in historical writing, anecdote, and even gossip—until certain families have become generally acknowledged, however unofficially, as the closest American equivalent to a titled aristocracy. Relations among the Cabots, the Lowells, and God, for example, require no retelling here, and great American families need no introduction. They do, however, deserve closer study and a finer appreciation than our native interest in genealogy has so far provided.[1]

The special role of the family in helping to explain a human being and his or her achievements has often been discussed, but remains to be fully understood. Those difficulties that obstruct the clear analysis and demonstration of family influences are, of course, substantial. Communication between siblings and between generations, for one example, sometimes takes very subtle forms such as attitude and gesture, of which no permanent record has been kept. Still, where such problems have been conscientiously studied, investigation—even though tentative—has provided evidence for the firm belief that the family exerts the broadest and most powerful kind of influence or force in the lives of individuals. As one observer has written of modern British life:

> Clearly certain families produce a disproportionately large number of eminent men and women. But equally clearly this study shows that men of natural but not outstanding ability can reach the front ranks of science and scholarship and the foremost positions in the cultural hierarchy of the country if they have been bred to a tradition of intellectual achievement and have been taught to turn their environment to account. Schools and universities can so train young men, but such training has a far stronger command

over the personality when it is transmitted through a family tradition.[2]

Certainly, the lives and literature of the Massachusetts Adamses prove that a single family could be just as influential in America. For more than a century, beginning about 1775, its members played leading roles in national and international affairs.

The chapters which follow study the Adams legacy as it was passed down to Henry Adams (1838–1918), the most illustrious member of the fourth generation of prominent Adamses. Before turning to that subject, however, we should remind ourselves that the Adamses hold a unique position in American history. Writing more than forty years ago, one historian remarked that the family "is the most distinguished in the United States. Suddenly passing from village obscurity into international fame in the latter part of the eighteenth century, it has ever since maintained a preeminent position, due neither to great wealth nor to hereditary title, but to character and sheer intellectual ability."[3] Today we might ask for a more exact definition of "character" and "ability," but we do not deny that, for more than four generations, the most outstanding Adamses compiled an impressive catalogue of high achievements, especially in politics, philosophy, history, and literature. In fact, no other American family can claim such a record: two Presidents of the United States, three ministers to England, and at least half a dozen productive writers, who authored and preserved in the Adams Papers the largest and most valuable collection of family records in our national history.

In those pages of family writings and in innumerable volumes of American history, detailed accounts of the chief Adams successes may easily be read. Here, no new summary will be attempted. Still, it should be useful to remind the reader that, like every other family, the Adamses also counted among their number some less-than-famous persons, who shared the stage if not the spotlight with Presidents, ministers, and eminent writers and historians, and who also helped to make the family a continuous source of powerful influence and living tradition. Chief among these were the Adams women, especially Abigail Smith (John Adams's Abigail), Louisa Catherine Johnson (John

Quincy's wife), and Marian Hooper, the wife of Henry Adams. Each of these women was remarkable in her own right, and each helped to shape the course of the male line. Yet, we shall be able to touch upon them only briefly in the following pages.[4] Then too, there were other male Adamses, like the brothers of John Quincy and Charles Francis Adams, whose lives can only be pieced together now from scattered references in family papers. They were the otherwise forgotten Adamses—the family failures. As such, they claim no place in American history, although the pathos and tragedy of their biographies still belong to any full account of family fortunes. But, in the version of family history that the more successful family members learned, these men represented merely an embarrassing counterpoint to the dominant theme of grand achievement.

Certainly, the price of being an Adams was often high, perhaps too high. When John Adams's second son, after a promising start at Harvard College, gave way to dissipation, the father's stern judgment left no doubt about his attitude: "I renounce him. King David's Absalom had some ambition and some enterprise. Mine is a mere rake, buck, blood, and beast."[5] Or, consider the history of the third generation, in which the third son, Charles Francis Adams, was left to pursue a political career amid the wreckage of his two older brothers' lives. The eldest, George Washington Adams, while still in his twenties, ended his life in an apparent suicide. "He had been a sensitive boy with artistic and literary tastes, and his father's constant admonitions to duty and perseverance had left him confused and disturbed."[6] Less dramatically, a second brother, John Adams II, simply "fled from the responsibilities of the family name: to die as a failed businessman in 1834."[7] As he grew to manhood, every male Adams learned enough about his family to see which examples to avoid as well as which to emulate.

Of course, during the lifetime of a fourth-generation heir such as Henry Adams, the most powerful truths of the family tradition emerged as living facts. Throughout almost the whole of his life, Henry was surrounded by memorials to the earlier Adamses—his great-grandparents, grandparents, and parents—in the forms of people, houses (some symbolic, like the White House, across the park from Henry's Washington home, yet practically inaccessible to the Adamses of his generation), history books, and almost everything associated with the national past. For Henry and his brothers and sisters, then, "it was impossible not to be conscious of the heritage which was theirs."[8] More important, that special Adams heritage was not merely a passive subject of historical interest to Henry; it powerfully influenced him in thought and action. In fact, the Adams heritage largely made Henry the man that he became; thus, a study of that heritage should help us to understand not only that man but also the literature which he wrote. But first, we must begin by identifying some of the forces that operated in unique combination on the Adams descendants of Henry's generation.

The Adams Papers show that the American Adamses soon became a family with sharply defined principles and interests. Each principle was set down in family writings, to be read and reread as both precept and warning. In this way, an important idea gradually took shape as a kind of magnetic pole, which attracted an increasing amount of thought and comment as family history grew longer; until finally, the family had acquired a traditional point of reference for every generation. Later thinkers and writers, in turn, would acknowledge, review, reinforce—but also sometimes importantly alter—the existing content of family thought. In fact, this intellectual process among the Adamses was always dynamic. Even ideas that remained essentially unchanged in content were still given new vigor and meaning in the exercise of re-expression, using the idiom of a new time. In substance, with some principles, very little change took place, and a family principle, reasserted over 150 years, was solidly established. In other cases, however, the course of family thought did not run smooth, and an idea that once formed a key part of the credo of John Adams might, by the time of Henry, three generations later, have been given an ironic twist which effectively turned a family maxim into an open question about the value of the family itself, as later sections of this book will illustrate.

In general, over four generations, five Adams family interests were most pervasive: politics; religion and philosophy; education; science; and literature.

"Politics are the divine science after all," wrote John Adams in 1778, and for four generations politics seemed almost synonymous with the family name. Political and diplomatic service, at local, national, and international levels, became the path to fame and recognition for the Adamses, who were first of all political men and yet not political men alone. John Adams, from his direct observation of able leaders, beginning with Colonel Quincy in tiny Braintree, Massachusetts, and extending to the chief figures in Boston, Philadelphia, Paris, and London, drew a series of psychological lessons about the "springs of human action" for his own use. From his lifelong reading in political theory, he collected a set of political principles—from Locke and Montesquieu, for example—which in turn became the touchstones of family politics.

From the first the Adams political heritage was founded on a tacit paradox. Along with his age, John Adams accepted an enlightened faith in man's reason and in the optimistic possibility of using that reason as the chief instrument of national and individual self-government. He believed that, carefully drafted and wisely implemented, the American Constitution would serve to establish and sustain a government of laws—but not of men. For his experience also taught him skepticism about human nature. Adams always held serious objections against every notion of human perfectability, and he passed them down to his heirs, whose experience confirmed them anew. The Adamses felt that effective government, like other forms of human action, could derive only from a correct balance of powers. Thus, any system for good governance had to include sufficient checks and balances to guarantee that result. Drafting the Massachusetts Constitution of 1780, John Adams wrote: "In the government of the Commonwealth of Massachusetts the legislative, executive and judicial power shall be placed in separate departments, to the end that it might be a government of laws, not of men." A hundred years later, these very words were echoed by Henry Adams, as he made his plea for a return to stable, constitutional government in the corrupt era of President Grant.

Acting as a political man, John Adams nevertheless managed to retain a large measure of personal independence. He grew alarmed by development of factions and parties in American political life because he always thought of himself as a representative of high principles, rather than of a region or party. This commitment to independence had early roots in young John Adams's close study of Colonel Quincy, the great man of Braintree, who, in Adams's words, "had a high sense of his accountability to the Supreme Governor of the world for the trusts imposed in him, and studiously avoided an ensnaring dependency on any man, and what . . . should tend to lay him under any disadvantage in the discharge of his duty." [9] Here was John's ideal—the man of affairs who could yet remain truly independent—which became a personal goal for the Adams males in four generations. Perhaps the most successful case of imitation was that of John Quincy Adams, who has been fittingly characterized as "The Great Independent of American politics." Yet his career actually proved the last opportunity to combine effectiveness and independence; afterward, first his son, Charles Francis Adams, and then his four grandsons learned that the old ideal had lost its value and that they must abandon active politics if they hoped to maintain their independence in the age of political parties.

Much earlier, even while he acknowledged that politics was "the divine science," John Adams had also displayed a certain ambivalence about his own ambitions and rewards. To his wife, he wrote in 1776:

> Let me have my farm, family and goose quill, and all the honors and offices this world has to bestow may go to those who deserve them better and desire them more. I count them not. . . . I had rather build stone walls upon Penn's Hill than to be first Prince in Europe or first General or first Senator in America. [10]

In his diary as well as his letters home, the founder of the family dynasty set down this picture of his life as a matter of simple alternatives. First Boston, and later London and Philadelphia, stood for the larger personal challenges and rewards of politics; Braintree (later renamed Quincy), Penn's Hill, and his family homestead represented an almost idyllic alternative, the pastoral life of a country squire. Certainly a part of John Adams never left Braintree behind, no matter where he went; and in his own account, the polarities represented by his personal options (real or imagined) emerged clearly enough for his progeny to read and understand. Yet his personal example—that of an active politician and statesman—and even more the reinforcing example of John Quincy, who followed, weighed heavily on the side of political commitment and service. Not until the fourth generation of famous Adamses was this balance reversed, allowing private interests to outweigh public obligation, and to make Henry Adams a self-appointed "stable companion to statesmen" rather than a statesman himself.

Unlike modern secular politics, John Adams's "science of politics" was built upon a solid foundation of moral and ethical principles and a set of sincere religious and philosophical convictions. A Creator's presence could be identified in everything, as Adams was quick to acknowledge. Yet his God was not the God of Calvin. His religious beliefs led Adams to embrace the idea of human progress, dependent, of course, upon reason, even while he also agreed that human appetites had to be constantly kept in check. Man had been created as a creature of both good and evil. A careful balance in the individual therefore represented the best possible adjustment that a man could reach in a world watched over by a God of punishment and reward. "Men should endeavor at a balance of affections and appetite," John Adams wrote, "under the monarchy of reason and conscience, within, as well as at a balance of power without." Any personal surrender to passion would lead to an inner tyranny in man, a condition as harmful and destructive as political tyranny in the state.[11]

This often expressed philosophy—the doctrine of the balanced man—gradually became a commonplace ideal of Adams family thought. In the process, the long sustained family habit of rigorous self-examination, documented on page after page of the Adams diaries, and in such writings as Henry Adams's *Education*, actually took on special importance as a first step toward self-improvement. A careful personal inventory provided a sound basis for redress of an unsatisfactory human balance; as a man, by the use of reason, struggled to improve himself in the eyes of the world and of his God. No Adams male, over four generations, ever escaped from the conviction that he was primarily responsible for his thoughts and actions, even when his own religious persuasion seemed to differ from the views of his ancestors. And, in a similar way, the ideal of human balance provided a useful yardstick for evaluating other men, both those who were Adamses and those who were not. What Henry Adams made of such measurements, we shall see in the chapters which follow.

More generally, it is important to remember that some notion of progress always found a place in the family philosophy. John Adams often expressed his faith in human improvement—especially through education—and clearly he expected positive development (toward no absolutely certain or well-defined end, however) among his progeny as much as among other parts of society. Checks and balances were necessary within and without; yet his sense of necessity could be informed by an optimistic faith. As he told Abigail:

> I must study politics and war, that my sons may have liberty to study mathematics and philosophy. My sons ought to study mathematics and philosophy, geography, natural history and naval architecture, navigation, commerce, and agriculture, in order to give their children a right to study painting, poetry, music, architecture, statuary, tapestry, and porcelain.[12]

In that expansive moment, John Adams revealed a family plan that constituted nothing less than an outline of the American dream; but it was also a program for high familial achievement, based on hard work and effective education. Right reason, careful training in morality, and high thinking were indispensable ingredients of intellectual, moral, and even aesthetic progress. Education would show his sons (as it had shown John Adams) the way to grand achievements; in science and art especially, they would be greater than any he could claim for himself. In truth, the family debt to education over four generations would be difficult for us to overestimate. Beginning with John Adams, all the Adamses who rose to positions of national eminence did so by training their minds in a continuous process of formal (usually legal) and informal learning. They engaged in a lifelong education, in which Harvard College played its part for every generation, as did political and literary apprenticeship within the family, and afterward, a rigorous program of disciplined reading, study, and writing. Taken together, these experiences made up the typical education of an Adams male.

In the case of politics, family interest as well as its record of achievement, first advancing and then declining, may be traced with relative ease through four generations, almost like a line across a graph. Such is not the case with all family concerns, however: the Adamses' pursuit of science, to take one important example, shows quite a different history. To comprehend it, we must first appreciate a general fact about family life. For every Adams who followed the second President, the men and accomplishments in the family line could be viewed and measured in a divided way. On one hand there was the family view; on the other, the public image—what history seemed to record. Just as John Adams's fatherly renunciation of his failed son strikes us now as much too severe—surely unduly harsh and uncompromising—so the picture of any Adams that emerges from family papers alone often seems to conflict in content and proportion with the more official public portrait, which is based upon a popular, historical consensus. Clearly, at any time, much of what a man represents within his family can be at variance with his public image. So it was with many of the Adamses, and so it is with us today.

Chief among these disparities is the case of John Quincy Adams, a man known to history as the great Secretary of State who was largely responsible for the Monroe Doctrine; a far-sighted President; and afterwards, a hard-working congressman who lived on to defeat the obnoxious "Gag Rule" in the House of Representatives. To his heirs, however, John Quincy seemed important less because of his political deeds than because of his advanced scientific views and his literary accomplishments. To grandsons Henry and Brooks, in particular, John Quincy represented a peculiar example of the family devotion to science, which seemed notable only in alternate generations (second and fourth). True, John Adams and his grandson Charles Francis did what they could to maintain an intelligent and well-informed interest in science, but, by a kind of hereditary accident, only John Quincy and Henry were granted the talents necessary to appreciate science. As evidence for this view, John Quincy left behind when he died two outstanding scientific accomplishments: a classic scientific paper, the *Report on Weights and Measures* (1812), which detailed a plan for large-scale public support of scientific research; and, even more impressive, the Smithsonian Institution, which remains today a most visible monument to his determination to make science flourish in America. Grandson Henry, of course, has often been regarded as a pioneer of scientific history, although his real achievements in both science and history were actually far more complex than that label implies, as we shall see.

To the Adamses of Henry's generation, then, both the importance of science and the obvious pattern of a skipped generation between John Quincy and Henry came to be regarded as fundamental facts of their heritage. Just such facts, placed alongside their general acknowledgment of the increasingly scientific and technological environment outside the family—in the world around them—help to account for their own special appreciation of the Adams ancestors. In short, the traditional values of politics and of national history, the chief points so often held up to public view, did not alone determine the meaning of the Adams heritage for family members.

This conclusion is documented at great length in the massive collection of Adams Papers. Here, we can do no more than sample the commentary of four generations of Adamses about their family heritage, especially about men and ideas. Yet we must remember that their heritage included habitual activities as well as habits of mind: perhaps the most important of these was the habit of writing itself, the primary means by which their historical record was established.

The Adamses were a writing family. They told their story in thousands of letters, diaries, copybooks, essays, poems, histories, novels, biographies, and autobiographies—a story we are only gradually learning to read fairly and with satisfactory understanding. To the word portrait of the family, every adult member contributed in some measure; and all together, they thoughtfully provided a massive response to the tacit question that still fascinates us today: What does it mean to be an Adams? In this volume, it is Henry Adams's individual answer that concerns us. Still, the larger family record, about which, as we shall see, Henry was comprehensively informed, requires at least some preliminary consideration, as a way of introducing us to Henry Adams's writings.

First, it may be said without exaggeration that when John Adams began to keep his diary, he initiated four generations of incessant literary activity. And almost from that time, family literature was made to serve a dual purpose, as the Adamses authored two well-defined varieties of writing—a public and a private literature. Materials intended for general publication were always kept carefully separated from private, personal, and often self-analytical statements, which usually took the form of personal correspondence and the diary. What John Adams established, in effect, was the example, to be followed in turn by his sons and their sons, of a studious man of letters who continually throughout his life made both public and private use of his considerable skill with the pen.

Of course the public literature of John Adams and of his most famous descendants played an important part by helping to establish them as successful political and literary men in the eyes of the world. Without attempting to amass a detailed catalogue of family titles, we still should recall that the "Novanglus" letters, published in various newspapers; *Thoughts on Government* (1776); the *Defense of the Constitutions of the United States* (1787f); and other public statements provided the foundation of John Adams's political career. And his heirs never lost sight of the model. The act of writing for a general public, in short, steadily held a place in the family definition of high achievement, a definition that neatly combined politics with literature.

Although the role of private literature in the family was much more subtle, the effects were no less real. In the third generation, for example, Charles Francis Adams became concerned because the characters of his presidential forebears (and their wives) had already been subjected to serious historical distortion. The history in which they appeared had been based solely upon documents already published; while the private, unpublished papers of the Adamses remained virtually unknown. The result was an historical injustice:

> The great men of the Revolution, in the eyes of posterity, are many of them like the heroes of a mythological age. They are seen, for the most part, when conscious that they are acting upon a theatre, where individual sentiment must be sometimes disguised, and often sacrificed, for the public good. Statesmen and generals rarely say all they think or feel. The consequence is, that, in the papers which come from them, they are made to assume a uniform of grave hue, which, though it doubtless exalts the opinion later generations may entertain of their perfections, somewhat diminishes the interest with which they study their character.[13]

In Charles Francis's view, his Adams ancestors deserved a better fate. To guarantee that result, Charles decided by 1840 that private family letters should now be published, because "they furnish an exact transcription of the feelings of the writer," which was "susceptible of no misconception."[14] The new combination of public notices with expressions of private feeling added up to a larger, truer history: "We not only see the record, but the private commentary also; and these, taken in connection with the contemporaneous histories . . . will serve to transmit to posterity the details for a narration in as complete a form as will in all probability ever be attained by the imperfect faculties of man."[15] Here, Charles recognized his duty to the family. Acting in the role of archivist-editor, he began the task of editing and printing several volumes of letters and papers drawn from the rich private holdings of the Adamses. In this way he made himself the chief defender of family honor, and his activities enlarged upon the examples of John and John Quincy by adding new responsibilities to the old family conception of the man of letters. Charles's literary activities, moreover, provided his sons with a new Adams example and even with a much more sophisticated form of literary apprenticeship, when they were recruited to assist him in his labors. Of the four boys, Henry proved especially receptive to his father's ideal of historical completeness, and of course he later made good use of his training as an editor and writer.

Most of this book is devoted to studying precisely what Henry Adams learned about his place in the family, and how he shaped that knowledge. At this point, it should be useful to summarize briefly the contents of the Adams heritage as he knew it. First, by the time of the fourth generation, Henry and his brothers were inducted by their Adams birth and their early training, in school and at home, into a literary tradition that had already proved to be as forceful and compelling as their political heritage. They were naturally made responsible for preserving and using the private writings of the family, especially as a means to defend, explain, and even protect other family members at the bar of history. Next, in this way and others, every Adams was also made aware of his special place in the contemporary world, even in a world that had significantly changed since the time of his famous ancestors. More than most Americans, in short, an Adams knew that his life was founded on a family tradition. Finally, an Adams learned early that he had been born into a heritage that not merely offered, but actually imposed upon him, the special conditions of a living family philosophy that included a set of particular interests, as in education, science, literature, and politics. For him too, these things came to be defined by the experiences of his own life, in terms that only other Adamses could fully comprehend. No wonder then, that even so successful a New England politician and writer as John F. Kennedy felt compelled to remark, after reviewing the Adams heritage, "I feel that the Adams family intimidates us all."[16] And so it does.

Over four illustrious generations, the Adamses devoted themselves to serving a special set of ideals and examples (although not without some changes and variations, as we have already noted). Like Quentin Compson in Faulkner's *Absalom, Absalom!*, an Adams had been born to what he knew, as most of us have not. Yet we can distinguish certain unmistakable characteristics of the Adams heritage:

1. A generous (and sometimes obsessive) use of mental and physical energy in the service of high ideals: statesmanship, leadership, literary craftsmanship.
2. Elevation of the single ideal of public service over all possibilities for private gain.
3. Conscious insistence on a national, rather than merely regional or partisan, point of view on all matters of consequence; and to international or universal standards for judging men and issues.
4. An optimistic faith in the possibility of human and national progress, but always tempered with a skeptical view of human nature.
5. A heavy reliance on education as the chief means of progress; and the conviction that life is an educative process.
6. A commitment to private writing as a useful method of personal record keeping, to show especially in a diary and letters the progress of the individual and to guarantee at least some personal vindication in the future.
7. A parallel commitment to public literature, especially writing and editing, primarily to help provide for the education (but also the entertainment) of other human beings.
8. A supreme conviction that duty and not pleasure is the divinely appointed business of human life—duty to the Creator, but also to nation and family. For an Adams, neglect of this duty could only be judged as total human failure.

Reduced in this way to a list of abstract ideas, the Adams heritage has been robbed of all those dynamic qualities that worked to make it a unique way of life. To learn about the real force and power of the family, we must turn away from this analysis, to study instead the influences of the family as they are revealed in the primary sources, the writings of the Adamses. Better than any set of dry principles, a letter of Henry Adams, sent from Paris in 1891 to Elizabeth Cameron, will illustrate the intellectual benefits of family membership:

A century ago, more or less, President Washington sent my grandfather, before he was thirty years old, as minister to the Hague, and my grandfather was fond of music to such an extent that, if I remember right, he tried to play the flute. Anyhow . . . when he [John Quincy Adams] was turned out of the Presidency he could think of nothing, for days together, but "Oh, Richard! Oh, mon roy, l'univers t'abandonne;" and as I had never heard the opera, I thought I would see it now that it has been revived at the Opéra Comique. . . . I tried to imagine myself as I was then—and you know what an awfully handsome young fellow Copley made me [in a portrait]—with full-dress and powdered hair, talking with Mme. Chose in the boxes and stopping to applaud. . . .[17]

In these lines, Henry Adams imaginatively relives the experience of John Quincy Adams, briefly reviewing his career, touching upon the Copley portrait, yet responding most of all to the particular operatic tune that became the sixth President's only effective solace after his defeat by Andrew Jackson in the election of 1828.

But the real source for Henry's empathic flight of fancy, buried deep in his memory and never acknowledged anywhere in his letter, was a passage from the diary of John Quincy Adams, which his grandson had often read and certainly taken to heart. In an entry for November 7, 1830, John Quincy Adams tried—for the first time in his personal diary—to explain his "agony of mind," caused first by "the failure of my re-election" and then intensified by an unspecified "domestic calamity" of which Henry makes no mention in his letter. As John Quincy recalls:

In the French opera of *Richard Coeur-de-Lion*, the minstrel, Blondel, sings under the walls of his prison a song, beginning:

O, Richard! O, mon Roi!
L'univers t'abandonne.

When I first heard this song, forty-five years ago . . . it made an indelible impression on my memory, without imagining that I should ever feel its force so much closer home. In the year 1829 scarce a day passed that did not bring it to my thoughts.[18]

As Henry Adams proved when he took his grandfather's diary for his own text, an Adams could not help but read passages from family papers with a special appreciation. For, as much as any artistic expression in music and art, the written words of a model forebear—with whom the reader knew he shared the experience of being an Adams—held a peculiar power to convey a rare and private meaning: "its force so much closer home."

1.

The Great Inheritance

It was a great inheritance. . . . It was an inheritance of which the possessors, unless false to all that is best in human nature, could not fail to be proud, one which any man might justly envy and desire; so pervading in its influences that a biographer of any one of the fourth generation might well make his theme a study in heredity. Yet at the same time it must not be forgotten that this remarkable heritage brought to those who received it burdens as well as honor.

—Henry Cabot Lodge, "Memorial Address,"
Charles Francis Adams: An Autobiography

For Henry Brooks Adams, the family past was American history personalized. He lived and wrote as a fourth-generation member of America's most illustrious family, who had used their best energies throughout three generations to help shape the political and social world into which Henry was born. Over the course of a long career, he learned to record his sensitive consciousness of family, and he showed a special awareness of the powerful and mysterious influences that formed parts of his Adams birthright. In his mind and on his written pages, this fourth-generation son gradually traced out a developing pattern, until from a miscellany of impressions, facts, and questions, a single outline of understanding emerged. Finally, the investigation of his debt to the family took shape as a literary goal, and personal acknowledgment became an artistic quest. In short, Henry sought to discover and set down in his own unique way all that it meant to be an Adams. For he knew that, from the beginning, his life had been made something different and quite extraordinary by the forces and circumstances that were important parts of his family heritage.

Yet Henry Adams was also his own man, a man of thought rather than of action. Freed from the usual economic necessities, this patrician New Englander could well afford to experiment with his life by playing various roles: teacher, reformer, politician, world traveler, and sage historian. Always the gentleman, he remained uncommitted finally to any single specialized profession, preferring to consider himself a serious amateur in everything. But more than anything else, Adams became a conscious literary artist who, from his days as a Harvard undergraduate until he was disabled by a stroke in 1912, willingly accepted the traditional family duty of setting down his thoughts in various literary forms—fiction, nonfiction, and poetry. First, Adams the observer and critic used essays to intensify his personal impressions; next, the historian capitalized on his remarkable ability to organize and interpret records of the past in sophisticated and novel ways; and later, the caustic prophet attempted to surprise as much as to inform his audience by forecasting the future with a degree of accuracy that still excites us today. Adams's desire to express himself, to make these versions of his personal experience into matters of public record, marked his last and highest calling—that of experimental autobiographer—a favorite role that allowed him to exercise all his skills as a mature writer. In particular, the chief result and the foremost product of Adams's art, *The Education of Henry Adams*, shows a mastery of form and style equalled in the author's generation only by the most notable literary artists, such as his friend Henry James. Finally, then, it was in literature that Henry Adams achieved most, and to his writings we must turn if we are to understand him.[1] First, however, it is necessary to appreciate those special qualities that helped to shape both the man and his art, to study the Great Inheritance itself in terms of paramount family interests.

Politics

As a matter of American history, in Henry's generation the separation of the Adams family from all positions of real political power became for the first time unmistakable and certain. John, the eldest son, dabbled a bit in political waters by becoming a perennially unsuccessful candidate for state offices; Brooks, the youngest, spent his life as a teacher and writer of history, especially family history; and the fourth brother, Charles Francis II, turned away from an early start in political journalism, first to business and later to historical writing, ending his life in a mood of disenchantment with all politics. Finally Charles declared that he had learned from "the experience of my family for a hundred years" that political activity could never make him "happy or contented" because "I love literary work for its own sake." Meanwhile, Henry Adams carried the family principle of independence as far as any of his brothers. An early letter to Charles, written in 1869, when Henry was still surveying the possibilities for a useful career, reveals that sense of Olympian aloofness that he never relinquished— the studied detachment of a man who always preferred to stand apart from the real battles of politics and to spare himself such painful defeats as those his forebears had experienced in the presidential elections of 1800 and 1828:

> I will not go down into the rough-and-tumble, nor mix with the crowd. . . . My path is a different one; and was never chosen in order to suit other people's tastes, but my own. . . . I have told you before that I mean to be unpopular, and do it because I must do it, or do as other people do and give up the path I chose for myself years ago. . . . You like the strife of the world. I detest it and despise it. You work for power. I work for my own satisfaction. You like roughness and strength; I like taste and dexterity. For God's sake, let us go our ways and not try to be like each other.[2]

Even while acknowledging the seductive temptations of power, the letter writer managed to put on the record the larger stamp of his complex personality, as he noted reservations strong enough to determine his conduct. At most, Henry Adams made himself a political amateur in one of America's most professionally political families; he never held political office, elective or appointive, and of course he did not, in the usual economic way, need to. In fact, his financial independence removed from his life one of the chief problems that had plagued John and John Quincy (although not Charles Francis Adams), who had claimed that public service amounted to personal sacrifice in the name of patriotic duty. Nevertheless, Henry Adams did not escape the feeling that political service represented an obligation owed by every Adams to both family and country, a kind of promisory birth-debt which he must in some way satisfy. Thus, the financial independence of his position actually operated to deny him a subtle measure of personal satisfaction, by eliminating the most common family argument for self-justification, based upon financial sacrifice in favor of political ideals. Henry was forced to search for other themes to use in telling about himself, when he sought to make his case as a worthy heir in a distinguished line.

In general his most important ideals came to him from his family: a deep-seated concern with political morality and a disapproval of everything he thought to be corrupt, such as the modern system of political spoils; a vast respect for the American Constitution and the political theories upon which it was built; a correspondingly great antipathy to the institution and forces of slavery, which, in his view, had worked to destroy the Constitution and with it, his family throughout three generations, and which in fact had produced the historical tragedy of a Civil War and its aftermath—social and political chaos. In essays, novels, and biographies, Henry returned again and again to these themes, which he invoked in order to study events and men against a usable standard of established quality. By Henry's time, politics for an Adams, had become inescapable. Yet, because he had consciously chosen a role as detached observer, his political concern showed itself more clearly in his writings than in his life. Adams's good friend, Henry James, drawing on his own keen powers of perception, best described this unusual position when he portrayed Henry and Marian Adams as the Bonnycastles of Washington, D.C.: "Her husband was not in politics, though politics were much in him."[3]

Religion and Philosophy

Though the withdrawal from active politics remained always unsatisfying and intellectually ambiguous, this lifelong problem troubled him less than did another deeply rooted but more private matter, his religious inheritance. Adams family belief had been planted with the seeds of New England Puritanism, and despite three generations of open-minded interest in new ideas, this fourth-generation heir found himself unprepared for life in a secular age. As early as 1858, in his Harvard Class Day Oration, young Henry gave evidence of a powerful will to believe—an early signal of that ardent desire for complete faith that would show up again and again throughout the remainder of his long life. In fact, the residual force of family obligation prepared this Adams to accept any version of universal order that could satisfy his rational skepticism. In family terms, his position simply reversed the earlier overbalance of faith against doubt, found in the testimony of John Quincy and Charles Francis Adams, who had refused to surrender their belief in a moral universe watched over by a benevolent Creator. Henry's conception of religion, appearing first on Class Day and in the early essays, and further developed in *Esther*, grew gradually more skeptical until it emerged as a dominant theme in the *Education*, where the author declared: "Of all the conditions of his youth which afterwards puzzled the grown-up man, this disappearance of religion puzzled him most."[4] The enigma remained to the end. Adams found that he could accept neither the Buddhism he found in the East nor the Catholicism of Chartres as a personal solution to the modern religious dilemma. Yet he kept searching for what he could never find—an intuitive faith strong enough to put to rest the skeptical doubts generated by a powerful mind.

All the while, evidence of his spiritual torment filled Adams's letters, which over the years took shape as the most complete record of his own experience—a worthy substitute for the usual Adams diary. His most revealing letters help to establish the most characteristic refrain of his life (which is so familiar to readers of the *Education*), the reiteration of personal failure and defeat and an insistence upon the writer's unworthiness. Of course this theme is not original with Henry or even with the earlier Adams writers; but his words nonetheless constitute an unmistakable echo of his forebears. "Down Vanity," John Adams had cautioned himself again and again, and, like John Quincy and Charles Francis, Henry took the message seriously. All the Adamses knew that excessive self-esteem often worked to destroy human character, as it had in the case of John Randolph, whose biography Henry Adams wrote. But most of all, they came to fear the corruptive power of vanity in their own lives, the possible damage to themselves. In learning this lesson, of course, Henry held one important advantage: he could draw upon a longer family history for evidence, one that told a repetitive story of destruction among his Adams forebears as much as among outsiders, and in doing so, provide himself with sharper tools for self-interrogation than any his great-grandfather or grandfather had used. With that enlarged self-consciousness, Henry made greater demands upon himself in both his life and his writing.

He studied the particulars of human character just as avidly as had his forefathers, but with a new and modern scientific motive—to test psychologically the traditional Adams theory of human nature. Where, he asked, was the scientific evidence of human improvement that would clearly demonstrate general progress among men and in society? Adamses over three generations had committed themselves to an optimistic view of human possibility, the same view that Henry Adams endorsed in some of his first published writings. Yet he was also aware (and again to a greater degree than any of his forebears) that another part of his heritage encouraged a negative assessment. Gradually, Adams's studies in politics and history confirmed this original grain of skepticism. His writings grew more detached in point of view, and his own sense of personal involvement (but not his interest) lessened, until, as an old man, he looked back only to mock his earlier role as a sincere advocate of reform and improvement. To the end of his life, however, some hope for human progress still remained. Faint and elusive as the personality of the author, it shows itself in small patches of sunlight, scattered here and there among the expanses of dark shadow in the *Education* and his letters.

Adams's personal goal actually represented a compromise between a faith in old-fashioned moral order and the conflicting demands of modern chaos; throughout his life he sought to attain the grand ideal of intellectual and emotional development he had inherited from his family: to become a balanced man. This was the man John and John Quincy Adams had always hoped to be, the man who would combine in himself just the right mixture of perceptive thought and effective action. Of Henry's three most famous forebears, however, only Charles Francis Adams had actually succeeded in achieving such a balance, and then only for a short time. His ministry to England represented a nearly perfect practical application of human power, both emotional and intellectual, effectively used to resolve apparent contradictions. The Civil War minister in London stood for a neat historical conjunction of man and moment—a case of human effectiveness that was lost when Charles Francis returned to America.

Much as he admired his father's one great achievement, Henry knew that he would never be able to equal it. In confessing his failure, he placed most of the blame upon himself, but he also looked for some alternative explanation, one that would downgrade his personal responsibility. Finally, Henry sought a deterministic principle in modern science persuasive enough to supplant the old family faith in individualism—a determinism that would render obsolete the inherited formula of balanced human character, and replace it with a better understanding of the modern nonmoral and nonreligious universe.

Education

This search called for education, which had become by Henry Adams's time, of all family concerns, the most heavily invested with optimistic hope and expectation, as the title of his autobiographical account demonstrates. His own intellectual training was traditional, and, on the surface at least, yet another reward of special privilege. Tutored by his father as a youth, Henry went on to Harvard and then to Germany, where he first read law and later began the rigorous program of self-education that continued for the rest of his life. Even though some of his letters seem to cast serious doubt on his personal achievements, Henry Adams never lost the family faith in relevant education. On balance, almost the whole of his active career offers testimony to its pervasive strength. As a youthful essayist, he undertook to instruct a whole nation in rudimentary political science; as a Harvard professor, he introduced the seminar system and a new method of Germanic graduate training, which emphasized original research and close study of source documents; as an editor, he hoped to evaluate the effectiveness of education as a force in national life, calling for an essay that could provide "a thorough analysis of what America has and has *not* done for education. . . ."[5] Here as elsewhere, Henry Adams hoped to advance the cause of public instruction, just as, in their days, John and John Quincy had sought to promote and improve all kinds of education. The fourth-generation son was acknowledging a debt to the earlier Adamses as much as to the first President when he wrote in 1875: "All our best Presidents wanted a national University, and I regret much that Washington's recommendation was not adopted."[6] But Henry was also well aware of the very different example of his father, who had employed his education finally for private rather than public ends, for literary instead of political purposes.

For the son, each phase of his education ended with an exercise in personal evaluation, in some form of literary composition: his undergraduate career was summed up in the *Harvard Magazine* essays and the Class Day oration; his early studies of British finance in a series of articles for the *North American Review*; the historical studies in biographies, the *History*, and his later books and essays. From each "experiment" in education Adams derived both personal satisfaction and some measure of intellectual and artistic growth. Every presumption of personal progress, moreover, was regularly tested by the act of writing up what he had learned.

Of course, literature also brought its special share of discouragement and disappointment to Adams, who keenly felt the failures of his highly didactic political essays and of his *History* to attract and influence a large public audience. As a result, by the time he came to write the *Education*, the chief testimony on the subject, Henry Adams had already begun to view all possibilities for general human enlightenment with deep skepticism. Here, as on other counts, the book simply does not square with the historical facts of Adams's life. Instead, the *Education* makes a subtle and complex statement, which depends for its effect upon a unique pedagogical strategy. Using a mixture of accuracy and distortion, irony and sincerity, in which the didactic tone may always be distinguished, the author tells a repetitious tale of failure in education—but without ever losing hope of finding better success. In effect, the *Education* constantly reinforces the reader's faith in progress through new means of education, which might be passed along from generation to generation, just as the Adams faith had been passed to Henry.

Science

By Henry's time no other part of family education had changed so much as had the knowledge and practice of science. John Adams had written confidently about learning "the science of government"; now Henry Adams found that he must attempt to understand a new universe of scientific knowledge, which threatened to make obsolete every traditional principle of politics, religion, philosophy, and education. Of course, as we might expect, this confrontation with modern science also affected Henry's attitude toward literature. Some of his early writings display the scientific interest that Professor Louis Agassiz had first inspired in the Harvard undergraduate, and the last essays show how this interest had grown with the man, into a speculative fancy for scientific history. Yet, as we study the record, there is a danger in forgetting that, early and late, Henry Adams remained always a scientific amateur, perceptive and thoughtful but never expert or profoundly knowledgeable. For him, the central problem was not to become a scientist, but simply to learn to accept science as a field of investigation for its own sake, rather than merely as a means of finding evidence to help bolster a preconceived truth of politics or religion.

Finally, it was left to Henry Adams to make old family views fit new circumstances, at a time when science suddenly loomed large as both an explanation and a force. Alone among the fourth-generation Adams brothers, he seemed to understand the transition from the old age to the new. "Among my father's sons not one save Henry had any aptitude for science," declared Brooks Adams; he correctly singled out Henry as the only true heir of John Quincy Adams, the most scientific mind in the earlier line: ". . . in Henry the instinct which he inherited from his grandfather showed itself strongly and early." For Brooks, heredity served to explain much of what brother Henry wrote, beginning with an early review of Lyell's *Geology*. However, this unique scientific portion of his heritage did not take distinct shape in Henry's own mind until his later years, when he began to discuss their family with Brooks, who had grown up ten years after Henry, in a much more science-conscious age, filled with post–Civil War technology, and yet who claimed to lack any real comprehension of the scientific problems that fascinated his older brother.[7] This exchange of ideas, especially on the subject of scientific John Quincy Adams (a biography of whom Brooks wrote but never published, after receiving Henry's caustic critique), actually added new richness to Henry's self-understanding, as he was led to identify himself even more closely with his grandfather.

By the time he came to write the *Education*, then, Henry was able to treat John Quincy Adams's interest in science with a sophisticated mixture of humor and respect, which imposed upon the writer the need for a special idiom, to express the puzzled feelings of a boy. His grandfather's primitive biological and horticultural experiments, for example, evoked nostalgic memories, designed to hide all possibility of scientific criticism in a cloud of sentimental delight. The modern-minded grandson simply put aside the best science he knew when he recalled that, as a boy, he had

> penetrated the President's dressing-closet where a row of tumblers, inverted on the shelf, covered caterpillars which were supposed to become moths or butterflies, but never did. The Madam bore with fortitude the loss of the tumblers which her husband purloined for these hatcheries; but she made protest when he carried off her best cut-glass bowls to

plant with acorns or peachstones that he might see the roots grow, but which, she said, he commonly forgot like the caterpillars.

At that time the President rode the hobby of tree-culture, and some fine old trees should still remain to witness it, unless they have been improved off the ground; but his was a restless mind, and although he took his hobbies seriously and would have been annoyed had his grandchild asked whether he was bored like an English duke, he probably cared more for the processes than for the results, so that his grandson was saddened by the sight and smell of peaches and pears, the best of their kind, which he brought up from the garden to rot on his shelves for seed. With the inherited virtues of his Puritan ancestors, the little boy Henry conscientiously brought up to him in his study the finest peaches he found in the garden, and ate only the less perfect. Naturally he ate more by way of compensation, but the act showed that he bore no grudge.[8]

The charm of recollection here outweighs every suggestion of disapproval. Antique science makes a winning claim to a place in the personal history of Henry Adams, but with complicated results which the reader does not begin to understand until the author cries "failure" later in his book.

Much more important, yet largely obscured by such nostalgia, is the comparison between John Quincy Adams and his grandson, which provides the real key to the author's attitude. A "restless mind" and a concern "more for the processes than for the results" represent shared qualities that unite the two Adamses by means of their common "instinct." In this passage early in the book, Henry has already begun to explain—by reference to his intellectual and instinctual heritage—his own search for method or "process" which comes to dominate later sections of the *Education*. Elsewhere, Henry Adams acted out his kinship with John Quincy in other ways, as by accepting the familiar role of interpreter or popularizer for science. He tried to help the public understand the ideas of scientific men like Sir Charles Lyell and Willard Gibbs by giving them exposure in popular literature and by championing their work whenever he

could. In Adams's view historians, educators, politicians—
everyone who was not a true scientist—had to be made better
informed about science.[9]

As in politics, Adams himself was left to function in the role
of observer rather than as doer. He moved among men like
Clarence King and Samuel Langley, listened to his fellow
members of the Cosmos Club, and read within the limits of his
scientific understanding. These encounters, personal and intellectual, provided Adams not only with a justification for the old
family attitude of open-minded interest in science but also with
important new evidence on the question of human progress.
When he attempted to employ scientific methods in his thinking,
Adams was also forced to reject some old family notions and
often to break sharply with the family past. In Henry's mind,
science no longer could be conceived of in John Adams's
simplistic terms, as a handmaiden of religion. Clearly, science
had achieved a sovereignty and power of its own, and scientific
thought demanded special attention.

As the old centers of power had shifted, political education
in the family had become as obsolete as the Adams scientific
inheritance. When principled eighteenth-century leaders gave
way to pragmatic nineteenth-century political parties, the
Adams heirs were left outside the magic circle of political power.
Determined to remain independent, Henry Adams knew that he
could never hope to operate the machinery of modern politics,
nor even, it seemed, to take a useful part in what was going on.
As he demonstrated in "Civil Service Reform" and more clearly
in *Gallatin* and the *Education*, the problem of exerting effective
control over events had grown too large. No longer was it a
sufficient solution to place and keep in office a group of high-
minded statesmen of the type that the earlier Adamses represented. Political power had escaped from the control of
individuals—even of the best politicians and statesmen—
perhaps from the control of political parties as well, to become
an ominous impersonal force. To Henry, this force seemed less
political than scientific; scientific training was required simply
to understand and even more to control it, if it could be
controlled at all. As the *Education* tells us, just this type of
training, which the earlier generations of Adamses had never

been obliged to consider a proper part of education, represented something that Henry Adams knew he had never received. In that omission, he saw the roots of the paramount "failure" of his life.

Literature

His almost theatrical cries of "failure" aside, Henry often admitted that he had gained richly from being an Adams of Massachusetts. He knew that his was a great inheritance, especially in literature. For three generations, the act of placing words on paper had served family members well as a means of self-definition and self-discipline, and even more as a way of controlling (at least temporarily) the hostile outside environment. Now in Henry's time, his increasing skill with the pen gradually blended with his scientific persuasions until he achieved a new style of exposition that successfully imitated the experimental techniques of modern scientific research. As he learned about life, Adams's statements became tentative rather than absolute, provocative instead of authoritative, hypotheses in place of conclusions. To his readers, meanwhile, Henry Adams conceded less and less. They must learn to "jump" in order to follow his lead, while on his part he labored to offer them more than any of his family had before him. It should come as no surprise to us that the best of his writings require some special understanding of just those experimental methods that he found necessary to make his meaning clear. Like his forebears, in short, Henry placed high value on literary artistry when he accepted the traditional duty of an Adams to be a man of letters. But his success as a writer was based on qualities far greater than familial pietism. Taking what earlier Adamses had bequeathed him in their manuscripts and their examples, he added his own brand of genius so that the best of his work stands alone—an achievement unequalled in the entire family line.

2.

Apprenticeship and Early Writing

... As I look back upon the Uncles, I see them as always writing—Uncle Charles in a nice square house just below his own on President's Hill, ... which he called the "Annex." Uncle Henry when he was in Quincy commanded undisputed possession of the Stone Library, while Uncle Brooks reigned in John Adams's study on the second floor of the Old House. It used to puzzle me what they all found to write about, for my father [John Adams] never seemed to write at all—but when I asked him about it, he said, "I suppose it amuses them!" When I asked why he too did not write, he said that he had done all his writing when he was young and had nothing more to say now.

—Abigail Adams Homans,
Education by Uncles.

The literary apprenticeship of Henry Adams began very early in his life, among the books and papers in his father's house on Mount Vernon Street, which contained the largest private library in Boston.

Here also as a boy he first beheld the labor of the file when he patiently held copy for his father's edition of the works of his great-grandfather. With what double emphasis must the words of John Adams have entered his mind as he sat beside his father, the sounding rhetoric reviving old controversy and recalling to father and son the legacy of political responsibility which was theirs. No classroom could have

31

made so deep an impression upon a sensitive boy as this room where the mental life of all the generations of the Adamses came to a luminous focus. . . .[1]

First at home and later at Harvard, where he wrote essays for the *Harvard Magazine*, Henry's apprenticeship helped to make him feel the peculiar weight of his Adams heritage, and this family consciousness, once implanted, never afterward disappeared from his mind. It had obviously taken deep root just a few months after graduation, when he explained to his brother Charles, "There are two things that seem to be at the bottom of our constitutions; one is a continual tendency towards politics; the other is family pride; and it is strange how these two feelings run through all of us."[2]

Such family pride, more than any other motive, showed Henry Adams the way to making his literary career. He began by preparing for the press a biography of his grandmother, Louisa Catherine Adams, constructed on the foundation of family papers, mainly her letters. But this task was never completed, as Henry turned instead to a literary defense of grandfather John Quincy Adams: *Documents Relating to New England Federalism, 1800–1815* (1877), in which were printed for the first time private papers that helped to refute the political charges against the sixth President raised both by his contemporaries and by such later historians as Herman Von Holst. By clearing the Adams name, Henry was fulfilling a duty he had acknowledged as early as 1859, when he told Charles: "I don't know whether you had it in your mind or not when you wrote, but it seems probable that the duty of editing our grandfather's works and writing his life, may fall on one of us, and if it does, that alone is enough for a man, and enough to shape his whole course."[3] Henry never explained exactly how this project might "shape his whole course" in life, but certainly he was contemplating a career as a writer and editor who would concentrate upon the Adams family as his chief subject.

Perhaps because he felt that his father had preempted that choice in 1860, Henry occupied himself instead with letters to the newspapers, writing first from Washington and later from England. These letters were intended to aid Charles Francis, the

Minister to England, by influencing public opinion in favor of the Union cause. At that time, letters were usually printed without the writers' names; so that when, in 1862, Henry Adams was identified as the author of "A Visit to Manchester," a critical review of British social life, the uproar in the British press shocked Adams into recognizing that his family connections, especially his father's diplomatic position, made him peculiarly vulnerable to attack by anyone who disliked the Adamses or America. As he told the American historian John Gorham Palfrey, "I was roasted with pepper and salt by the English press. . . . My own Anglicism is somewhat wilted."[4] Of course, the sensitive young man may have exaggerated the damage, but even so, Henry never forgot the unpleasant incident, which started him searching for a less risky form of self-expression, such as the historical essay.

Meanwhile, among the fourth-generation sons private literature was changing in other ways. The diary habit effectively disappeared; but the family obligation to record one's life and thoughts still remained potent. One of Henry's letters to brother Charles, written in 1860, makes this clear: "I propose to write you this winter a series of private letters to show how things look . . . to me it will supply the place of a Journal."[5] Taken as a whole, Henry's correspondence came to represent the most impressive survival of private literature in the fourth generation, as well as a comprehensive reminder of the earlier Adams diaries. Like the diaries, the correspondence contains considerable self-examination. In 1862, for example, the twenty-four year old social butterfly, apparently so formidable a member of London society, set down private feelings that his English circle would never have suspected:

> I've disappointed myself, and experience the curious sensation of discovering myself to be a humbug. How is this possible? Do you understand how, without a double personality, *I* can feel that *I* am a failure? One would think that the *I* which could feel that, must be a different *ego* from the *I* of which it is felt.[6]

Much later, in his fine poem "Buddha and Brahma" (written in 1891 and first printed in 1915) and in the *Education*, Adams would return to this notion of his "double personality," to treat the idea with greater complexity and sophistication. In the private letters of his young manhood, however, the writer could only begin to discuss the possibility of a divided self.

Apart from reporting private feelings, the letter form also served Henry Adams in the traditional family way, to make him something of a public figure, even when he was reluctant to be identified. In fact, having once been "roasted" by the English press, he afterward displayed a lifelong ambivalence toward his reading audience, alternating between interest and disdain, which helps to explain the unusual publication histories of all his major works. As early as 1867, for example, after publishing three articles in the highly respected *North American Review*, Adams might have been expected to congratulate himself on beginning a successful career. Instead, his private evaluation, contained in a letter to brother Charles, takes a much different view:

> The triumph of earning $240 in paper in one year does not satisfy my ambition. John is a political genius; let him follow the family bent. You are a lawyer and with a few years' patience will be the richest and most respectable of us all. I claim my right to part company with you both. I never will make a speech, never run for office, never belong to a party. I am going to plunge under the stream. For years you will hear nothing of any publication of mine—perhaps never, who knows. I do not mean to tie myself to anything, but I do mean to make it impossible for myself to follow the family go-cart.[7]

The deep sense of personal insecurity expressed in almost every line grew out of the writer's uncomfortable respect for his great family history, an appreciation he could expect his brother to share. Only when Henry could rely on such a sympathetic reception did he feel free to confess a deep distrust of self. Forty years later, the original, hand-picked audience for the first printing of *The Education of Henry Adams* would be composed of just such readers.

Grandfather John Quincy Adams had always denied that personal ambition motivated him to write newspaper articles; he insisted instead that he was exercising the good citizen's right and duty to express himself on all public matters. In his own apprenticeship, Henry Adams hoped to expand on this notion of duty by treating the old sense of obligation as a source of modern power, the power to influence public opinion. As he explained to brother Charles, "One man who has real ability may do a great deal, but we ought to have a more concentrated power of influence than any that now exists."[8] The instrument remained the same—literature, especially expository writing in the form of essays. His subjects naturally included politics, about which fellow Americans seemed badly in need of proper instruction; but he wrote about science, religion, and education as well. By 1870, when Henry ended his literary apprenticeship by leaving journalism and Washington for a teaching post at Harvard College, he had completed three key statements that must be regarded as touchstones for his later and more mature works.

"Captain John Smith"

The first really significant event in Henry Adams's literary career was the publication of "Captain John Smith" in the *North American Review** for January 1867.[9] The unsigned essay had been started in 1862, while Henry was living in England. This early draft was revised and rewritten until 1866, when Charles Eliot Norton finally accepted the article for publication. With some further changes, the essay was reprinted in *Chapters of Erie* (1871) and *Historical Essays* (1891).

"Captain John Smith" has frequently been interpreted as simply a fourth-generation contribution to the family campaign against slavery and an assault upon a principal ancestral figure of the slave-holding South. Yet the facts suggest neither a merely topical statement of moral indictment, a hastily contrived defense of the Adamses against an old family enemy, nor even a

*Cited below as *NAR*.

noncombatant's contribution to the Union cause, although certainly the essay did absorb something of the author's partisan feelings. The material for "Captain John Smith" was not purposely selected as an extension of wartime sentiments; rather, the author was making a conscious attempt to overcome present circumstances by turning experimentally to the past. The idea for the essay was first suggested by John Gorham Palfrey, who mentioned during a visit to the London home of Minister Adams his own doubts about the authenticity of the famous Pocahontas legend.[10] This hint of historical error fell upon Henry Adams just after he had been publicly exposed as the author of "A Visit to Manchester," and he remained embarrassed by the publicity. To Palfrey he wrote, "my pen is forced to keep away from political matters, unless I want to bring the English press down on my head again."[11] So he took up a new "literary toy," as he called the Pocahontas project. Before he finished, it proved more than a "toy" because Pocahontas gave him a first addictive taste of serious historical writing, based upon scholarly research. However, the project brought him troubles almost at once.

The youthful Adams, as yet an uncertain practitioner of both research and writing, could not satisfy himself with his first attempt to find the truth about Pocahontas and Smith. He was driven first to identify and then to ponder the contradictions and limitations of the historical record, all the while learning to be a critical user of literary evidence from the past and a thoughtful critic of his own work. Indeed, even after Professor Palfrey showed satisfaction with Henry's efforts and advised him, in 1863, to publish, Adams remained reluctant, preferring instead to keep his article close by in manuscript. But three years later another motive prevailed, and Adams finally determined "to win my spurs" in literature.

The first published version of the essay applies the traditional family view of man-centered history. Adams begins by analyzing the chief actors and then shifts his focus to consider the "veracity of Captain John Smith" (*NAR*, 2). In form, the article purports to be a review of two then-recent books: Charles Deane's 1866 edition of Smith's *A True Relation of Virginia*, and Deane's 1860 edition of Edward Maria Wingfield's *A Dis-*

course of Virginia. Adams justifies his method by using the Wingfield work to help explain the deficiencies he finds in Smith's report. The reviewer's attention, naturally enough, remains upon Smith, as Adams reprints side by side passages from *A True Relation* (1608) and from Smith's later *The General History* (1624), and then goes on to point out differences between the two—noting especially a "character of exaggeration" in the later account. The chief discrepancies concern the Pocahontas legend, which was not mentioned in *A True Relation* but which is prominent in *The General History.*

Adams's doubts about Smith's accounts reflect his own inherited skepticism concerning human character and motivation. In his first letter to Palfrey, Adams wrote of Pocahontas:

> What her motive was I cannot understand, for she was a mere child, only twelve years old, and could hardly have had a sentimental attachment to Smith; yet her services ceased when he left the province; and she went off to live with a relation on the Potomac. Perhaps it was some wild-Indian semi-lunacy that drove her to it, for I confess I am very sceptical about any pure philanthropy in an Indian child that would drive her through a forest in mid-winter many miles in order to betray her father. Such an act implies strong motives.[12]

As he went on with his research, the apprentice historian arrived at harsher judgments. Working during the American Civil War, which had already split the Union and endangered the future of the Constitution—two cherished ideals in the Adams political system—the young man would give no quarter either to Southern character or to the legendary forces of slavery, for slavery had been held odious by Adamses of every generation, and Henry would not relent in a time of crisis. Writing out of his own set of biases, familial and regional, he hoped to cast doubt on the noble motives proclaimed in the accepted version of John Rolfe's marriage to Pocahontas. With little charity toward the South and even less historical objectivity, he wrote: "I confess, this seems to me to show a degree of self-devotion on his part that does not talley with my idea of the character of the Virginia settlers. It belonged rather to the latitude of New England."[13]

As Adams planned it, his essay would make a timely contribution to the family war against slavery and the South. Behind Virginia and the figure of Pocahontas stood John Randolph, an old family enemy and the defender of the antebellum South. Adams well knew that Randolph liked to brag about his descent from Pocahontas. Thus, to its author, "Captain John Smith" represented something more than merely a correction of the historical record: ". . . it is in some sort a flank, or rather a rear attack, on the Virginia aristocracy, who will be utterly gravelled by it if it is successful."[14]

In effect, the essay brought the weight of moral judgment to bear upon Captain Smith with as much force as John Quincy Adams had once used to castigate Andrew Jackson. Smith was pictured as a dishonest historian; and his motive showed itself to be the worst any Adams could imagine: excessive personal ambition. The additions and distortions in his later accounts resulted from an ardent desire to achieve fame and fortune. John Smith, "smarting under what he considered undeserved neglect," made an "ambitious" appeal "to the public" by writing up his experiences for a second time (*NAR*, 29–30). Poor George Bancroft and other historians were taken in by Smith because of their optimistic view of human nature, but Henry Adams could not be so easily fooled. As a perceptive student of mankind, he well understood the character of the man who had written *The General History*: "In this work he embodied everything that could tend to the increase of his own reputation. . . . Pocahontas was made to appear in it as a kind of stage deity on every possible occasion, and his own share in the affairs of the Colony is magnified at the expense of all his companions"(*NAR*, 30).

Yet this lesson in human nature was not the only one that young Adams tried to teach. Certainly, as a man, Smith had suffered from overvaulting ambition; even more important, however, as a writer he had been responsible for a more damaging error, a distortion of the historical record, lasting from 1624 until "the present day." Henry Adams believed, in short, that through the corrupt character and actions of this single man, the whole American nation had suffered, for his false record of the

UNIVERSITY OF WINNIPEG
LIBRARY
515 Portage Avenue
Winnipeg, Manitoba
DISCARDED

past could not be used to provide clear lessons for the present. Unlike an Adams forebear, Smith had written only to establish a "tyrannical sway . . . over the intelligence of the country" (*NAR*, 14). No Adams could possibly forgive such intellectual tyranny.

"*Lyell's* Principles of Geology *(10th ed.) a review*"

An important fringe benefit of being an Adams in America or abroad was the company one could keep. Just as a visit from Professor Palfrey gave Henry the idea for "Captain John Smith," so his friendship with a prominent English scientist prompted the American to develop an interest in science, especially geology. Sir Charles Lyell, "a frequent visitor" to the American Legation, "on terms of intimacy with the entire family," and a close associate of Charles Darwin, induced young Henry Adams to join the chief debate of the age—between religion and modern science.[15] Early in 1867, Lyell confided a desire to have the recently published tenth edition of his *Principles of Geology* given intelligent critical notice in America, and Adams offered his services. His review-essay appeared in the *North American Review* for October 1868.

While working on it, Henry engaged himself in the basic research that would eventually grow into his lifelong fascination with "geologizing"—at Wenlock Abbey, in the Rocky Mountains, and on the coral reefs of the Pacific—as well as his celebrated friendship with the professional geologist, Clarence King. The essay, finished a year and a half after the original conversation with Lyell, constitutes the most important piece of family writing concerned with science to appear since John Quincy's *Report on Weights and Measures*. Moreover, this article was signed with its author's full name, showing that Henry Adams meant to use the essay as a public declaration of literary intent. As he wrote, he knew that he had begun to make a reputation in American letters, and also that his work was heavily indebted to what he had learned in Professor Agassiz's science classes at Harvard College. Agassiz's catastrophic explanation formed one side of the scientific controversy about the origins of the earth—an explanation to which the uniformitarian concepts of Lyell and Darwin were sharply opposed. Adams recognized the fundamental nature of the debate. But in his essay he hoped to provide a clear-cut exposition of the problem, rather than to take one side or the other in the argument, with the risk of being proved wrong later on. To Charles Eliot Norton, editor of the *North American Review*, he explained:

> ... I shall try to express more valuable opinions than my own, though I don't wish to be controversial. . . . My own leaning, though not strong, is still towards them [Lyell and Darwin]. . . . It is not likely that I should handle the controversy vigorously—the essay would rather be an historical one—but I should have to touch it.[16]

When it appeared, the essay did show Adams's ability to locate "more valuable opinions" in the works of Hutton, Darwin, Heer, Lamarck, and others, as well as in earlier editions of the *Principles* and the ideas of Agassiz. Certainly the apprentice scholar had also benefited from Palfrey's help with "Captain John Smith." Now, in his determination to avoid being "controversial," Adams actually converted the review form into a lengthy discussion of the two sides of the geological debate—but he made no attempt to decide the issue for the reader. The old family ideal of the balanced man had been translated into a balance of content and form, as the author used information from his research to point out deficiencies in the evidence offered by both parties.

As his letter to Norton disclosed, Adams's real sympathies lay with Lyell and uniformitarianism; nonetheless, he gave full credit to Agassiz and the glacial theory, taking note of their important contributions, which had already influenced the study of geology and forced Lyell to alter his original theories at some points. In his carefully conceived role as amateur expositor of professional science, Adams explained: "The discovery of this climatic element in geology was one of more importance than can yet be fairly estimated. . . . But the glacial theory is not complete, it lacks indeed its most essential side . . . cause" (*NAR*, 475). Elsewhere in the essay the author makes it equally clear that Lyell's alternative proposals are themselves not fully sufficient to answer every criticism. Finally, the whole field of geological science remains as yet incapable of providing a sufficient explanation for the origins of life. Above all, what emerges most clearly from his essay is the author's absolute determination to avoid taking a side in the popular conflict between science and religion. In Adams's mind, geology as a scientific discipline and a field of knowledge should restrict itself to the available evidence. Science must be studied in the physical, rather than the spiritual, world. The most useful paths for further scientific research had been marked out, largely by the willingness of scientists themselves to accept these limitations. Lyell (following Hutton, in the exploration of inorganic matter) and Darwin (in the study of organic) both agreed; and taken all together their work proved that "Nature never moved by leaps, but that all her steps would, if properly studied, show a logically rigid sequence" (*NAR*, 483).

Without as yet being fully conscious of the implications, young Adams penned a conclusion that pointed to the path of his own intellectual development. The search for proper method and "sequence" became the pattern of his future thought and the key to the best of his later writings. More than thirty years after the review of Lyell first appeared, its author was still arguing the value of "geologizing," which he came to see as a logical extension of his lifelong concern with history: "After all, Geology is but History, and I am only carrying my field a little back of T. Jefferson. . . ."[17] Even more to the point, the "logically rigid sequence" of nature composed a modest preview of Adams's method in his *History*, where the historian sought to trace "only . . . facts in their sequence." Whether studying history or science, then, the intelligent observer must remain detached and uncommitted: "Extremely little is as yet known with certainty on the subject, too little to warrant any unscientific person in becoming a partisan of either opinion . . ." (*NAR*, 496). The young man had begun to build a case for personal indecision as much as an artistic argument for a literary method of balanced presentation. "Lyell" ends in a series of speculations, its author having failed to endorse either partisan geological interpretation. Finally, Adams asks, what more can I be expected to do, so long as real scientific authorities "agree no better than this in regard to the meaning of their own discoveries"?

Such diffidence aside, as evidence of its author's concern for science, "Lyell" is far more valuable than the sum of its criticisms and speculations. For it shows us much of what the young Henry Adams thought about the man of science—the human type that would appear years later in the *Education* as the representative of intellectual evolution, the thinker best equipped for life in the twentieth century. First, however, in the earlier essay, the scientific man shows up (as a partial portrait, only) in the figure of Lyell himself. Once the limitations of geological evidence have been duly noted, Adams shifts his focus to the effects of rigorous analysis upon the mind of the practicing scientist. Then the author attempts a personification of scientific method, as he extends the traditional family concern with the close study of men, within and without the family, into the modern scientific era. But to comprehend the full meaning of the picture presented in "Lyell," we must also keep in mind the less attractive self-portrait that Adams had sketched a few years earlier:

> The more I see, the more I am convinced that a man whose mind is balanced like mine, in such a way that what is evil never seems unmixed with good, and what is good always streaked with evil; an object seems never important enough to call out strong energies till they are exhausted, nor necessary enough not to allow of its failure being possible to retrieve; in short, a mind which is not strongly positive and absolute, cannot be steadily successful in action, which requires quietness and perseverance.[18]

When that was written in 1862, mental balance had seemed to guarantee failure in the introspective letter-writer; yet by 1868, Adams had been forced to recognize that, in the scientist at least, just such a balance represented the chief prerequisite for any real success.

Lyell the man proved as important to Adams as Lyell the geologist. A "methodical" and "disinterested" mind kept Lyell free from the "exaggeration" of which John Smith had been

convicted in the earlier essay. In fact, the obvious limitations
that Adams observed in Lyell's nature and method showed up to
be the true sources of his special genius. For, while

> few students can resist the fascination of building geologi-
> cal castles-in-the-air, he seems to feel a certain amount of
> pleasure in lopping away fanciful excrescenses which other
> men foster, and in treating the earth's marvelous history in
> that coldly scientific spirit which admits only what is
> enough, and no more than enough, to produce the result
> observed (*NAR*, 467).

In such economy of thought, Adams finds the best reason for
the success of Lyell's scientific work. Instead of responding
defensively with a furious display of temper, as John and John
Quincy Adams had so often done when their opinions were
challenged, Lyell kept himself free to modify his earlier views,
and to accept the usable ideas of Lamarck and Darwin. His
open-mindedness led to a better scientific theory—and improved
geological theory, in turn, resulted in better science—already in
Adams's mind an important part of human progress. All such
progress required balanced minds and men like Lyell, who
could help to guarantee that science would remain free of such
errors of record as historians had perpetuated in the matter of
Pocahontas. But an equally important key to such progress
emerged from Lyell's method and not alone from the man. The
study of an outstanding geologist and of geological method
taught young Henry Adams what might be expected when a
powerful mind has been made to do useful work within strict
bounds of thought. It was a lesson he never forgot.

"Civil Service Reform"

Despite the political setback Henry Adams suffered when
the British press revealed his hand in "A Visit to Manchester,"
his retreat proved to be only temporary. The "tendency towards
politics" he had noted in himself asserted its force almost as soon
as the young essayist returned from England after the Civil War

to confront the sordid spectacle of Reconstruction. In Washington, Adams found the new American politics of the Grant administration, and out of his shocked response came the most impressive of his apprentice writings, the essays concerned with political reform. They are the best testimony to his painful awareness that the Adams family no longer could claim a place in national affairs. Yet even as he wrote "Civil Service Reform," his most comprehensive political statement of that time, Henry remained true to the ideals of his forebears. Whenever an inherited principle could be applied, the fourth-generation heir knew exactly where he stood. If he was confused and uncertain in matters of history and science, the young writer shaped answers to political questions with a masterful control of both his material and his convictions. This fact was evident when he published "Civil Service Reform" in the *North American Review* for October 1869.[19]

Adams's essay pinpointed the inherent dangers of Grantism, treating it essentially as a threat to the principles of sound government set forth in the Constitution. The position he took in 1869 actually favored conservative reform—some change to meet new conditions, but change that would not needlessly destroy the old ideals. American government, Adams believed, should remain a system of divided and balanced powers deriving from the Constitution. By moving to shift the power to appoint federal officials from the executive branch to the legislative—a transfer directly attributable to the growing influence of political parties, which the Adams Presidents had always warned against—elected leaders were threatening the whole system of sound government and betraying their own responsibilities. Rulers of all sorts, John Adams once had declared, are under "the most solemn and the most sacred moral obligations . . . to exert all their intellectual liberty to employ all their faculties, talents, and power for the public, general, universal good of their nations, not for their separate good, or the interest of any party."[20] Now, Henry Adams told his audience, Grant and the spoils system made a mockery of all moral principles in politics. Even more, the old checks against corrupt human nature were being rendered useless at a most crucial time, when the character and ability of the men who held office seemed increasingly open to question. National catastrophe was imminent.

Thus alarmed, Adams turned his political review into a spirited plea for better men in government and improved national conduct. Much like the argument he would make years later, in the pages of *Democracy*, his case for Civil Service reform revealed a heavy debt to Adams family beliefs. Without mentioning John Quincy Adams by name, for example, the essayist dated the decline in the moral influence of the presidency from the inauguration of Andrew Jackson, John Quincy's victorious opponent in the election of 1828. In fairness, Henry quickly goes on to point out, however, that "Congress first began to claim as a right [rather than a privilege] the nominating power" only "within the last ten years" (*Essays*, 103). During that time the Senate, the "seat of their [party organizations'] intrigues," was primarily to blame for "controlling the executive patronage"; thus, in the workings of that body, Adams located the chief threat to moral government. All of this, of course, merely echoed the common themes of earlier family thought. In fact, the same problem had long before been explored in a passage of President John Quincy Adams's diary (to which his grandson makes no reference): "Efforts have been made by some of the Senators to obtain different nominations, and to introduce a principle of change or rotation in office. . . . A more pernicious expedient could scarcely have been devised." Two generations later, Henry knew that his kinsman's judgment had been proved sound.

What had changed was the presidency itself. The modern power of political parties now made it difficult if not impossible for a Chief Executive to exert effective leadership or to imitate the actions of a strong President like John Quincy Adams, who had retained many of Monroe's appointees, declaring, "I determined . . . to renominate every person against whom there was no complaint which would have warranted his dismissal." The political men around Henry Adams in 1869 displayed no such strength or independence, although just those virtues had characterized "the early administrations, from the time of Washington to the time of Jackson," a span including the terms of both Adams Presidents (*Essays*, 101). Now, instead of political independence, the "pliability" of Mr. Boutwell made him a modern politician in the style of the times; while his opposite number Judge Hoar, Grant's Attorney General and an anachronistic figure of a statesman, "indifferent to opposition whether in or out of his party, obstinate to excess . . . belonged in fact to a class of men who had been gradually driven from politics, but whom it is the hope of reformers to restore" (*Essays*, 109–110). There could be little doubt which type of New Englander Adams's forebears represented in the mind of the writer.

But the most serious national problem centered on the voting public, who simply did not comprehend the true nature of modern politicians. Unlike generations of well-tutored, skeptical Adamses, most Americans had been fooled because they did not study human nature closely enough. Thus, Adams described the popular view of Grant in 1869:

> The new President had unbounded popular confidence. He was tied to no party. He was under no pledges. He had the inestimable advantage of a military training, which unlike a political training, was calculated to encourage the moral distinction between right and wrong . . . almost the entire public, expected to see him at once grasp with a firm hand the helm of government, and give the vessel of state a steady and determined course. The example of President Washington offered an obvious standard for the ambition of Grant. It was long before the conservative class of citizens, who had no partisan prejudices, could convince themselves that in this respect they had not perhaps overrated so much as misconceived the character of Grant.[21]

Such ignorance was fatal, for even with all the apparent advantages of independence, sound moral education, and strong public support, Grant had failed to do his presidential duty and the nation seemed imperiled.

Elsewhere in "Civil Service Reform" Adams went beyond this kind of historical description to draw a clearer lesson about Grantism for the readers' benefit. Because patronage had become the accepted spoils of the winning party, Grant had found himself unable to withstand the demands made on him: "It is folly to suppose that the executive can maintain itself while such a right is conceded or even theoretically acknowledged" (*Essays*, 105). Power that reigned unchecked, especially power in the hands of political parties, could lead only to corruption; for the operation of checks and balances still remained the only sure protection against the weaknesses of human nature. Somehow the realistic wisdom of John Adams and the other Founders had been cast aside in the post–Civil War era. Fortunately, his great-grandson was left to plead the old family case: "Men must strip from the subject all imaginary distinctions, and confront face to face the bald and disgusting fact that members of Congress cannot be honest with such a power in their hands" (*Essays*, 104). For Grant and his administration had provided a political spectacle so threatening and sordid that even the stoical Henry Adams was alarmed: "There seems to be no limit to the elasticity of respectable men's consciences when their interests and their pride are involved" (*Essays*, 101). Writing in that prophetic voice that would become characteristic of his later works, the young author sadly insists, "It is equally folly to imagine that the government itself can endure under a strain which would have broken the Roman Empire into fragments" (*Essays*, 105).

Everywhere in the essay, Adams's discussion of political men serves to explain the fallen state of American government since Jackson, and to dramatize the need for a quick return to sound constitutional principles. Man and government are symbiotic. Unchanging human nature makes it necessary for the nation to respect and apply rules of good government based upon a knowledge of human weakness. Naturally when the essayist turns away from men to consider valid political principles, he locates these principles in the ideas of writers who were not themselves confused by "imaginary distinctions," authorities whose understanding of human nature was thorough and complete. To document the general principles of sound government, for example, Henry relies upon the public writings of his great-grandfather. The essay begins with a quotation from "The Massachusetts Bill of Rights" expressing the principle of separation of powers, John Adams's most important contribution to the Massachusetts Constitution: "*to the end it may be a government of laws and not of men*" (*Essays*, 97; italics Henry Adams's). Henry Adams felt that the chief danger in 1869 could be equated with the old family fear that men would usurp the authority of law. A few pages on, when he repeats his warning against popular disregard for the principle of separation of political powers, his words are drawn from John Adams's *Defense of the Constitutions of Government of the United States of America*: "If the executive power, or any considerable part of it, is left in the hands either of an aristocratical or a democratical assembly, it will corrupt the legislature as necessarily as rust corrupts iron or as arsenic poisons the human body; and when the legislature is corrupted the people are undone." Later, the essayist rephrases the opening quotation and reminds us, in conclusion, that "the whole subject of civil-service reform is reduced to a single principle,—the same which is asserted in the thirtieth article of the Massachusetts Bill of Rights" (*Essays*, 126).

Despite these references, at no point in the essay is there a specific attribution to John Adams. Perhaps the writer had determined to forestall any possible criticism of his essay as merely an exercise in ancestral pietism; this diffidence he would carry over to the writing of his *History* and *Education*, as we shall later see. In any case, it should be clear that "Civil Service Reform" stands upon the foundation of earlier family examples and family principles. But the essay goes beyond mere reaffirmation of past ideals. Looking around him, Henry Adams has to acknowledge that the old family ideal of political independence no longer can protect the office of the President (regardless of the man) from the overwhelming pressures exerted by political parties. Yet even so, Henry believes that real reform does not depend upon making better use of those parties. Rather, he rests his hopes for improvement on the alternative power of public opinion, an enlightened new force of independent criticism and reform, of which his essay is meant to form a part:

> Nothing remains but to act outside of all party organizations, and to appeal with all the earnestness that the emergency requires, not to Congress nor to the President, but to the people, to return to the first principles of the government, and to shut off forever this source of corruption in the state (*Essays*, 113).

In an age of party politics the duty of an Adams remains a lonely one—to work as an independent teacher and critic of politics, past and present. Divorcing himself from both the power and the corruption of modern political life, Henry Adams was attempting to exercise an indirect power to influence public opinion. In the nineteenth century unlike the eighteenth, he felt, this power alone could bring about real reform, by means of "the creation of such a sound public opinion as will hold future Presidents more closely to their charge" (*Essays*, 113).

As a youthful essayist, Henry Adams always worked to educate his readers, using the most effective rhetorical techniques he could command. Most often he depended upon repetition to make his points clear; and, for proof, he appealed to acknowledged authorities in history, science, and political theory. Bancroft, Lyell, and John Adams, for example, were cited with critical respect, based upon Henry Adams's own extensive research, but without servility; they were used, as in "Civil Service Reform," to buttress the theoretical aspects of Henry's argument. Again, by writing on many different subjects, Henry Adams learned (as his father had before him) how to achieve control, if not yet mastery, over a variety of literary methods. These would later serve him much more effectively when he turned away from the essay form to history, biography, and the novel. The Lyell review was an exercise in logical analysis, in which the scientific subject was neatly complemented by a scientific method of exposition and coldly scientific prose. It marked a step toward Adams's best historical style—a flexible tool for use with any subject that required factual presentation and where apparent impartiality would be valued.

The less restrained prose of "Captain John Smith," on the other hand, marshals a frontal attack on the character of Smith, who had, after all, exercised a "tyrannical sway . . . over the intelligence of the country." Adams's no-holds-barred approach here might be passed off as merely youthful exuberance; however, he would later employ the same vitriolic style in his full-length biography of John Randolph. More important, the "Smith" essay shows Adams's ability to use source documents skillfully; he begins to make his case by providing the reader with two conflicting accounts of Smith's activities and then relies upon the documents themselves to support his own conclusions. This treatment points the way to Adams's method of organizing both *Gallatin* and the *History*.

"Civil Service Reform" shows the essayist already in possession in 1869 of the stylistic and rhetorical devices that are commonly associated only with Henry Adams's later works. The mark of the future novelist, for example, stamps the passage in which Adams pictures conditions in the capital just after Grant took office, only to surrender himself to the evils of patronage. Emotive words and images, rather than logical exposition, carry the burden of meaning:

> The President gave way. Then began those cruel scenes which for months reduced the city of Washington to such a condition as is caused by an ordinary pestilence or famine. Private suffering is of small consequence where the nation is the chief sufferer. It matters little how many miserable women and worn-out men, the discarded servants of the Republic, are to be ground to death under the wheels of this slow-moving idol of faction, since their tears or agony are as little likely to save others as they are to help these in their supplications to the inexorable appointment-clerk (*Essays*, 106).

When he shifts his attention from setting to character, Adams makes use of a more personal attack, just as he did in "Captain John Smith." Here, however, the sharp wit and the seemingly charitable pose hold the reader until the didactic spokesman completes his message with a threat:

> There is little satisfaction in striking at a fallen man, and Mr. Hale is now fallen so low that an assailant must stoop far to reach him. It would be pleasanter now to pass him by and abstain from pointing a moral at his expense; but in this case Mr. Hale was the representative of a class which must be struck wherever it can be reached, by every legitimate weapon, until it is beaten into insignificance, or the hope of reform may be abandoned at the outset (*Essays*, 117).

By far the most famous of Adams's rhetorical techniques—
usually associated only with the *Education*—is a mordant irony.
Already in "Civil Service Reform," however, the careful reader
can detect signs of the master ironist. Developing his attack on
the party of patronage, Adams first factually narrates the activities of the Grand Army of the Republic, which gathered evidence
against employees of the government who were already in office
when Grant became President. Then, with no real warning, the
essayist begins to shift from factual reporting to ironic judgment:

> [The G. A. R.] . . . then made a formal demand upon the
> United States government, through the heads of depart-
> ments, denouncing, like Jacobins of the reign of terror, the
> criminals thus condemned without a hearing, and demand-
> ing their removal for the benefit of soldiers of the Grand
> Army.
>
> If there is anything in the most liberal view of this
> action that can be made to palliate or excuse the outrage, it
> would be well to make it known. The government owes it to
> its own dignity, if not to decency, to repel the idea that it
> could ever have tolerated any approach to such interference
> with its duties, while the mere suggestion that its action
> could have been affected by such a means is in itself so near
> an insult that it would not be fitting for the pages of this
> Review.

Of course "dignity" and "decency" had long before disappeared
from government, as the writer tells the reader elsewhere in the
essay. Nonetheless, Adams writes as though there might be still
some doubt about the guilt of the present government until, at
the last moment, he destroys this false suspense and dramatically
closes his case by playing the trump card. As a part of the essay,
he reprints the text of the document that the "Grand Army"
circulated to demand wholesale replacement of officeholders, a
demand to which every branch of government except the Treasury acceded.[22] In Adams's view the "Grand Army of the Republic" had scored a Pyrrhic victory by defeating the real
interests of the Republic from which it took its name. The irony
stands complete.

3.

Biographies and Novels

My wishes are for a quiet and literary life, as I believe that to
be the happiest and in this country not the least useful.

—Henry Adams,
Harvard College *Life Book,*
Class of 1858.

When in 1877 Henry Adams left Harvard and Boston to take
up a new career as a biographer and historian in Washington, he
felt that he was being drawn, as if by a powerful magnet, to the
real center of American power. Washington was the political
city where his ancestors had struggled with ambition and for
reputation. Once he had settled there, Henry felt comfortable
enough to call it home for the remainder of his life. But he did
not return the Adams family to power, at least not to the familiar
forms of political power; instead, Henry's presence in Washington signaled a new chapter in family history. This Adams was
present on the political scene only to act as an observer and
critic. Henry Adams came home to Washington to make his
mark not as a politician or statesman but as a serious man of
letters.

The most impressive single testimony to this high
ambition—Adams's nine-volume *History of the United States of
America During the Administrations of Jefferson and Madison,*
completed in 1891—requires extended discussion, which will
appear in the following chapter. Between 1877 and 1891, Adams
also wrote *The Life of Albert Gallatin* (1879), *John Randolph*
(1882), a lost biography of Aaron Burr, and two novels, *Democ-*

racy: An American Novel (1880) and *Esther: A Novel* (1884); and he edited *The Writings of Albert Gallatin* (1879). Of these, the two published biographies and the two novels are especially significant because they illustrate their author's development toward full mastery of complex literary strategies and reveal the persuasive vitality of Adams family thought.

The fact of Henry's being an Adams actually played a key part in the decision of Albert Rolaz Gallatin, the only surviving son, to commission him to write the first biography of Jefferson's Secretary of Treasury. Since his father's death in 1849, the younger Gallatin "had not been able to find anyone competent to write his history and with whom I was willing to trust his papers. Your name of Adams was all sufficient for me to place the most implicit confidence in your discretion, integrity and talents." [1] The finished *Gallatin* brought another invitation, this time to write a life of John Randolph for the American Statesmen Series. Together, the two biographies, in many ways so different, took their place finally as a handsome complement to the more ambitious *History*. In all these studies, Adams benefited from his unique advantage of free access to that rich treasury of family opinions and ideas that he had at hand in family archives. For John and John Quincy Adams had shared their historic times with Gallatin and Randolph, and all four had helped to influence events in the *History*.

In the family documents, Albert Gallatin first appeared as a leading opponent of President John Adams's administration. He was viewed with distrust, and even suspected of dark intrigues, by John and Abigail Adams, who labeled him "the sly, the artful, the insidious Gallatin." [2] A generation later, however, John Quincy found in Gallatin a man of supreme ability and, more particularly, of controlled emotions—a man whose superior balance of character the Adams diarist noted with admiration. Analyzing his own conduct at Ghent, for example, John Quincy found that he had too often given way to "temper" and "irritability," while the diplomatic Gallatin "throws off my heat with a joke." A few years later, however, John Quincy, ever skeptical, began to suspect that Gallatin was moved by the same forces of personal ambition that all the Adamses recognized in themselves. When Gallatin opposed the Monroe administration by advocating naval and financial support for Greece, Secretary of State John Quincy Adams thought he detected hidden reasons:

> I look for the motives of this strange proposal, and find them not very deeply laid. Mr. Gallatin still builds castles in the air of popularity, and, being under no responsibility for consequences, patronizes the Greek cause for the sake of raising his own reputation.[3]

Yet, despite political differences, Gallatin was clearly a man of special talents, which impressed themselves upon all of the Adamses in turn. John Quincy's son, Charles, described the family's reactions to a political dinner with several congressmen present: "These men disgusted us all, even my father was out of patience. Mr. Gallatin's wit was thrown away upon hogs and I should scarcely have blamed him had he taken his invitation to meet such company as an insult to his character."[4] Called on to be Gallatin's biographer, then, Henry Adams was prepared to offer, even before he began any additional research, a well-documented consensus of family views: though he sometimes opposed the interests of the Adamses, Albert Gallatin was a man of sound character and great ability, who had proved his value in American politics.

In the case of John Randolph, on the other hand, the family papers painted a far less flattering portrait—from the time of the second President, Randolph had been marked down as an enemy to all the Adamses. John Adams labeled this follower of Thomas Paine a "disciple of Terrorism," and accused him of "treating me, with the Utmost Contempt." The violence and irresponsibility of Randolph's frequent attacks puzzled Adams, who claimed he could not "sound . . . the Language of John Randolph and Major Sheffey." Indignantly, Adams exclaimed to Jefferson, "What do these ignorant Boys mean by the 'Profligacy of John Adams's Administration?' Randolph and Sheffey accuse John Adams of Profligacy!"[5] The thought was too much to bear in silence. John Quincy Adams, in his turn, studied Randolph as a fellow congressman and declared in 1804 that "Mr. John Randolph has been raving all this session."[6] Over the next twenty-five years, the tone of the diary entries became decidedly more bitter, as the heir of John Adams observed this strange specimen of man, who used "tricksy humors to make himself conspicuous" and resorted to "besotted violence," which "excluded him thenceforward from all right to personal civility from me." With a conviction that denied all appeal, John Quincy summed up the Southerner in a diary entry for July 26, 1828: "Randolph is the image and superscription of a great man stamped upon base metal."

Randolph and those who willingly followed his lead betrayed every Adams ideal. They represented a continuing threat to the principles of the Constitution. "Clay's project is that in which John Randolph failed, to control or overthrow the Executive by swaying the House of Representatives."[7] Even more, they enjoyed the demagogic power of controlling or "swaying" other men, an especially dangerous threat to democratic government because it elevated the use of persuasive rhetoric over all appeals to logic and reason. Just that power in Randolph disgusted John Quincy Adams, who recorded his account of the Virginian's histrionics in words that no later biographer of Randolph could easily ignore:

> His speech, as usual, had neither beginning, middle, nor end. Egotism, Virginian aristocracy, slave-scourging liberty, religion, literature, science, wit, fancy, generous feelings, and malignant passions constitute a chaos in his mind, from which nothing orderly can ever flow. . . . It was useless to call him to order: he can no more keep order than he can keep silence.[8]

Again when Charles Francis Adams visited his father in Washington, the son could not escape a kindred fascination with the persuasive force of Randolph: "He makes beautiful speeches, there is more of real parliamentary eloquence in him than in any one in the House." Of course Charles was too much an Adams to be taken in by mere rhetoric; nor was he ignorant of the antipathy that the Southerner had so often displayed toward the Adams family. Yet, in spite of both considerations, the diarist described John Randolph with more pity than bitterness:

He is a man with no argument, but a great deal of shrewd
observation and cutting satire. . . . I am obliged to consider
him a great man although he has been a violent opponent
to my race. . . . We look at him as a crumbled pillar,
mourning over the loss of it's [*sic*] own beauty and jealous
of the more modern and perhaps less pure ones.[9]

Many years later, when Charles Francis Adams described to
Charles Francis II the qualifications of the ideal statesman, he
listed: first, the "mastery of the whole theory of morals," and
second, "the application of the knowledge thus gained to the
events of his time in a continuous and systematic way." By these
criteria, John Quincy Adams represented, in his son's view, "the
only picture of a full grown statesman that the history of the
United States has yet produced." John Randolph, to the contrary, always remained in Charles Francis's opinion the foremost
of political "failures," who "never acquire sufficient certainty of
purpose to be able to guide their steps at all"; he was, in fact, a
"mere sport of fortune."[10]

For his own part, John Randolph never spared the feelings
of the Adams family. He raged bitterly about the "American
House of Stuart," as he labeled the Adamses. He fought the
Presidents, father and son, and sought to repay every protest of
theirs with his own ration of contempt for the New Englanders.
In short, he made it quite impossible for any Adams who was
stirred by family pride to undertake the task of writing a
biography of Randolph without assuming the position of a
disputant in the long-standing family feud.

The Life of Albert Gallatin and *John Randolph*

In addition to the rich historical record—public and
private—that Henry Adams used in writing his biographies, he
also employed a more specialized set of beliefs concerning the
study and practice of history. These conscious and unconscious
attitudes grew from his experiences as student, teacher, essayist,
and, most of all, as an Adams. His letter to a favorite Harvard
pupil, written in 1873, explained: "America or Europe, our own

century or prehistoric time, are all alike to the historian if he can only find out what men are and have been driving at, consciously or unconsciously."[11] *Randolph* and *Gallatin* were meant to be historical in just this way. Both books were written as case studies, although of very different men. Each man, in turn, could be seen as the representative of a largely unchanging type of human character, and each life provided adequate literary material for a modern morality, taught to readers of the author's own day.

For Adams, John Randolph emerged as a potentially great man, flawed by a fatal inner division that ultimately doomed him to political failure and made his story finally incomprehensible: ". . . one is forced to believe that in this Virginian character there were two sides, so completely distinct that the one had no connection with the other."[12] His actions violated every principle that he professed, and his "self-contradictions" constantly brought Randolph to grief. According to Adams,

> . . . between his Anglican tastes and his Gallican policy he was in a false position, as he was also between his aristocratic prejudices and his democratic theories, his deistical doctrines and his conservative temperament, his interests as a slave-owner and his theories as an *ami des noirs*, and finally in the entire delusion which possessed his mind that a Virginian aristocracy could maintain itself in alliance with a democratic polity (*Randolph*, 33).

While showing real sympathy for Randolph's principles when they seemed noble, Adams could not overcome his shock at seeing them so often perverted in action. Such a mind without logic and a character without balance (both qualities that so often had figured in the pages of earlier Adams family journals) offered the biographer no real basis for portraiture except that of enigma: "Or, to sum up all these questions in one, was Randolph capable of remaining true to any principle or any friendship that required him to control his violent temper and imperious will?" (*Randolph*, 136).

Yet to answer for Randolph only would be to mistake the biographer's real purpose. Adams's apparent fascination with

Randolph's character actually masks an obsessive desire to understand the Southern politician—a type utterly different from the Adams breed of New England statesmen and from the class of pioneer scientific administrators represented by Albert Gallatin. Gallatin's contemporary evaluation of Randolph, for example, was remarkably similar to Henry Adams's own: ". . . the eccentricities and temper of J. Randolph soon destroyed his usefulness. . . ." [13]

Whereas Adams shaped *Randolph* into the case study of a human type that puzzled and disgusted him, the feelings behind *Gallatin* were exactly opposite. The later biography gave its author the opportunity to admire in a detached way a man who more than measured up to family standards, whose life offered many useful lessons for Adams's own time. Twenty years after the book was first published, the author confessed just how highly he rated Gallatin, after meeting with a descendant of "old Albert Gallatin, to whose sacred memory I've shown a respect and devotion that I never thought proper to show my own kith. . . ." [14]

Unlike Randolph, Gallatin possessed the advantages of good education, severe (Genevan) moral training, and a family tradition of public service. The biographer, working with a figure so much like a member of his own family, soon realized that he had undertaken a twofold job: first, to establish Gallatin's greatness; and second, to show what had happened to this man of outstanding ability and character during a particular period in American life. Early in the book, Adams foreshadows his completed tragedy when, in describing the young Gallatin on the verge of leaving Geneva for America in 1780, he paints a picture familiar to every reader of the Adams diaries and letters, a picture of self-sacrifice:

> The act [of leaving] was not a wise one. That future which the young Gallatin grasped so eagerly with outstretched arms had little in it that even to an ardent imagination at nineteen could compensate for the wanton sacrifice it involved. There is no reason to suppose that Albert Gallatin's career was more brilliant or more successful in America than with the same efforts and with equal sacrifices it might

have been in Europe; for his character and abilities must have insured pre-eminence in whatever path he chose (*Gallatin*, 18).

Adams goes on to show that Gallatin's great abilities served his high principles during every phase of his career. He braved personal danger to defy rebellion in the Pittsburgh meeting of 1794, became a party leader in Congress by 1801 and later the foremost Secretary of the Treasury after Hamilton, and finally ended his career as a diplomatic envoy in Europe—all with great distinction, according to Adams, but not with unbroken success. Yet the biographer remains less concerned with recounting Gallatin's political triumphs and defeats than with analyzing those personal qualities that made him generally useful to his adopted nation. Speaking of the statesman's congressional career, 1795–1801, Adams says, "In some respects it was without a parallel in our history," because Gallatin, a foreigner by birth, was able to seize and hold the leadership of his party "by the sheer force of ability and character, without ostentation and without the tricks of popularity . . ." (*Gallatin*, 154). With a fine touch of ironic drama, Adams is able to prove that such mastery by "ability and character" contrasts sharply with a less admirable type of power, the force personified in John Randolph of Virginia, who maintained his mastery in debate and over his party by his "dogmatic and overbearing temper and . . . powers of sarcasm or invective" (*Gallatin*, 154).

Gallatin's power, not surprisingly, had very different roots: "His power lay in courage, honesty of purpose, and thoroughness of study. Undoubtedly his mind was one of rare power, . . . a mind for which no principle was too broad and no detail too delicate; but it was essentially a scientific and not a political mind" (*Gallatin*, 154). This "scientific mind" had sometimes led Gallatin into political trouble because the usual business of government was anything but scientific. As an example, Adams cites Gallatin's opposition, based on principles of sound finance, to the construction of the naval frigates "Constitution," "Constellation," and "United States." In principle, this opposition had been entirely justified, but Adams shows that Gallatin's position finally did not accord with higher national interests.

Politics and history proved Gallatin wrong when the three frigates later provided America's only shred of "national dignity" in the sea-wars with France and England. Good science and good politics were not necessarily identical.

Just as Randolph's irrational and vindictive temper often led him to serious mistakes and inconsistencies, so too great a reliance on scientific qualities of logic and close-reasoning proved to be Gallatin's major fault.

> . . . government has to deal with beings ruled not only by reason but by feeling, and its success depends on the degree to which it can satisfy or at least compromise between the double standard of criticism. Mr. Gallatin habitually made too little allowance for the force and the complexity of human passions and instincts. Self-contained and self-reliant himself, and, like most close reasoners, distrustful of everything that had a mere feeling for its justification, he held government down to an exact observance of rules that made no allowance for national pride (*Gallatin*, 171).

Another part of the "pride" for which Gallatin failed to allow sufficiently was regional; he did not fully comprehend the potent forces of American political regionalism, especially as regionalism showed itself in the Senate during the period when Gallatin was serving in the executive branch.

To explain Gallatin's plight, Adams turns the clock back to consider a parallel situation in the administration of John Adams, when the threat of a national conflict seemed equally ominous:

> It was not unlike the great contest of ten years before between John Adams and a similar group of Senators; it went through a similar phase, and in each case the result was dependent on the question of war or peace. There are few more interesting contrasts of character in our history than that between the New England President, with his intense personality and his overpowering bursts of passion, confronting his enemies with a will that could not control or even mask its features, and "the Genevan," as the Aurora

called him, calm, reticent, wary, never vehement, full of
resource, ignoring enmity, hating strife. Perhaps a combination of two such characters, if they could have been made
to work in harmony, might have proved too much even for
the Senate; and, if so, a problem in American history might
have been solved, for, as it was, the Senate succeeded in
overthrowing both (*Gallatin*, 411).

What is most significant here is not the appeal to past history,
even family history, to explain Gallatin's difficulty. Henry
Adams goes beyond the obvious point of historical similarity,
first to contrast their characters, while suggesting the idea of
limitations in both men, a notion which implicitly underlies the
fact that each "contest" developed to a point of national crisis;
and second, to teach Adams's own contemporaries a lesson in
practical politics.

Put briefly, an harmonious combination of the qualities of
Albert Gallatin and John Adams would have provided just that
"balance" that each lacked alone—a balance that "might" also
have insured their success and prevented their failure. At the
same time, this ideal balance of qualities "might have" provided
a solution to the continuing "problem in American history."
The author's tentativeness is worth noting. His final sentence is
prefaced with "perhaps" and twice qualified with "might"; and
once the hypothesis has been introduced, the biographer simply
retires from his essay in conjecture, to resume the narrative of
Gallatin's life. He does not decide the point for his reader. In
making the more general suggestion that Gallatin's real power
did not depend upon the sordid business of practical politics,
Adams was of course restating the family position in favor of
personal independence. For, in the biographer's view, Gallatin
never considered himself a party man. He had served in Congress
when "there was no such party tyranny as grew up afterwards in
American politics" (*Gallatin*, 214). When his principles seemed
about to be overruled by party policies, he simply withdrew from
the Treasury and from all politics. His biographer once had
hoped for effective reform from Grant because "he was tied to no
party" and from the political independents who could effect
reforms in the party system. In each case Henry Adams believed

that some kind of personal detachment was absolutely necessary to the political reformer, as much as to the revisionist historian, who wrote (as in "Captain John Smith") to correct mistakes in the historical record. Perhaps because he saw in Gallatin a kindred spirit, separated from the cruder energies of life, the biographer turned Gallatin's story into something of a mirror for himself. Gallatin's life took shape as almost a textbook lesson about what might happen if Henry Adams chose to follow the political path.

When Adams turned his attention away from the men themselves, he made of *Gallatin* and *Randolph* a series of capsule essays on questions of politics, past and present. As in the later *Education*, here the supple handling of apparently time-bound questions is truly remarkable; the author manages to point his discussions both backward, to moments in the Adams family past, and forward, to his own day, all the while keeping his biographical focus clear. Perhaps the easiest approach to Adams's artistry in the biographies is to study his treatment of a few key political topics, such as the question of slavery. Certainly no other political subject dealt with by Adams has received so much attention from his critics, who have even suggested that "Captain John Smith" and *John Randolph* should be read as strategic battles in the four-generation Adams family crusade against slavery and slaveholders.[15] Yet this view fails to appreciate the consistent antislavery argument found in Henry Adams's other works, among them *Gallatin* and the *Education*. Beginning with his earliest legislative service, Adams tells us approvingly, Albert Gallatin always stood for the abolition of slavery. His moral condemnation of that peculiar institution was unmistakably identical to the position of the Adams family; Gallatin's official report of 1790, which his biographer reprints in part, could easily have appeared in the pages of an Adams diary: "Slavery is inconsistent with every principle of humanity, justice, and right, and repugnant to the spirit and express letter of the constitution of this Commonwealth [Pennsylvania]."[16] By 1880, when Adams told the story, the moral and constitutional questions had been decided—in favor of the Adams-Gallatin principles.

Yet other important constitutional questions remained unresolved, such as those the author had considered earlier in "Civil Service Reform." In fact, the dangerous perversion of John Adams's old constitutional principle of balance of powers between the executive and legislative branches now loomed larger in Henry Adams's mind, and he feared a wholesale increase of congressional power at the expense of all executive control. Already, in foreign affairs, for example, the Senate had taken from the President those treaty-making powers that had provided the key to the success of Jefferson and Gallatin at the time of the Louisiana Purchase of 1803.[17] By telling the story of that achievement, Adams hoped to show why the American system was currently threatened. Randolph had always attacked executive power (and with it, the Presidents Adams) and sought to weaken all centralist interpretations of the Constitution. In Henry Adams's view, Randolph stood for the "prostitution to the base uses of the slave power" of an otherwise legitimate doctrine of states' rights, when between the two, there was "no necessary connection" (*Randolph*, 178-79). Perfected by Calhoun, this egregious doctrine first led to the treason of secession; next, to the even more irrational test of the Civil War; and finally, to those postwar perversions of the Constitution that Henry Adams found in the politics of his own day. At the source of this long causal chain, he placed the illogical mind of John Randolph.

But Adams also knew that Gallatin shared much of Randolph's distrust of executive power:

> . . . Mr. Gallatin never changed his opinion that the President was too powerful; even in his most mature age he would probably have preferred a system more nearly resembling some of the present colonial governments of Great Britain (*Gallatin*, 79).

Yet there was one important difference, traceable to the superior quality of Gallatin's mind. His distrust became a principle that he could act upon in 1796, by opposing the Federalists and Jay's treaty, but that he pragmatically reexamined and sometimes had to ignore after taking executive office himself in 1801. Adams identifies this conflict between constitutional principle and personal action as the grand irony of Gallatin's career. Speaking of his situation in 1799, Adams says:

> The time came when Mr. Gallatin and his present opponents [Federalists] stood in positions precisely reversed, and when he was compelled by the force of circumstances to ask for powers quite as dangerous as those he was now arguing against. Congress granted them, and he exercised them, greatly against his will and amid the denunciations of his Federalist enemies (*Gallatin*, 220).

And Gallatin was not alone. For after taking power, the Jeffersonians, including Gallatin, were driven to adopt new courses of action, until, by the time of the Embargo Act of 1808, the Republicans and Federalists "had completely changed their position . . ." (*Gallatin*, 379).

Finally, then, Adams uses the negative and positive values of Randolph and Gallatin to teach a single overriding lesson in constitutional interpretation—the lesson of necessary change. Just as "Civil Service Reform" had pointed out the practical limitations of applying John Adams's principle of balanced powers in a later age, so the biographies acknowledge that historical necessity sometimes dictates a change of principles to national leaders, as in the case of the Louisiana Purchase. Of course, in reaching this conclusion, the biographer had himself been forced to modify his original beliefs. The idea of retaining indefinitely the original limits of power no longer seemed sufficient after the Civil War, and in 1870 Adams publicly confessed that he found "little doubt that the great political problem of all ages cannot, at least in a community like that of the future American, be solved by the theory of the American Constitution."[18] For the great-grandson of John Adams, this was an important concession. His strict constructionist philosophy had been overcome by his perception of new forces at work in American life, new forms of power, undreamed of during John Adams's eighteenth century. Now, America's giant corporations controlled the power to "trample on law, custom, decency, and every restraint known to society, without scruple, and as yet without check." Moreover,

> Under the American form of society no authority exists capable of effective resistance. The national government, in order to deal with the corporations, must assume powers refused to it by its fundamental law,—and even then is exposed to the chance of forming an absolute central government which sooner or later is likely to fall into the hands it is struggling to escape, and thus destroy the limits of its power only in order to make corruption omnipotent.[19]

Gallatin and Randolph too had watched the operation of "social forces" that had wrought "fatal changes in the Constitution." Randolph had failed to respond in action or belief; thus his biographer treats the last half of the Southerner's life as nothing more significant than a tale of human waste: "To follow him through five-and-twenty years of miserable discontent and growing eccentricities would be time thrown away" (*Randolph*, 130). And twenty pages later: "To pursue Randolph's course farther through the meanderings of his opposition would be waste of time" (*Randolph*, 156). Three of the last four chapters in the book are titled: "A Nuisance and a Curse," "Eccentricities," and "Faculties Misemployed." Clearly, the career of this Virginian finally displayed no progress toward those human ideals the biographer had learned to respect. In Gallatin, on the other hand, Adams found "essentially a scientific and not a political mind," a subject who seemed well equipped to control and use the forces of change that entered his life. In fact, the best abilities of the man showed themselves only in his later years, when Gallatin renounced politics and devoted himself instead to the new sciences of his day:

> Perhaps one might not wander very far from the truth if one added that these pursuits [scientific] were, on the whole, his most permanent claim to distinction . . . he was the father of American ethnology, and there has been no time since his death when the little band of his followers have forgotten

him; there never can come a time when students of that subject can venture to discard his work.

The reason of this steadiness in the estimate of his scientific reputation is simply that his method was sound and his execution accurate . . . (*Gallatin*, 643-44).

More than anything he achieved in politics, Gallatin's late activity in science provided the real source for the biographer's admiration. And the final lines of the passage, moreover, present an important key to Adams's judgment. For his own training as an historian and biographer had made him appreciate the values of the scientific method, even while he remained reluctant to engage in a discussion of science itself.

What seems strange today is that the biographer made so little use of the acknowledged superiority of Gallatin's science over his politics. In part Adams's own lack of familiarity with science might have been to blame, except that the example of the Lyell review showed his ability to grapple with the complexities of scientific theory when he set himself to the task. Instead, Adams's pessimistic inclinations led him to insist upon treating the story of Gallatin not as the tale of a scientific hero who only late in life found his proper vocation but rather as the human tragedy of political failure, an admirable man whose career neatly paralleled the lives of Henry's own forebears. Finally, Adams used Gallatin to prove that men of good character and great ability should expect to be defeated in the political arena by the impersonal forces of time and change. In "Civil Service Reform" Adams had recognized that political power no longer served morality; rather, power had become a function of party, a change which Randolph, who "prided himself on independence," simply failed to comprehend, thus opening the way to his pitiful end. But Gallatin's story was different and far more complex. Most of all, it offered a series of lessons that the biographer could not ignore, lessons that other statesmen besides Gallatin had learned in painful fashion:

He [Gallatin] had yet to pass through his twelve years of struggle and disappointment in order to learn how his own followers and his own President were to answer his ideal, when the same insolence of foreign dictation and the same violence of a recalcitrant party presented to their and to his own lips the cup of which John Adams was now draining the dregs (*Gallatin*, 266).

As Adams describes him, Gallatin had lost "that sublime confidence in human nature which had given to Mr. Jefferson and his party their single irresistible claim to popular devotion. His statesmanship had become, what practical statesmanship always has and must become, a mere struggle to deal with concrete facts at the cost of philosophic and *a priori* principles" (*Gallatin*, 560). Once the evidence had been set down, Adams concluded with a moral epigram worthy of his forebears: "There are moments in politics when great results can be reached only by small men" (*Gallatin*, 432).

A parallel case could be found in the diary of grandfather John Quincy Adams, who recorded his own disillusionment over the success of English Minister Bagot, a man of inferior abilities, and a polar opposite to Gallatin: "the mediocrity of his [Bagot's] talents has been one of the principal causes of his success. This is so obvious that it has staggered my belief in the universality of the maxim that men of the greatest talents ought to be sought out for diplomatic missions." When Gallatin came to review his career, he also fixed upon this inability to translate his own principles into meaningful actions. In a letter to a lifelong friend, he observed: "As to the world, I have been, like you, disappointed in the estimate I had formed of the virtue of mankind and of its influence over others. Every day's experience convinces us that most unprincipled men are often most successful."[20]

Looking closely at John Randolph's career, Adams could locate the cause for failure in a debilitating lack of emotional and intellectual balance, the effect being an almost total destruction of character and mind. Randolph provided an awful warning, a confirmation by negative example of the family truism: the effective statesman must be a balanced man. His fundamental deficiencies in character, then, much more than any enmity to the Adamses, finally limited Randolph's usefulness as a comparative case for either John or John Quincy Adams. In

Gallatin, on the contrary, the biographer found it easy to measure his subject by the standards of the Adams family, sometimes to the advantage of John or John Quincy and at other times to demonstrate Gallatin's superiority. Commonly, the author paired Gallatin with John Quincy Adams because the two had so often shared the same political scene. Despite six years' difference in age and differences in temperament and background, "there was nevertheless a curious parallelism in the lives and characters of the two men, which, notwithstanding every jar, compelled them to move side by side and to agree in policy and opinion even while persuading themselves that their aims and methods were radically divergent" (*Gallatin,* 496).

To Henry Adams, J. Q. Adams and Albert Gallatin represented a single type of high-minded statesman, now rendered obsolete by the catastrophic changes in American politics since their day:

> During nearly twelve years they continued to work together in the management of our foreign relations. The irruption of President Jackson and his political following threw them both out of public life; . . . Both were then non-partisan; both held very strong convictions in regard to the duties and the short-comings of the day; both died near the same time, the last relics of the early statesmanship of the republic (*Gallatin,* 497).

The best proof of their combined value to the nation showed up during the negotiations at Ghent in 1814, which Henry Adams described chiefly by relying on his grandfather's diary:

> The negotiation with the British commissioners was, however, much more simple than the negotiation with one another; of the first the diplomatic notes and protocols give a fair description, but of the last a far more entertaining account is given in the Diary of John Quincy Adams. The accident which placed Mr. Gallatin at the foot of the commission placed Mr. Adams at its head,—a result peculiarly unfortunate, because, even if the other commissioners

had conceded respect to the age, the services, and the tact of Mr. Gallatin, they had no idea of showing any such deference to Mr. Adams. From the outset it was clear that Messrs. Bayard, Clay, and Russell meant to let Mr. Adams understand that though he might be the nominal mouth-piece he was not the autocrat of the commission, and their methods of conveying this information were such as in those days Mr. Clay was celebrated for successfully using. Mr. Adams had little of Mr. Gallatin's capacity for pacifying strife; he was by nature as combative as Mr. Clay, and before the commission separated there were exciting and very amusing scenes of collision, in one of which Mr. Adams plainly intimated his opinion of the conduct of his colleagues, and Mr. Clay broke out upon him with: "You *dare* not, you *cannot*, you SHALL not insinuate that there has been a cabal of three members against you!"

In this affair Mr. Gallatin's situation was delicate in the highest degree. All recognized the fact that he was properly head of the mission; his opinion carried most weight; his pen was most in demand; his voice was most patiently heard. The tact with which he steered his way between the shoals that surrounded him is the most remarkable instance in our history of perfect diplomatic skill; even Dr. Franklin, in a very similar situation, had not the same success. In no instance did Mr. Gallatin allow himself to be drawn into the conflicts of his colleagues, and yet he succeeded in sustaining Mr. Adams in every essential point without appearing to do so. When the negotiation was closed, all his four colleagues were united, at least to outward appearance, in cordiality to him, and Mr. Adams had reason to be, and seems in fact always to have been, positively grateful. If Mr. Clay felt differently, as there was afterwards reason to believe, he showed no such feeling at the time. The story as told in Mr. Adams's Diary proves clearly enough that this delicate tact of Mr. Gallatin probably saved the treaty (*Gallatin*, 521–22).

This passage is quoted at unusual length because it represents such a rich sampling of the biographer's art. Adams's treatment includes a weighing of public and private accounts in order to reach a more nearly objective consensus on individual character; comparison of an event with a parallel drawn from family history—here, the "very similar situation" of 1778, when as part of the American Commission to France, John Adams and Franklin acted together as official negotiators despite their great personal differences, many of which John Adams indignantly recorded in his own diary; and finally, an acknowledgment of Gallatin's greater usefulness as a practical statesman at Ghent, a fact that finally both John Quincy (in his diary) and Henry Adams (in *Gallatin*) were willing to concede. Like so much of *Gallatin*, the passage pays a handsome compliment to a superior statesman.

In *John Randolph*, Adams insisted on the superiority of the New England statesman type (including the Adams Presidents) over the Virginia politician.[21] In the Gallatin biography, however, Adams was not bound by the problem of a family feud nor by an obvious case for regional prejudice. Gallatin was a Genevan by birth, and this independence of American regional limitations, especially in political attitudes, actually functioned to his advantage; he was able to decide political questions without being influenced by any sectional bias. His unusual freedom of thought, in turn, accounted for much of Gallatin's effectiveness as a statesman and helped him to develop what Adams chose to call a truly "scientific" mind. Even more to the point, Gallatin's advantage opened to the biographer much greater opportunities for a free play of his own historical speculation than any regional subject could have provided. In both books, of course, the writer's prejudices played an important part. But the difference between the two is unmistakable: Gallatin filled the biographer's preconceived ideals of the statesman; Randolph did not.

Adams summed up *John Randolph* in these words: "I am bored to death by correcting the proofs of a very dull book about John Randolph, the fault of which is in the enforced obligation to take that lunatic monkey *au sérieux*."[22] Of *Gallatin*, Adams always held a different view:

> To do justice to Gallatin was a labor of love. After long study of the prominent figures in our history, I am more

than ever convinced that for combination of ability, integrity, knowledge, unselfishness, and social fitness Mr. Gallatin has no equal. He was the most fully and perfectly equipped statesman we can show. Other men, as I take hold of them, are soft in some spots and rough in others. Gallatin never gave way in my hand or seemed unfinished. That he made mistakes I can see, but even in his blunders he was respectable.[23]

From the facts about this complex man, Adams selected out for retelling all that was needed to complete a timeless moral and intellectual drama, from which one lesson emerged most clearly:

To my mind the moral of his life lies a little deeper than party politics and I have tried here and there rather to suggest than to assert it. The inevitable isolation and disillusionment of a really strong mind—one that combines force with elevation—is to me the romance and tragedy of statesmanship. The politician who goes to his grave without suspecting his own limitations, is not a picturesque figure; he is only an animal. . . . Gallatin was greater, because he could and did refuse power when he found out what vanity it was, and yet became neither a cynic nor a transcendental philosopher.[24]

Probably no other subject outside of his own family could have taught the biographer so much about the meaning of being an Adams.

Democracy and Esther

By themselves, Henry Adams's studies in biography and history were not sufficient to satisfy his interest in literary expression; thus he also tried his hand at fiction, writing two novels, Democracy (1880) and Esther (1884).[25] Both books center on female characters; the two may be read together as the author's most extensive commentary on the value and influence of the feminine presence in the world prior to the publication of Mont-Saint-Michel and Chartres. The biographies and the

History did not offer Adams much of an opportunity to study historical women, and Henry, in part because of his own marriage but also because he had long admired the women in his family, such as Abigail and Louisa Catherine Adams, certainly regretted the omission in his literary representation of American life. He felt that the Adams women had never received full public credit or appreciation and that the family tradition had always unfairly emphasized masculine achievements and ideals. In his novels, he had an opportunity to explore the warmer world of distaff values and to pay a chivalrous compliment to the Adams women (not the least impressive of whom was his wife). These women provided examples, past and present, of benign human force caught up in a hostile social and intellectual environment. Much in the manner of *Gallatin*, the story of Adams's novelistic heroines was also the story of himself, as we shall see. When each heroine fails to win out or even to adjust satisfactorily her ideals and hopes to surrounding circumstances, she is showing the reader a real or imagined plight that their author pictured as his own. Almost as much as the later *Education*, the novels tell us about Henry's failure to make of his Adams heritage a sufficient rationale for effective action in the world. As the Horatio Alger stories provided programmatic explanations of how to succeed, so Adams's novels taught the lesson of how to fail.

Adams sought to hide his authorship of both novels from all except his closest personal friends. His secret pleased him not only because it served to protect his reputation as a serious historian but also because it kept him free of the notoriety surrounding the immensely popular *Democracy*. Instead, authorship became something of a private joke, played upon in letters to John Hay, who shared the secret. Yet Adams was fundamentally serious about keeping this secret; his annoyance when he feared that a careless friend had revealed his authorial identity was real enough.[26] But another part of Adams wanted public acclaim; as late as 1905, he was still bragging about the only work of his (the *Education* was not yet written) to achieve some measure of popularity: "The wholesale piracy of *Democracy* was the single real triumph of my life."[27] Four years after *Democracy*, Adams published *Esther* under the pseudonym

Frances Snow Compton. Adams claimed that book was an "experiment," a test of the reading public (as "Civil Service Reform" had tested the political power of public opinion) to see whether a serious novel could find a sizable audience without the benefit of advertising or a well-known author's name. "My experiment has failed," Adams declared in 1885, but in the same letter he also called for an English edition of *Esther*.[28] In 1886, just after the death of his wife Marian, who had helped him to plan *Democracy* and whose special qualities of character and personality found their way into the heroine of *Esther*, Adams explained both his strong personal attachment to that novel and his desire to protect the secret of its authorship:

> Perhaps I made a mistake even to tell King about it [*Esther*]; but having told him, I could not leave you out. Now, let it die! To admit the public to it would be almost unendurable to me. I will not pretend that the book is not precious to me, but its value has nothing to do with the public who could never understand that such a book might be written in one's heart's blood. Do not even imagine that I scorn the public, as you say. Twenty years ago, I would have been glad to please it. Today, and for more than a year past, I have been and am living with not a thought but from minute to minute; and the public is as far away from me as the celebrated Kung-fu-tse. . . .[29]

The reading public certainly had not been so far from the author's thoughts in 1880, when *Democracy* first appeared, offering a fictional treatment of recent, post–Civil War politics in Washington. In fact, the book analyzed the political situation of Adams's own day almost schematically, for the benefit of both the heroine and the reader, who shares in her political education throughout. In brief, the story combines Madeleine Lee's search to find the real meaning of democracy with a conventional tale of romance—a contest for Madeleine's hand, waged between two political men of sharply contrasting types: Ratcliffe, the modern politician who wields the power to make government work; and Carrington, the old-fashioned Southern statesman, now left without political position or power, a political idealist rather than a pragmatist. Madeleine Lee arrives in Washington having already rejected the sterile intellectual atmosphere of Boston and the crass business life of her native New York. She has also suffered personally through the death of her husband and of their only child, and now at the age of thirty she feels herself to be as hard and as unyielding as "pure steel." She is altogether ready to undertake a new and far more ambitious role at the center of American politics: "What she wanted, was POWER" (*Democracy*, 9).

Drawn like Adams himself to the seat of power, Madeleine discovers that her best opportunity to exercise real political power is represented by the prospect of a marriage to Senator Ratcliffe, who in the course of the book becomes Secretary of the Treasury (surely an echo of *Gallatin*) and who leaves no doubt about his ambition to be President. Intelligent, wealthy, and attractive, Madeleine soon finds herself getting deeper and deeper into politics; she begins as an observer and quickly becomes a participant, a key figure in a developing political drama. What seems at first her dispassionate study of power, carried out in a detached spirit of intellectual curiosity, soon threatens to destroy Madeleine's emotional and intellectual stability, and finally her most basic moral being. For her, the price of political education is high, perhaps too high. By telling her story, Henry Adams, the incorrigible political moralist of "Civil Service Reform," managed to piece together in his novel a much more forceful and pessimistic protest against the fate of Adams family ideals in an age of Ratcliffean politics.

In the novel, Adams weaves some of the materials from his earlier writings into a richer, more imaginative fabric. The moral and political hero of *Democracy*, for example, is Carrington, an impoverished Southerner, who first appears defeated and politically powerless in post–Civil War Washington—but who, despite temptations, remains throughout a man of principle. He is simply not for sale in a world where other men are all too easily bought and delivered. Of course, as a fictional character Carrington can be portrayed as Adams's ideal of the noble Southerner: Carrington is a loyal Virginian, but never a secessionist; a former Confederate soldier who fought bravely for his region and his political beliefs, but never for the cause of slavery. He is, in short, an admirable representative of the Old South—

the South of George Washington and Mount Vernon—or better, of that part of the south that shared with old New England the principles epitomized in the classic correspondence between Thomas Jefferson and John Adams.

Because of his rigid adherence to the old code of personal principles, Carrington has been defeated in past politics and now seems to be almost politically impotent. Yet even though he appears to be beaten by Ratcliffe's skillful maneuvering, Carrington at least has power enough to move Madeleine Lee to reject all that Ratcliffe offers her. Carrington's letter revealing that Ratcliffe has accepted a bribe makes Madeleine realize the true nature of her suitor: his total lack of moral principles, personal and political, turns her away from his offer of marriage and power. As Adams tells us, "Carrington was very well aware that the weak side of the Senator [Ratcliffe] lay in his blind ignorance of morals" (*Democracy*, 59-60). But both Madeleine and the reader have to be taught the real price of such ignorance.

The author of *Democracy* insists that the old regional values—like archaic personal principles—should not be simply forgotten in the postwar period. In particular, he choses to emphasize the similarities between pre–Civil War New England and Virginia; writing as an historian turned novelist, Adams shows that the fullest possible understanding of the past, including the human origins of character and action, still provides the most useful key to the present and the future. The political drama of the novel is acted out by characters who help us to measure how much American life has changed, since the Civil War most obviously, but since the time of the Adams Presidents as well. Ratcliffe, Carrington's chief opponent, represents not New England, where he was born, but his present home on the Western frontier, where a new political power is already emerging. This "Prairie Giant of Peonia" has displaced the old New Englander in power; he now seems ready to dominate the whole of the Republic. Again, a contrast in moral character between the Southern idealist and Western pragmatist works (together with a somewhat mechanical manipulation of setting) to establish Adams's point: The South that only recently presented itself as an enemy to the Union now seems to offer the best hope for a much-needed renaissance in American political life.

The contest for the hand of the heroine thus becomes a

struggle to determine the future course of the nation. Madeleine Lee's problem—to perceive and understand the moral and psychological makeup of her two suitors—represents the attempt of the novelist to evaluate the historical significance of the regions for which Carrington and Ratcliffe stand.

Most of all, Adams tries to demonstrate that Madeleine cannot simply be told the truth; she must be made to see for herself. Only gradually does she gain this personal understanding, until she arrives finally at a correct estimate of Ratcliffe:

> . . . The audacity of the man would have seemed sublime if she had felt sure that he knew the difference between good and evil, between a lie and the truth; but the more she saw of him, the surer she was that his courage was mere moral paralysis, and that he talked about virtue and vice as a man who is color-blind talks about red and green; he did not see them as she saw them; if left to choose for himself he would have nothing to guide him. Was it politics that had caused this atrophy of the moral senses by disuse? (*Democracy*, 194).

At this point in the novel, for the reader as much as for Madeleine, the ironic characterization of "The Prairie Giant of Peonia" has done its work. Ratcliffe, like John Randolph, is a regressive figure, a degenerate successor to President Washington (or a President Adams). Ratcliffe provides Henry Adams's affirmative answer to the question that Madeleine asks.

Ratcliffe's political power derives from a confident analysis of other men, his understanding of their motives, and from a pragmatic skill in managing their actions to suit his interests. Within the limits of politics, he is successful, even in manipulating a President. Yet, because he is morally "color-blind," he badly misjudges Carrington and Sybil (Madeleine's sister) and underestimates their power to protect Madeleine—all because their motives are not political. In the final, climactic scene, Ratcliffe encounters Madeleine alone, and, exerting all his charm and magnetic fascination, he offers the highest prize of which he can conceive, the greatest within his own system of purely political values: to become the wife of a President and the most powerful woman in the country. Her determined rejection shows the reader a different set of values, totally alien to Ratcliffe's life and thought: "Mr. Ratcliffe, I am not to be bought" (*Democracy*, 200).

Madeleine has renounced her ambition for power to join with Carrington and Sybil in actively affirming traditional moral principles. Defeated by this alliance of past and present, Ratcliffe loses his famous self-control, and suddenly bursts into a violent fit of temper, once the chief weakness of John Randolph and a flaw in character well understood by every reader of the Adams diaries. As he confronts the failure caused by his own misjudgment of human nature, Ratcliffe destroys every vestige of personal balance and creates a scandalous public scene, destined to end his career, by scuffling with a foreign diplomat on a public street. Like his hopes for marriage to Mrs. Lee, his chances for the presidency are dashed. Again, the derangement of Ratcliffe's faculties also shows itself in the crucial interview with Madeleine: a "heartless coquette," he twice calls the heroine, and in that epithet Adams's sense of irony finds its voice. For Ratcliffe's evaluation provides the final proof of his moral color-blindness, his inability to interpret human actions except by political motives. No label could be less appropriate for the sympathetic character of Madeleine Lee which Adams has developed. Already she has demonstrated "heart" by sacrificing all romantic interest in Carrington to Sybil, and now her denial of the temptation to wield power constitutes a final rejection of Ratcliffe on the very grounds of her heart—a heart that must be reckoned much larger than his.

The portrait of "The Honourable Silas P. Ratcliffe" offers modern evidence for John Adams's old belief in the inherent depravity of man. Ratcliffe's own immorality, moreover, is compounded by his failure to understand human nature and by an inability to view human character in any except a narrowly political way. Madeleine's moral success (which is almost undermined by her excessive ambition) rests upon a larger vision and better understanding. Even though the ending of the book is inconclusive, there remains at least a shred of hope in the hint of a forthcoming union between Madeleine and Carrington. For Adams, of course, the pending resolution of Madeleine Lee's problems, the best chance for her future, represents a public hope as well. The readers who share her point of view are the same public who should appreciate his message. But, like Madeleine, the public must first learn to judge political men as they really are, not as they claim to be. Here, the readers are helped along toward a rejection of merely pragmatic political values by Adams's inclusion of other figures who represent higher personal standards—such as the characters of Nathan Gore and Carrington himself—both of whom embody the older principles of personal honor and high moral conduct, which defined the political code of the Adams family.

In the contrast between Ratcliffe and Carrington, the novelist manages to build a strong case against the corrupting forces of change that by 1880 had perverted the older politics of principle, the traditional Adams politics. "The Prairie Giant of Peonia" is destroyed by his own overweening ambition; his object never grows beyond a selfish desire to exercise a crude domination over the country and over Mrs. Lee as well. As in the case of John Randolph, Ratcliffe's most effective weapon is irresponsible rhetoric; again, the power of persuasion masks deeper weaknesses in reasoning, and, far more important, the absence of any fixed "theory of morals"—that asset which Charles Francis Adams had once singled out as the first requirement of a statesman.

Unlike the admirable Gallatin, Ratcliffe is a mere creature of a political party, lacking every vestige of independence. When Madeleine inquires, "'Have you never refused to go with your party?' 'Never!' was Ratcliffe's firm reply" (*Democracy*, 47). This corrupting obeisance to party provides him with a convenient excuse for immoral actions. Attempting to explain away his part in the bribe, for example, he tells Madeleine that he has acted not upon his own judgment but out of a disciplined loyalty to party leaders: "Their declaration, as the responsible heads of the organization, that certain action on my part was essential to the interests of the party, satisfied me" (*Democracy*, 193).

Such pragmatic opportunism could not satisfy Henry Adams. He underscores his objections to Ratcliffe's stand by setting this display of modern corruption against the old Adams ideal of duty, thus showing that Ratcliffe lacks not only all knowledge of the true "springs of action" in men unlike himself, but the willingness to search out his own motives as well. The modern politician has lost every sense of personal accountability for his actions: "Like most men in the same place, he did not stop to cast up both columns of his account with the party, nor to ask himself the question that lay at the heart of his grievance: How far had he served his party and how far himself?" (*Democracy*, 84). No member of the Adams family, placed in a position of power and public trust, had ever failed to conduct an intensive self-examination, especially on the point of personal ambition. To an Adams, self-restraint and self-control were as important in personal behavior as political balance of powers was in national government.

In contrasting Carrington to Ratcliffe, the novelist makes good use of his opportunity to demonstrate the vitality of three-generation-old Adams ideals.[30] Although the Southerner's lack of financial independence limits his freedom, because he cannot flee from Washington and politics altogether, he never becomes a slave to party, nor is he willing (any more than the wealthier Madeleine, once she sees the light) to be bribed by Ratcliffe. Carrington's ideals and principles are lost to view in Washington life but effectively recovered in the scenes set at Mount Vernon and Arlington; they are the principles of George Washington and the Constitution, of Lee and the Southerners who fought in the Civil War out of duty to their states and not in defense of slavery, the old Adams anathema. As Henry portrays him, Carrington represents the frail surviving hope for a renaissance of idealism in American politics, and for a better national future. His suit for Madeleine never appears to be strong alongside Ratcliffe's, but his single attempt at action proves at least decisive enough to educate, if not to captivate, the elusive heroine. Still, at the end of the story Ratcliffe remains in power at the capital, and Adams's generally pessimistic judgment on modern democracy has not been overturned.

More than any other character, of course, the heroine expresses the convictions of Henry Adams. "'I want to go to Egypt,' said Madeleine, still smiling faintly; 'democracy has shaken my nerves to pieces. Oh, what rest it would be to live in the Great Pyramid and look out for ever at the polar star!'"

(*Democracy*, 203). The mingled suggestions of disappointment and hope in this concluding speech tell something of the complexity that the author insists upon. Because Madeleine Lee, unlike Ratcliffe but like Adams himself, is introspective, she cannot escape from complications regardless of which course of action she chooses to follow. To make the point clear, the novelist once again uses the device of contrasting characters: Madeleine and her younger sister Sybil work together in tandem, helping to define each other, much as Carrington and Ratcliffe do. Briefly, their differences in personality and attitude point up both the positive values and the personal handicaps that the novelist had already discovered in the introspective habits of the Adams family.

Madeleine's problems were familiar enough to a fourth-generation heir, who understood that each of his forebears had lived as a divided being, torn between principles and ambitions, attractions and repulsions. Unlike Sybil,

> Madeleine dissected her own feelings and was always wondering whether they were real or not; she had a habit of taking off her mental clothing, as she might take off a dress, and looking at it as though it belonged to someone else, and as though sensations were manufactured like clothes. This seems to be one of the easier ways of deadening sorrow, as though the mind could teach itself to lop off its feelers. Sybil particularly disliked this self-inspection. In the first place she did not understand it, and in the second her mind was all feelers, and amputation was death. She could no more analyze a feeling than doubt its existence, both which were habits of her sister (*Democracy*, 119–20).

Her habitual introspection does lead Madeleine to a larger understanding of herself; but that in turn brings greater weakness and confusion:

> She had not known the recesses of her own heart. She had honestly supposed that Sybil's interests and Sybil's happiness were forcing her to an act of self-sacrifice; and now she saw that in the depths of her soul very different motives had

been at work: ambition, thirst for power, restless eagerness to meddle in what did not concern her, blind longing to escape from the torture of watching other women with full lives and satisfied instincts, while her own life was hungry and sad (*Democracy*, 184).

For Madeleine and for Adams, no end was yet in sight. Still, the novelist, like his diary-writing forebears who had filled their pages with self-interrogation, knew that the introspective habit often brought its own bitter reward: ". . . the worst was not in that disappointment [of ambitions], but in the discovery of her own weakness and self-deception" (*Democracy*, 184). It was left for the *Education*, however, to make self-discovery a central, rather than merely a contributing, literary theme.

As she becomes aware of her own complex nature, Madeleine Lee also finds that the outside world no longer seems so simple nor the guides to action so well marked. A younger Henry Adams had treated the chief political issue, in "Civil Service Reform," as a clear-cut matter of morals; now, for Mrs. Lee political questions have been complicated by the romantic attraction she feels toward Ratcliffe and by her own ambition for power. The Senator himself tells Madeleine that effective reform "is utterly hopeless, and not even desirable," because it would interfere with the practical functioning of governmental machinery (*Democracy*, 41). Yet even the pragmatic politician recognizes the bare possibility that once had motivated Adams the essayist and that the novelist still holds out for Mrs. Lee and her nation. As Ratcliffe is forced to admit: "Purify society and you purify the government. But try to purify the government artifically and you only aggravate failure" (*Democracy*, 42).

To the maturing author, his earlier view seemed in retrospect to offer a clarity and simplicity now hopelessly lost. Madeleine's education—like his own historical study—had become an unpleasant introduction to the paralyzing complexities of modern politics. Every thoughtful person who completed the course simply learned too much: details became hopelessly confused, and values disappeared, until only stark, polar opposites, like Mount Vernon and the Senate, or George Washington and Silas P. Ratcliffe, offered any clear meaning. Change, of course, always served to confound the observer, just as the changes in post–Civil War America had confounded Charles Francis Adams and his sons, and helped to influence their withdrawal from active political life, a withdrawal not unlike Madeleine's flight from political power. Her final retreat from Washington, with all her moral values yet intact, teaches a lesson that Adams, at about the same time, was also offering in private to an ex-student from his Harvard seminar, now an aspirant to public office. As Adams wrote in 1881 to Henry Cabot Lodge:

> I suppose every man who had looked on at the game has been struck by the remarkable way in which politics deteriorate the moral tone of everyone who mixes in them. . . . Politicians as a class must be as mean as card-sharpers, turf-men, or Wall Street curbstone operators. There is no respectable industry in existence which will not average a higher morality.[31]

Both this letter and the novel tell us much about Henry Adams's self-justification for his failure to climb aboard the "family go-cart" of politics. Using the freedoms offered in the world of fiction, he chose to dramatize the same real-life forces that had caused his own bittersweet rejection of an active political career.

Once he had told this political story, Adams felt free to dramatize the play of other social forces he saw in the world, especially religion, science, and art. *Esther*, his second and last novel, studied just these matters, drawing particular attention to the question of the survival of religious faith in the society of Henry Adams's day. The book represents an extension of the family's serious religious concern, already recorded for three generations; moreover, *Esther* forms an important part of Adams's total statement concerning his personal religious experience, to which *Mont-Saint-Michel and Chartres* and the *Education* would also contribute. Aside from the treatment of religion, however, *Esther* leaves the traditional Adams family values far behind. It was the most experimental work that Henry

Adams had yet written, a speculative look at modern American life, especially intellectual life. Previewing the *Education*, *Esther* measured the past against the present, using a comparative method that owes something to the earlier "Lyell" review. Again, the author sets down a series of logical arguments for his reader's consideration, and then ends his work without ever reaching any final conclusions. Yet, in *Esther*, unlike "Lyell," the conflict between science and religion does receive full and frank attention, as Adams first explores their differences by employing representative characters to show both views, and then dramatizes the intellectual contest between scientific and religious thought in the form of a romantic competition for the heroine, an echo of the plot he had used in *Democracy*.

Interesting as the ideas may be, *Esther* must be regarded as both a flawed and a dated novel. It survives chiefly as a repository for Adams's thoughts; there is little action, and the characters seem to be brought together mechanically, by the cooperative project of decorating a New York City church. The heroine's father dies (reflecting the real-life loss suffered by Marian Adams), and the book ends on the familiar note sounded by *Democracy*, as Esther rejects her two suitors and is left to search for more satisfactory answers to her questions about life. For its appeal to readers, the novel depends almost entirely on an intellectual debate concerned with those nonpolitical questions omitted from *Democracy*. *Esther* offers, in short, a test case for three quite distinct modes of individual education, each one presented as a possible alternative to the political-historical training the author knew best. These different types of education are represented by characters drawn at least in part from Henry Adams's real-life contemporaries, who become fictional spokesmen for art, science, and religion. To their blandishments, the novelist adds the responses of his heroine, who acts as a passive sounding board for the debate, in her self-defined role as a seeker after truth. Unlike Madeleine Lee, Esther covets knowledge and not power. Each of her friends has arrived at some personal resolution for her dilemma, which takes the classic form of the conflict between faith and reason, instinct and intellect.

For Esther, however, acceptance of any of these solutions proves difficult and finally impossible. She is not traditional; she is the modern "American type" that lacks "ideas" as Wharton, the spokesman for traditional art, acknowledges:

> "I hesitate before every thing American . . . I don't know— you don't know—and I never yet met any man who could tell me, whether American types are going to supplant the old ones, or whether they are to come to nothing for want of ideas. Miss Dudley is one of the most marked American types I ever saw" (*Esther*, 222).

For this "marked American" type, no form of conventional education can be entirely satisfactory. Adams's conclusion would be turned into a more personal demonstration in the pages of the *Education*.

Meanwhile, the novelist's reliance on representative characters to teach his lesson to readers shows a debt to the mental habits of his ancestors, who so often made the moral stand for the man (or woman) in their diaries and letters. Applying the old technique to fiction rather than history or biography, Adams still sought what he had hoped for from "Lyell" and his other essays: to set forth clearly, in some popular form, the most significant ideas of his age. But once again, he was disappointed with the results; there was no popular demand for his book. As a kind of fictional treatment of ideas, *Esther* could offer only flat characters and abstract debates about religion, science, and art. By eliminating the political values of a character like Ratcliffe, the novelist had sacrificed much of his strength, based on those political themes about which he knew most. In consequence this nonpolitical novel appears to us clumsy and uncertain in its arguments and inconclusive overall. Like the life of John Randolph, at some point *Esther* seems to fall apart.

Earlier, when Adams had written "Lyell," his primary purpose had been to study the alien mind of the scientist and to make general observations about the processes of scientific thinking. In *Esther*, he more ambitiously tries to describe the operation of three distinct types of mind, as well as to measure their effects upon a fourth—the mind of Esther, his heroine, who keeps in her own head a running tally of her tutors' intellectual successes and failures. Esther, in short, is both observer and actor, much in the manner of Madeleine Lee. But she is also the "American type," and the novelist attempts to suggest the special complexity of her situation by contrasting her with a far different "type"—in Catherine Brooke, the youthful innocent, who stands outside the intellectual arenas of art, science, and religion. Her mind and spirit remain free; she is almost totally uneducated and equally untroubled by the questions that beset Esther. Catherine displays a sturdy moral character and a powerful imagination, both unaffected by the corrosive influences of skepticism or introspection. Using her as a point of reference, Adams is able to show the high price that Esther has paid for the development of a disciplined, logical mind: "she had some rather more serious cause for disquiet about herself, in regard to which she did not care to consult her cousin or any one else" (*Esther*, 258).

By sketching the history of each representative character, the author is able to explore the useful limits of rationality—in art and science, as well as religion, faith must come to the aid of reason. Otherwise belief and confident action are impossible. Just as her teachers cannot will Esther's acceptance of the ideas each in turn offers, so she cannot will her own faith in any of their doctrines. Her despair at the prospect of resigning herself to a religion in which she does not believe serves to make the point:

> "I want to submit," cried Esther piteously, rising in her turn and speaking in accents of real distress and passion. "Why can't some of you make me? For a few minutes at a time I think it done, and then I suddenly find myself more defiant than ever. I want nothing of the church! Why should it trouble me? Why should I submit to it? Why can't it leave me alone?" (*Esther*, 319).

The Adamses of earlier generations would have castigated such a declaration as patent evidence of personal vanity and pride. In the next few lines of *Esther*, however, the scientific suitor, George Strong, shows us that the nineteenth century of Henry

Adams had broken all ties with the earlier era of intellectual unity—when science, art, and religion were unified in thought and when belief could be strictly enforced:

> "What you want is the Roman church," continued Strong mercilessly. "They know how to deal with pride of will. Millions of men and women have gone through the same struggle, and the church tells them to fix their eyes on a symbol of faith, and if their eyes wander, scourges them for it" (*Esther*, 319).

As a modern scientist, rather than a medieval priest, Strong cannot condone any such suppression of the intellect in the name of religion. He is forced to break off the interview when he sees that the price of such a faith for Esther would be her own self-immolation:

> "Come!" said he coolly, as he forced her to give up the crucifix; "my little bluff has failed. I throw up the hand" (*Esther*, 319).

At the time that he was writing *Esther*, Henry Adams could go no further toward explaining nineteenth-century American life. The writer's neat symbolic conjunction of unity and multiplicity in the virgin and the dynamo still lay ahead. For the moment, his mind remained speculative and not dogmatic on the religious issue; his faith in science had yet to be confirmed; and that in art was even less certain. It should not surprise us, then, that his "experiment" in the novel form was destined to fail, because his method of setting down all sides of complicated intellectual questions demanded a special kind of reader, who could balance in his mind all these conflicting points of view and still be satisfied with suspended judgment. As a novel, the book simply does not work because the intellectual questions of the nineteenth century had so far provided the writer only with grounds for an endless debate.

In a far more personal way, Adams managed to make of his second novel a revealing continuation of his fictional autobiography. His heroine's dissatisfactions actually revealed the mind of the author himself; moreover, her character owed a large debt to Henry's wife, Marian Hooper Adams, whose tragic suicide led the novelist to declare: "I care more for one chapter, or any dozen pages of *Esther* than for the whole history, including maps and indexes; so much more, indeed, that I would not let anyone read the story for fear the reader should profane it."[32] *Democracy* treated public rather than private matters, real enough to anyone who looked around in the external world, or who read the news from Washington. *Esther*, on the other hand, dealt with internal conflicts, rooted in the mind and the emotions. They were intensely personal to Adams, although he chose to treat them with a seemingly impersonal, nonconfessional manner, which heightened the impression of detachment and objectivity.

Put simply, the principal difference between the two novels showed itself in the shifting concerns of the writer: from politics, the old stock-in-trade of Adams family life, he had moved on to psychology and its implications for modern philosophy. As the scientist explains in *Esther*:

> "The thing is simple enough. Hazard and I and every one else agree that thought is eternal. If you can get hold of one true thought, you are immortal as far as that thought goes. The only difficulty is that every fellow thinks his thought the true one" (*Esther*, 355).

Henry Adams proved no exception to Strong's rule. His novels document an attempt to "get hold of one true thought" and then to make it seem convincing to his reading public, many of whom expected to find a higher degree of truth or certainty than the author could claim for himself. In *Esther* as in "Lyell," the absence of simple answers dictated the author's refusal to be either direct or didactic. "Civil Service Reform" and *Democracy*, on the other hand, taught their lessons with obvious conviction and authority. But these were attitudes that Henry Adams could not adopt while he remained uncertain—whenever, in fact, his literary searches carried him beyond the intellectual limits of the family heritage.

4.

History of the United States During the Administrations of Thomas Jefferson and James Madison

> ... and was it modesty that determined Henry Adams to begin his history where his great-grandfather had ceased making it, and to close it before he should chronicle the profound tragedy of his grandfather's administration?
>
> —Henry Steele Commager, "Introduction" to Henry Adams, *History of the Administrations of Thomas Jefferson and James Madison* (New York, 1930).

For many readers the only satisfactory distillation of Henry Adams's wit and learning, the consummate display of his literary skills, is to be found in the *History of the United States During the Administrations of Jefferson and Madison.*[1] Certainly the *History* stands apart from all other of Adams's writings. It is at once an unique experiment, a classic American achievement, and its author's personal tribute to the greatness of America's historical past. Adams rightly felt that these nine volumes contained the choicest fruits of his study of both history and life. In them, the gentleman-historian carefully constructed, on the foundations of previously unused source materials, an ambitious narrative account of America during the years 1800–1817. When he finished polishing his manuscript, he believed that he had produced a serious American rival to Gibbon's masterpiece, *Decline and Fall of the Roman Empire.*

88

But instead of popular acclaim Henry Adams was rewarded only with public apathy and neglect. So the *History* actually became for him a symbol of personal defeat—a sharp blow to his ego that not even the playfully disparaging reminiscences in the *Education of Henry Adams* could entirely conceal. His years of hard work did not open to Adams an illustrious career as a literary diplomat (on the model of George Bancroft or James Russell Lowell). Nor was the book recognized for what it really represented: the first important example of "scientific" history written in America.

Adams's late estimate notwithstanding, the *History* remains today a rich and rewarding study. Its pages display Adams's literary and historical intentions and attitudes, as well as fine examples of his philosophy and method. And, like its author, the *History* is various and complex; it may be profitably examined from many points of the intellectual compass. For that reason, the discussion in this chapter must necessarily be limited; there is no attempt to arrive at an overall evaluation of the historical merits of the book or of "scientific history" in general. These pages focus instead upon the debt that the *History* owes to the Adams family, particularly to Henry Adams's understanding of the part that the Adamses had played in American history. For, whatever the other values of the *History* (and they are many), we should recall that the book was conceived and written during important years in the life of its author, 1878-1888, years in which Adams attained a greatly enlarged appreciation of personal as much as national history. His own motives and prejudices, as much as the mass of documentary sources, provided material for his book. As he grew to recognize these special feelings within himself, Adams used them in his writings sometimes openly and sometimes guardedly, but most often in the service of the old family need—self-justification. Even acting the part of a scientific historian, Henry remained, first of all, an Adams.

Sources and Method

The *History* demands recognition on grounds of ambition and magnitude. The breadth of intellectual interests displayed in these nine volumes certifies the book as one of the "pioneer attempts at social history"[2] at the same time that it demonstrates the lofty position that Henry Adams reached as a serious thinker. To this self-development, his family heritage had contributed a grand standard of measurement for the human mind, the broad intellectual range so often exemplified by the men of the Adams line. In the *History*, the author shows himself to be the true intellectual heir of his most gifted forebear, John Quincy Adams, even though the figure of John Quincy plays only a minor role in the narrative; while his grandson seems to attribute greatness of mind—not to any Adams but to Thomas Jefferson.

In Henry Adams's view the habit of Jefferson's mind was to "widen every intellectual exercise." These words exactly describe the author's attitude toward the historical problem he had set for himself in the *History*, where the men and events of a limited chronological period are portrayed against the broadest backgrounds of European and American life. Accordingly, the effects of human action can be traced into every geographical area of America and along each identifiable path of historical "force." Moreover, throughout this whole intellectual exercise, the historian's mind seems to radiate mental energy, as he attempts to bring the fullest documentation, the keenest insights, and the most sophisticated mode of narration together into an inclusive demonstration of what history at its best should be.

The tiny kernel of the *History* lies hidden in the diary of John Quincy Adams. A portion of the entry for 20 October 1821 reads:

> Jefferson and Madison did attain power by organizing and heading a system of attack upon the Washington Administration, chiefly under the banner of States rights and State sovereignty. They argued and scolded against all implied powers, and pretended that the Government of the Union had no powers but such as were expressly delegated by the Constitution. They succeeded. Mr. Jefferson was elected President of the United States, and the first thing he did was to purchase Louisiana—an assumption of implied power greater in itself and more comprehensive in its conse-

quences than all the assumptions of implied powers in the twelve years of the Washington and Adams Administrations put together. Through the sixteen years of the Jefferson and Madison Administrations not the least regard was paid to the doctrines of rejecting implied powers, upon which those gentlemen had vaulted into the seat of government. . . .[3]

Only the barest bones of an intellectual skeleton emerged from John Quincy Adams's page, to be fleshed out later with the complicated mix of details, documents, attitudes, and skills that characterize Henry Adams's *History*. For even though the problem had been recorded in the thoughts of an ancestor, it still remained for his descendant to exhume from the past the usable materials for a more complete present and to extend the old lines of time and force into a new generation.

When he began to write his *History*, Adams was already an accomplished historian, who had displayed his talents in essays and biographies, as well as in the classroom at Harvard. Ever restless in matters of the mind, Professor Adams had drifted from an early concern with medieval history into the colonial period in America, and later into the more recent American past, teaching in turn each of these subjects to his students. In an age before narrow academic specialization, Henry Adams's command of history was certainly great enough to insure his opportunity for choice when he sat down to write—choice of an appropriate subject for the most ambitious literary enterprise of his entire career. In a later generation, the question of Adams's motives for this choice has appealed to careful readers. As Henry Steele Commager asks,

> . . . was it modesty that determined Henry Adams to begin his history where his great-grandfather had ceased making it, and to close it before he should chronicle the profound tragedy of his grandfather's administration? Or was it a recognition that the democratic experiment, the moulding of national character, was to be made despite rather than through the presidencies of John and John Quincy Adams?[4]

Some consideration of Henry Adams's family will help us to avoid simplistic answers.

The *History* deals with the period 1880–1817, a notable hiatus in family power, flanked on both sides by the more glorious chapters of Adams history. The historian selected for special study two of the three American Presidents who served between the terms of John Adams (1796–1800) and John Quincy Adams (1824–1828). To make the withdrawal of family participation more clear-cut, John Adams had recalled John Quincy from a diplomatic post in Berlin just before Jefferson took office, so that, for the next thirteen years, the younger Adams remained isolated from executive power, serving first in the Senate and then abroad. Only in 1817, at the close of Madison's presidency and after the period covered by the *History*, did John Quincy assume a major role in formulating national policy, when he became Secretary of State under President Monroe. Once the limits of his study were established, the historian realized that his choice had also made it possible to write an anatomy of American change, the story of national development in a transitional period, during which political control shifted from New England to Virginia, as the New England philosophy gave way to the theories and practices of Virginia Republicanism. Even more important, Henry Adams had found a way to analyze this change in power without being forced to sit in judgment of his Adams forebears.

Nonetheless, the study of American history still presented some difficulties. Adams had already learned that neither men nor events opened themselves to simple or definitive analysis and understanding; thus, the modern reader of the *History* is faced with evidence of the author's complex response to his mature view of what had occurred in America during the short period of seventeen years. In particular, the organization of the book, especially Adams's use of "frame" chapters to begin and end the nine volumes, demands special attention: the reader must keep the opening section of the "frame" (conveniently labeled "American Life in 1800") constantly in mind as he advances through the book, until he is finally able to complete his measurement of national change by comparing the opening section with the closing "frame" (which might have been titled "America in 1817"). Inside this generous overview, or "frame," the author relates incidents and describes his actors, expecting at every point that, because of his dynamic method, each one will be understood not in isolation but as a part of the larger fabric of national life. Among the first six chapters, the three concerned with separate geographic sections are especially open to misinterpretation, unless a total impression of American life is continuously kept in view. Otherwise Adams's account seems seriously prejudiced by his origins; the immediate context of his statements suggests a narrow New England regionalism—exactly the position the author seeks to modify or even to correct in the second and sixth chapters of the "frame," where he considers the nation not in terms of geographical regions but rather as a political and social whole.

This unusual narrative technique deserves close study. The "frame" chapters as well as those between are designed to make reading an active, imaginative exercise, not merely a passive entertainment. Only the reader's mental participation, his constant balancing of regional and national perspectives, can do full justice to the historian's method.[5] By using such a complex technique, Adams hoped to expand the inclusiveness of his coverage without sacrificing vivid intensity or interest in detail. He aimed at setting forth historical truth of a high order, and scholarship, historical insight, literary craftsmanship—all had something to contribute to great historical achievement. Nevertheless, objective history still lay beyond Adams's expectation: "Some misunderstanding must always take place when the observer is at cross-purpose with the society he describes" (*History* I, 172).

Most of the source materials for the *History* were already familiar at the time Adams began work on this most ambitious literary project of his life. He had edited and published the Gallatin papers along with a life of Gallatin. His biography of John Randolph belonged to the same period, and another work, *Documents Relating to New-England Federalism*, included several pieces relevant to the *History*, as did his manuscript biography of Aaron Burr, fated never to be printed. Gradually, as the author reworked these old materials, new themes and patterns began to emerge, until subjects that had once commanded attention in and of themselves now became parts of a larger and more complex whole. Of course there were additional sources too, chiefly batches of diplomatic papers, secured or copied from foreign archives and not previously available to historians. The official records of the British, French, and Spanish ministries were opened to Henry Adams, largely because of the magic of his family name.

The papers of the Adams family also played a notable part in the *History*, although their use is not conspicuous. Henry Adams preferred to hide his debt to the earlier Adamses, who had left behind at Quincy, especially in the writings of John Adams, many documents that influenced Henry's picture of American life in the age of Jefferson and Madison. But family influence went much deeper than the ink and paper of Adams literature. Henry Adams had served his first historical apprenticeship during the mid-1850s, when Charles Francis Adams and his son labored together over the proof sheets for the *Works* of John Adams. Now in the 1880s Henry was acting on his own as he poured over the papers of John and John Quincy Adams once again in preparation for the *History*. Yet despite the passage of time and Henry's advantage of familiarity with methods of Germanic scholarship, family attitudes toward the historian's task seem to have changed hardly at all. A clear echo of Charles Francis Adams sounded in the words of a son who recognized the necessary incompleteness of all attempts to reveal the secrets of human character from outside the self: "History is not often able to penetrate the private lives of famous men, and catch their words as they were uttered" (*History*, II, 34).

The old Adams intention emerged with renewed vitality; the historian determined to get at the truths behind public statements and public personalities, and thereby arrive at a more complete understanding of history. In particular, Henry hoped to measure with a new precision the impact of historic events upon the men who participated in them, and to show the psychological changes wrought by public actions. This Adams, with the complicated knowledge of the private and public sides of two Presidents already etched into his memory, was now prepared to find a similar complexity in the figure of a third President, Thomas Jefferson. The language of a Jefferson letter of 1807, for example, led Adams to remark: "The difference of tone between this letter and the President's public language was extreme" (*History*, III, 332). As the historian weighed details of language and conduct, harsher judgment crept closer to the surface of his remarks, and analysis often emerged as skeptical criticism. Small wonder, then, that Henry Adams preferred to keep two generations of his kinsmen outside of the limelight of his *History*, just as he would later choose to keep so much of his own life out of the *Education*.

In the *History*, Adams's reserve about matters of family was not based merely on a morbid sensitivity, born of a personal failure to gain recognition and distinction on the old family lines of politics and statesmanship. His earlier studies, coming once again under review as he prepared a new work from old materials, now seemed to prove the intellectual failure of all historical writing that was built upon prejudices in favor of regional or family position. Modern scholarship demanded something better. His new task in the *History*, as Adams understood it, marked a departure from the old historical business of special pleading. Rather, this book was to be an unbiased account, one that required of its author a more "scientific" set of attitudes than any that had been characteristic of family habits of mind, conditioned as those habits were by legal training.

The law and especially the adversary system of legal practice now seemed seriously at odds with what Henry Adams was trying to accomplish. All of his old objections to the formal study of law emerged anew, this time as an argument against making legal thinking the basis for modern history. Setting down his personal philosophy, the author showed his intention of producing a history free from the partisan prejudices that had flawed history in the past. At the same time, of course, Henry was also declaring his personal independence from a traditional form of family education. An Adams had always been trained in law before he began to make and write history. Yet,

The quarrel between law and history is old, and its source lies deep. Perhaps no good historian was ever a good lawyer: whether any good lawyer could be a good historian might be equally doubted. The lawyer is required to give facts the mould of a theory; the historian need only state facts in their sequence (*History*, III, 45).

On its surface, Adams's statement appears to be inconsistent with his later utterances about finding some scientific law or theory to explain history, and equally disparaging of attempts by his brothers and other legally trained historians to write good history. A few years after he finished his own *History*, Adams went on to expand his criticisms and to name some historians who had already been rendered obsolete, including Motley, Macaulay, and Carlyle. "None of them are worth reading now, for the whole school of history is altogether changed, and, compared with Motley, Thucydides is young, but good society won't find that out yet for another fifty years."[6] While he was writing the *History*, however, Adams still took seriously a duty to make the public understand. His experimental solution to the problem of re-creating for readers seventeen years of American life took shape in his mind as a scientific display of "facts in their sequence."

Once the "facts" had been established to his own satisfaction, Adams turned away from the usual demonstration of the veracity of sources, to concentrate instead upon the mentality and intellectual capacity of both the historian and his audience. Each party has to respond to "facts" by interpreting and reconstructing the "sequence" for himself. In this way, a special relationship between historian and reader is created, not in the limited confines of a Harvard classroom, but across the open pages of the *History*, and according to certain directions provided by the artistic historian. Earlier, Adams had experimented with parallel printing of the record in "Captain John Smith," and later, he would employ in the *Education* another experimental technique, but always with the intention of making the reader react in such a way that he would learn actively (rather than passively) from the text. Here, in the *History*, Adams sought to forge a durable link between author and reader by writing history "straight," by setting down "facts" with little or no expression of his personal attitudes and feelings. These "facts" could then operate upon the reader so as to increase his understanding   without   awakening   his   latent   prejudices.

Adams's real goal was a shared sense of objective history; his method, dispassionate recital. When he decried his "failure" in the years after the *History* had been published, he was assuming responsibility for a double disappointment. He had failed to convey the real "facts" upon which everyone could agree, and, in a larger way, his audience had failed to respond with the intellectual and critical vigor he had hoped to stimulate.

The Adams Ancestors in the History

By selecting inauspicious years in family political history, Henry Adams expected to free himself from exhibitions of family pride. He knew that he could keep John and John Quincy Adams in the background of the *History* and still measure them as statesmen and human beings against their chief antagonists, such as Jefferson (in these years), Timothy Pickering, and John Randolph. At the same time the earlier Adamses could be compared with men like Albert Gallatin, who represented high achievement in Henry Adams's mind, and even Napoleon, the dominant international figure on Adams's canvas. For the fourth-generation son, his book presented a rare opportunity to study the Adams family fair-mindedly if not with absolute objectivity.

To protect himself from pride, the author resorted to a curious and sometimes irritatingly evasive use of indirect references to the Adamses. Certainly he had no wish to stir the old fires of controversy, based upon inherited family feuds (although, as his critics made clear, he did not entirely avoid this danger). Before concentrating on the *History*, however, we should recall that, already, in 1877, Adams had tried to pay his debt to family honor by compiling *Documents Relating to New-England Federalism: 1800-1815*. This book answered the charges against both John Adams and John Quincy Adams made by Henry Adams's Harvard pupil, Henry Cabot Lodge, in his own volume of ancestral history, *Life and Letters of George Cabot* (1877). *Documents* pointedly ignored the accusatory, personal tone of Lodge's editorial voice in *George Cabot*, which may have reminded Adams of the youthful excesses in his essay on Captain John Smith. Ten years older and wiser, the historian-teacher marked out for himself a lofty and impersonal editorial stance, as he explained in *Documents*: "This volume has no controversial purpose. Under the ashes of half a century the fires of personal and party passion still glow in these pages; but only curious students in history care any longer to stir them."[7] Lodge, on the other hand, had stirred the coals at every opportunity. He attacked John Adams's "dark imaginings," his "jealousy," and his "fatal element: the rapid process of mental exaggeration"; Lodge also denounced John Quincy Adams's "torrent of personal hatred." In all, *George Cabot* represented a frankly partisan account, and one that, its author claimed, "my friend, Professor Adams" had reviewed in its entirety before it ever reached print.[8]

Lodge's reconstruction of the old Federalist case must have alerted Henry Adams to the historical vulnerability of John and John Quincy Adams to attacks based upon their personalities (rather than upon their abilities or achievements). Just this kind of attack seemed most modern and "scientific" in Henry Adams's day. The popularity of Darwin's theories and the study of genealogy both helped to make history personal, as Henry would demonstrate in his *Education*. But Lodge's attack and the whole school of history based upon personalities were examples of the bondage of the past, the kind of inadequate history that Henry Adams wished to supersede with his own reconstruction of the Jeffersonian era and even earlier, in *Documents*.

There, as he answered Lodge's "Preface," Adams managed to combine the feelings of a Harvard professor, dedicated to ideals of historical objectivity and completeness, with the special reluctance of a proud and sensitive family member, determined not to embarrass any of the Adamses, including himself:

> In order to furnish students in one mass with all the evidence as yet at hand to throw light upon the acts and motives of the characters in this curious scene of our history. . . . So far as the editor is concerned, his object has been, not to join in an argument, but to stimulate, if possible, a new generation in our universities and else-

where, by giving them a new interest in their work and new material to digest.[9]

Much like a modern "casebook," this collection of essays and correspondence seems to illuminate the historical problem by directing attention to new source materials. Yet the reader cannot entirely trust these words of his editor. For when he came to reproduce what he himself designated as the single most important document in the collection, John Quincy Adams's "Reply to the Appeal of the Massachusetts Federalists," Henry Adams felt compelled to depart from his declared ideal of completeness: "a few passages of a personal nature, relating to Mr. H. G. Otis, have been omitted." As editor, Adams explained that the "Reply" had been written "after six years of political strain," when John Quincy Adams "had at last been driven, in what he conceived to be disgrace and humiliation, from the Presidency, . . . smarting not only under the conviction that this was to be the end of a career which he had so earnestly longed to make useful to his country, but smarting, also, under a series of petty and exasperating attacks. . . ."[10] Under such circumstances, it was hardly surprising that the "Reply" conveyed a certain "bitterness." After reflection and consultation with his friends, John Quincy had "suppressed the publication," and his grandson was now printing the "Reply" (in an incomplete form, however) for the first time.

In substance, Henry Adams's remarks compose a justification and an excuse for his kinsman, rather than responsible editorial scholarship. By stressing John Quincy Adams's motives of high-minded public service (with no mention of personal ambition) and by loyally extending the moratorium on publishing the old complaint against Mr. Otis, Henry proved himself to be a proud representative of the Adams line.

Here and elsewhere, in many small but important ways, Henry Adams was able to try out in *Documents Relating to New-England Federalism* the dual role of ambitious historian and loyal family member that he would fill with greater success in the *History*, ten years later. In the latter book, however, the attention of the reader had to be focused upon Southern figures (especially Jefferson) and Southern ideas and policies, if the sequence of events was to be made comprehensible. A regional approach could not be avoided: "During the administrations of Jefferson and Madison, the national government was in the main controlled by ideas and interests peculiar to the region south of the Potomac, and only to be understood from a Southern stand-point" (*History*, III, 22). Of course, this regional focus actually aided the author in his attempts to direct the beams of historical investigation away from his family. Whatever their relationship to Federalism, the Adamses clearly did not belong to the South. But even so, the obliqueness of Henry Adams's references to John and John Quincy Adams is not consistent throughout the *History*; rather, the technique can be seen most clearly where the temptation to place an Adams at center stage is greatest, as in the treatment of the historical period just prior to Jefferson's assumption of presidential office, the final days of John Adams's administration, and in the coverage of the negotiations at Ghent, where John Quincy Adams's career in diplomacy reached its summit.

Before turning to these most significant crises in family history, however, it will be useful to note Henry Adams's general reticence about identifying his forebears by name in the *History*. For John Adams we find such substitutions as, "the retiring President," "Jefferson's predecessor," "Washington's successor," or "the last President." John Quincy Adams, appearing later in the account, is repeatedly called simply "a Massachusetts Senator."[11] And the reader is left to imagine the delight the historian must have felt as he inserted into his text the following capsule biography of John Adams: ". . . the actual President of the United States, who signed with Franklin the treaty of peace with Great Britain, was the son of a small farmer, and had himself kept a school in his youth" (*History*, I, 181).

There are other places in the *History* where even the author's conscious attempt to control family pride and loyalty could not insulate him from at least some involvement in apologetics. The often discussed matter of John Adams's bad manners when he refused to participate in Jefferson's inauguration led Henry Adams to adopt a strategy of quick shifts in narrative point of view, from that of John Adams, to Jefferson, to historical omniscience (characteristically introduced with a seemingly modest "perhaps"). This method allowed the historian to avoid rendering any real judgment, by turning attention finally to a questionable (to say the least) historical analogy:

> The retiring President was not present at the installation of his successor. In Jefferson's eyes a revolution had taken place as vast as that of 1776; and if this was his belief, perhaps the late President was wise to retire from a stage where everything was arranged to point a censure upon his principles, and where he would have seemed, in his successor's opinion, as little in place as George III would have appeared at the installation of President Washington (*History*, I, 191).

In this passage Henry Adams conceals his real sympathy for his great-grandfather. The historical point of view of John Adams is simply left out of the account, while the historian takes refuge, instead, in a narrative tone of nearly Olympian detachment. Here, in capsule form is a demonstration of the basic technique that allows the historian to appear to be writing from a position above faction, party, and family. Once this seemingly objective principle establishes control, the pervading ideal of detachment becomes firmly planted in the reader's mind, where it operates as a continuing balance or corrective for the author's occasional sallies into more personal commentary.

One notable effect of Henry Adams's treatment of John and John Quincy Adams is a deliberate merging of the two separate personalities, to make them representatives of a single "Adams" standard of political behavior. This technique leaves the reader with a clear idea of what the family stood for, but with no special understanding of each President's individual abilities and deficiencies. Of course, as we have noted, Henry Adams's selection of the 1800–1817 period made John Adams a matter of past history, rather than a present actor. But his great-grandson also chooses to underscore John's absence from the scene whenever possible, adding one indirect reference after another, to produce a composite portrait that might well be labeled "the misunderstood ex-President." Overall, the John Adams of the *History* owes a heavy debt to the author's familial pride. Consider the feelings of Henry Adams when he reprinted these lines from a letter written by A. J. Dallas: "I verily believe one year more of writing, speaking, and appointing would render Mr. Jefferson a more odious President, even to the Democrats, than John Adams."[12] These words had appeared earlier in *Gallatin*; now Henry Adams included the same quotation as a part of the subtle and disingenuous appeal made by the *History* for historical justice to John Adams.

One Adams or another usually appears in the *History* to provide a usable standard for measuring Jefferson or some other chief figure. Yet Jefferson remains always central to the book because, as leader of "the Virginia school," his influence extended throughout the administration of Madison as well as his own. He founded a "school" of political theory, much as John Adams founded a "school" of family philosophy, and, appropriately enough, Jefferson is the figure most often paired with John Adams. This method has a double usefulness: it functions to express a judgment of both partners in the description. In another passage, one of the most impressive demonstrations of literary versatility found anywhere in the *History*, the author shows how he can defend his ancestor against charges of unbridled temper (which John Adams often brought against himself in his diary and which Jefferson, Pickering, and other contemporaries helped to make a commonplace part of his historical portrait) by comparing Adams first with Jefferson and then with the irreproachable George Washington. As a critic of John Adams, Henry tells us, Jefferson showed almost no perception:

> Perhaps temper had more to do with Jefferson's reasoning than he imagined. Nothing could be better calculated to nettle a philosophic President who believed the world, except within his own domain, to be too much governed, than the charge that he himself had played the despot and had trampled upon private rights; but that such charges should be pressed with the coarseness of Luther Martin, and should depend on the rulings of John Marshall, seemed an intolerable outrage on the purity of Jefferson's intentions.

In such cases an explosion of anger was a common form of relief. Even President Washington was said to have sometimes dashed his hat upon the ground, and the second President was famous for gusts of temper (*History*, III, 452).

These lines contradict the author's earlier professions of neutral, scientific historiography. Here, Adams is playing the lawyer rather than the objective historian, offering a brief in defense of the "second President," John Adams. But at the same time the rhetorical thrust moves in another direction, to belittle Jefferson by bringing him within the limits of human fallibility and by suggesting, in a seemingly neutral tone, what Jefferson might have learned if he had been born to a tradition of honest self-interrogation, as every Adams had. Jefferson, unlike John Adams, suffered acutely from a failure to "imagine" enough about himself, or, simply, to know himself. John Adams, on the other hand, had recorded in his diary warning after warning about his need for self-control. Henry Adams could point to his kinsman's record and explain that each "explosion of anger" at least had provided some form of personal "relief." In Jefferson's case, the outlets for his unacknowledged anger had been different and perhaps darker. Jefferson "would never have shown his passion in acts of violence or in physical excitement. His sensitiveness relieved itself in irritability and complaints, in threats forgotten as soon as uttered, or in reflections tinged with a color of philosophic thought" (*History*, III, 453). The reader is left with a certain conviction that, on the whole, John Adams's outbursts of temper were preferable. In Henry Adams's hands character analysis, focusing upon intellectual and psychological explanation, rather than outward action, alters and refines the old Adams family interest in the study of men. The dangers associated with uncontrollable temper, for example, are now represented as matters of covert possibility as much as overt action. Thanks to the historian's interest in modern psychology, character and personality demand new and more complex forms of investigation.

More often than John Adams, it is John Quincy who becomes the family representative used for comparison or measurement in the *History*. Sometimes the author employs a technique of brief allusion, which usually manages to inject a note of sympathetic understanding and to set John Quincy up as an example for other men. By this method Henry Adams helps to establish the case for his grandfather without appearing to try:

> Governor Sullivan [of Massachusetts] was a man of ability and courage. Popular and successful, he had broken the long sway of Federalism in Massachusetts, and within a few months had carried his re-election against the utmost exertions of the Essex Junto; but he had seen John Quincy Adams fall a sacrifice to the embargo, and he had no wish to be himself the next victim of Jefferson's theories (*History*, IV, 255).

In other places, an Adams forebear is used not so much as an individual example of right conduct but more as a kind of standard against which to measure the gains and losses of national political change: "The relapse of Massachusetts to Federalism and the overthrow of Senator Adams in the spring of 1808 were the first signs of the political price which President Jefferson must pay for his passion of peace" (*History*, IV, 283). Here, the parallelism in syntax, the two subject phrases, magnify the importance of John Quincy Adams. His nominal image serves a representative function in quite a different way from that illustrated by the quotation above, where the name stands for the man whose example, Henry Adams asserts, influenced Governor Sullivan.

A better understanding of these passages also requires some consideration of another related technique, which contributes to the allusiveness of both references. In order to function as standards, whether individual or more largely representative, these brief citations depend upon the fully formulated descriptions and attitudes expressed earlier in his text by the historian, well in advance of the shorthand references. The technique, of course, was not new to Henry Adams's writing at the time of the *History*; but it deserves special attention here because his treatment of representative characters, literary symbols, and allusions plays a significant role in the *History*. The specific mention of John Quincy Adams in the passage above, for example, draws upon the larger demonstration of attitude set forth a few pages earlier:

> John Quincy Adams, at whose growing influence this letter [written by Timothy Pickering] struck, had been from his earliest recollection, through his father's experience or his own, closely connected with political interests. During forty years he had been the sport of public turbulence, and for forty years he was yet to undergo every vicissitude of political failure and success; but in the range of his chequered life he was subjected to no other trial so severe as that which Pickering forced him to meet. In the path of duty he might doubtless face social and political ostracism, even in a town such as Boston then was, and defy it. Men as good as he had done as much, in many times and places; but to do this in support of a President [Jefferson] whom he disliked and distrusted, for the sake of a policy in which he had no faith [the Embargo], was enough to shatter a character of iron. Fortunately for him, his temper was not one to seek relief in half-way measures. He had made a mistake in voting for an embargo without limit of time; but since no measure of resistance to Europe more vigorous than the embargo could gain support from either party, he accepted and defended it (*History*, IV, 239–40).

Although this complex defense of John Quincy Adams acknowledges his faults, the rhetorical emphasis upon self-sacrifice relieves John Quincy of much of the personal responsibility for the reversals in his career. His real error—weakness in judgment—is quickly passed over, as the account concentrates instead upon the context or situation, the old family feud with Pickering, begun in the time of John Adams and carried on against his son. Of course, Henry Cabot Lodge's recent revival of Pickering's old charges could have made Henry Adams especially reluctant to admit error among his family, even two generations after the fact. Yet this reluctance seems remarkably like that he had already displayed in his account of another family feud in *John Randolph*.

When he came to write the final volume of the *History*, on the other hand, an entirely different set of considerations, created by the absence of any such feud and by the dissimilar historical context of the Ghent negotiations of 1814, operated upon the historian to produce a very different portrait of John Quincy Adams. In these pages, Henry Adams admits to—and even enlarges upon—the weaknesses of his grandfather (especially John Quincy's frequent loss of intellectual and emotional balance, resulting from personal irritation and a failure to control his temper). At Ghent, John Quincy Adams had been surrounded by men of a different stamp from Pickering: thus, he had to be measured against Albert Gallatin, always the exemplary statesman and never a captious critic of the Adamses. As a result of the disparate situation, the historian's appraisal of this later period in John Quincy Adams's career reveals the higher degree of objectivity that Henry Adams could achieve at moments when family honor did not seem to be directly threatened:

> When the American commissioners discussed the subject [an Indian treaty] among themselves, September 20, [John Q.] Adams proposed to break off the negotiation on that issue; but Gallatin good-naturedly overruled him, and Adams would not himself, on cool reflection, have ventured to take such responsibility. Indeed, he suggested an article for an Indian amnesty, practically accepting the British demand. . . . His mistake in pressing such an issue was obvious to every one but himself, and would have been evident to him had he not been blinded by irritation at the British note (*History*, IX, 28,30).

The comparative merits of John Quincy Adams and Albert Gallatin have already received considerable attention in my earlier discussion of the biographies; a few additional comments will appear later. Here we should note that the portrayal of John Quincy Adams is not consistent throughout the *History*; the author's treatment varies according to the context or set of associations that influence a larger historical judgment. In particular, the portrayal alters according to the author's choice of figures to make up the sets or pairs he uses for comparison and contrast. The mental habit, showing itself as a narrative device, is characteristic of Henry Adams's work early and late, as my analysis of *Democracy* and the *Education* demonstrates.

In the much longer *History* Adams experiments with an extension of comparison-contrast by building a long chain of dualities, which become increasingly abstract and even symbolic representations of force as the book continues. This method can be described as an accretion of individual components into an acceptable causal chain.

For purposes of measurement and criticism, the historian pieces together a representative family position in matters of politics, morals, and character, ignoring meanwhile the individual strengths and weaknesses of John and John Quincy Adams. Thus, the important passage above illuminating John Quincy Adams's position on the Embargo also serves to establish a conjunction of political views in two separate generations of the family: "John Quincy Adams . . . had been from his earliest recollection, through his father's experience or his own, closely connected with political interests." Any more pronounced declaration of the family interest in politics might well have compromised the impartial position of the historian. Of course the circumstances of Pickering's feud with two generations of the Adams family made this inclusive use of two Adamses as a single point of view easy and natural. From the moment that the topic of the feud finds its way into the *History*, Henry Adams treats it as an historical influence or force, rooted in the period before 1800 (thus making necessary some reference, however indirect, to John Adams) but also a continuing power to affect the well-being of the nation.

John Quincy Adams enters the *History* at the time of his election to the Senate (1803), where he served alongside Timothy Pickering, the other Senator from Massachusetts. From this moment, the historian contends, their two courses in politics were fixed. It was John Quincy Adams " . . . whose father had but three years before dismissed Pickering abruptly and without explanation from his Cabinet. Neither of the senators owned a temper or character likely to allay strife. The feud between them was bitter and life-long. From the moment of their appearance in the Senate they took opposite sides" (*History*, II, 110). The apparent unwillingness of the historian to dramatize the feud seems appropriate to his larger subject; and as he continues his account, a carefully balanced analysis of both parties to the feud protects the writer against any possible charge of prejudice. His introduction (above) has been carefully understated; he traces cause ("dismissed") and effect ("strife," "feud"); finally, Adams describes the political result ("opposite sides").

By the time the historian has completed this story two volumes later, however, the sequential description has dramatically enlarged the feud from a modest dispute in Massachusetts politics to a representative example of national danger, a forerunner of the Essex Junto. As Adams draws out his line of historical consideration for the reader, the family feud develops startling implications: "Among the antipathies and humors of New-England politics none was more characteristic than this personal antagonism [between Pickering and John Quincy Adams] beginning a new conspiracy which was to shake the Union to its foundations" (*History*, IV, 173). By now, the earlier parity of "temper or character" which had marked the figures as they were first introduced has given way to the historian's charge of "conspiracy."

Elsewhere in the *History*, despite his declared intention to present "facts in their sequence," free of all prejudice, Henry Adams sometimes slips into personal expressions of regional and familial favoritism. W. R. Taylor has pointed to the New England bias hidden in the simple phrase "even in New England" as it appears in many comparisons.[13] Another inconspicuous clue to the author's real attitude shows up in his occasional disregard for the time limits he had set. Henry Adams was well aware that his two forebears had been turned out of office after a single term. Both Presidents Adams suffered from lack of sustained popularity; their political programs thus were weakened. Measured by public acceptance, Jefferson's career provided a marked contrast, of which the historian took special notice. In doing so, Henry Adams expanded the boundaries of his historical concern, in this way enlarging the scope and force of his criticism:

> Jefferson clung with touching pathos to the love and respect of his fellow-citizens, who repaid his devotion with equal attachment; but many an American President who yearned no less passionately for the people's regard would have died an outcast rather than have trafficked in their dignity and his

own self-respect in order to seek or save a personal popularity . . . the truth must be admitted that in 1808—for the first
and probably for the last time in history—a President of the
United States begged for mercy from a British Minister
(*History*, IV, 191).

A far more pathetic story remains unwritten here. It first came to
Henry Adams from the pages of John and John Quincy Adams,
whose diaries attested in alternate entries to yearnings "for
the people's regard" and to the Adamses' proud spirit of
independence—perhaps the best face that could be put on their
common loss of popularity. Now those expressions of human
feeling, so long unacknowledged in public, led the historian to
build his own case for the Adams family: neither the self-respect
of an Adams, even in defeat, nor our national self-respect had
ever been sacrificed under an Adams President to the merely
selfish needs of human personality or ambition.

If the American people had sometimes been blind to the
merits of the Adams breed, professional politicians showed no
less obtuseness. John Quincy Adams's nomination in 1809 as
Madison's Minister to Russia was blocked in the Senate at the
same time that Albert Gallatin's nomination as Secretary of State
met opposition there. This double proof of the lack of popular
appreciation for superior abilities led the historian to explore
another comparison-contrast, which ends in a foreshadowing of
the greater crisis of 1812:

Senators who rejected the services of Gallatin and John
Quincy Adams in order to employ those of Robert Smith,
Dr. Eustis, and Governor Hamilton could not but suffer
discredit. Faction which had no capacity of its own, and
which showed only dislike of ability in others, could never
rule a government in times of danger or distress (*History*, V,
12).

Here the historical lesson concerning John Quincy Adams is
taught by an ironic refutation of senatorial judgment. Although
his appointment was finally confirmed only after an embarrass-

ing display of factional politics, Minister Adams went on to achieve results that completely refuted his partisan critics: "Adams's diplomatic victory was Napoleonic in its magnitude and completeness. Even Caulaincourt, [Napoleon's Ambassador to Russia and John Quincy Adams's chief diplomatic adversary] whom he overthrew, good-naturedly congratulated him after he had succeeded, against Caulaincourt's utmost efforts, in saving all the American ships" (*History*, V, 419).

The Ghent negotiations marked the summit of John Quincy Adams's diplomatic career. Henry Adams evaluates Ghent by comparing it to a similar event in John Adams's life, his meetings with British representatives to draft the Treaty of Paris (1783). To justify this parallel treatment, which once again moves the historian outside his designated period of historical interest, Adams simply adopts a British point of view and suggests that very little had been learned from all past dealings with Americans:

> Experience had not convinced the British government that in dealing with the United States it required the best ability it could command. The mistake made by Lord Shelburne in 1783 was repeated by Lord Castlereagh in 1814. The miscalculation of relative ability . . . was not reasonable. Probably the whole British public service, including Lords and Commons, could not at that day have produced four men competent to meet Gallatin, J. Q. Adams, Bayard, and Clay on the ground of American interests; and when Castlereagh opposed to them Gambier, Goulburn, and Dr. Adams [not a member of the American Adams family], he sacrificed whatever advantage diplomacy offered; for in diplomacy as in generalship, the individual commanded success (*History*, IX, 14).

Where "the individual commanded success" history directs attention to individual ability and character. But here, Adams does not stop with a simple justification of his historical concern with important individuals; he goes further, to compliment the American delegations—of 1814 but of 1783 as well. Superior men, like John and John Quincy Adams, are facts; and such facts, placed in proper sequence, make history, or at least the history of diplomacy and "generalship."

Once this point is clear, Henry Adams feels free to suggest that history displays other parallels too. Issues and principles are created out of repetition as well as change; John Quincy Adams, who learned politics from his father, also learned loyalty to his father's political convictions. John Adams's chief contribution to the Treaty of 1783, for example, was the article guaranteeing fishing rights for New England, an article that his son later tried unsuccessfully to defend at Ghent:

> John Adams's persistence secured the article of the definitive treaty, which, without expressly admitting a natural right, coupled the in-shore fisheries and the navigation of the Mississippi with the recognition of independence. In 1814 as in 1783 John Adams clung to his trophies, and his son would have waged indefinite war rather than break his father's heart by sacrificing what he had won; but at Ghent the son stood in isolation which the father in the worst times had never known. Massachusetts left him to struggle alone for a principle that needed not only argument but force to make it victorious (*History*, IX, 45).

Thus, the personal cost of family loyalty could be high indeed. As their descendant realized, both Adams Presidents had suffered during their careers from a sharp drop in popularity and a resultant loss of political effectiveness. Principled conduct sometimes led to political failure. In Henry Adams's view, the political philosophy of the family, studied alongside the course of events and the alignment of forces in America since 1783, showed no real evidence of modification, compensation, or adjustment to meet changed circumstances. The result was an increasing irrelevance of the family position, and, on the part of family members, a stubborn determination to maintain Adams honor, even at the cost of obsolescence.

Later, Henry Adams would make the same point about his own Adams generation in the *Education*, where he identified himself as "an eighteenth-century man" displaced in the twentieth century. Here, in the *History*, he traces that pattern of displacement in the past and shows how personal failure became an inescapable consequence of the paradoxical situation in which the Adamses found themselves. The immediate subject is John Quincy Adams, but a general lesson also emerges:

> By a misfortune commonly reserved for men of the strongest wills, he represented no one but himself and a powerless minority. His State repudiated and, in a manner, ostracized him. Massachusetts gave him no support, even in defending her own rights; by every means in her power she deprived him of influence, and loaded him with the burden of her own unpopularity. Adams represented a community not only hostile to the war, but avowedly laboring to produce peace by means opposed to those employed at Ghent. If the Ghent commission should succeed in making a treaty, it could do so only by some sacrifice of Massachusetts which would ruin Adams at home. If the Ghent commission should fail, Adams must be equally ruined by any peace produced through the treasonable intrigues or overt rebellion of his State (*History*, IX, 16).

Ability and character had made John Quincy Adams one of the best of all American diplomatists; yet he found himself finally in circumstances over which he had little control and from which he could emerge only as a failure.

Once the outline of the negotiations has been set down, the historian is ready to look more closely at his grandfather's character, especially as it showed itself in the historical context of Ghent. Measured alongside the British delegation, as we have seen, John Quincy Adams seemed an impressive figure; compared with Gallatin, who was easily the first man among the Americans, however, Adams displayed serious limitations. The precedence of Adams's nomination to serve made him (rather than Gallatin) titular head of the American commission. The results, as his grandson dryly observes, were not propitious:

> Such a head to a commission so constituted needed all the force of character which Adams had, and some qualities he did not possess, in order to retain enough influence to

shape any project into a treaty that he could consent to sign; while Gallatin's singular tact and nobility of character were never more likely to fail than in the effort to make allowance for the difficulties of his chief's position (*History*, IX, 16-17).

Nor was the problem of personalities unacknowledged by John Quincy Adams himself. In a letter to his wife, which the historian reprints, grandfather Adams recorded his own analysis of strengths and weaknesses:

"Of the five members of the American mission, the Chevalier [Bayard] has the most perfect control of his temper, the most deliberate coolness; and it is the more meritorious because it is real self-command. His feelings are as quick and his spirits as high as those of any one among us, but he certainly has them more under government. I can scarcely express to you how much both he and Mr. Gallatin have risen in my esteem since we have been here living together. Gallatin has not quite so constant a supremacy over his own emotions; yet he seldom yields to an ebullition of temper, and recovers from it immediately. He has a faculty, when discussion grows too warm, of turning off its edge by a joke, which I envy him more than all his other talents; and he has in his character one of the most extraordinary combinations of stubbornness and of flexibility that I ever met with in man. His greatest fault I think to be an ingenuity sometimes trenching upon ingenuousness" (*History*, IX, 51).

Another letter, reprinted from "Adams MSS," expresses John Quincy Adams's view more simply: "Mr. Gallatin keeps and increases his influence over us all. It would have been an irreparable loss if our country had been deprived of the benefit of his talents in this negotiation" (*History*, IX, 50-51). Henry Adams, basing much of his account of Ghent on the family diaries and letters, remarks: "Whatever Adams thought of the treaty, his respect for at least two of his colleagues was expressed in terms of praise rarely used by him," and at another point the historian corrects his ancestor by stating flatly: "Gallatin never lost control of his temper or his tongue" (*History*, IX, 50; VI, 446).

Albert Gallatin and John Randolph in the History

The Albert Gallatin of the *History* is largely consistent with the portrait Adams had offered in his earlier biography. The chief differences may by explained by the author's need to place his old hero in a secondary position, as an executive aide to the Virginia Presidents, and by the effects of extending the portrait through nine volumes. Overall, Gallatin emerges more as a standard for measuring other men than as an actor in his own right. His character, actions, and ideas are all fully considered. But his own influence upon history is never allowed to become a dominant theme in the *History*. The reason seems clear: Gallatin simply was not, in Adams's view, truly representative of the Jeffersonian school. The historian takes every opportunity to underscore this point. In sum, he treats Gallatin as a noble figure cast in a supporting role. A few samples will illustrate:

> Gallatin's fitness was undisputed. . . . Any question of Gallatin's patriotism suggested ideas even more delicate than those raised by doubts of his fitness. . . . The men who doubted Gallatin's patriotism were for the most part themselves habitually factious, or actually dallying with ideas of treason (*History*, V, 6).

> Upon Gallatin, as usual, the brunt of unpopular responsibility fell (*History*, V, 178).

> . . . Gallatin redeemed the mistakes of his party. . . . Gallatin never failed to cover every weak spot in the Administration (*History*, IV, 148).

> So it happened that Jefferson gave up his Virginian dogmas, and adopted Gallatin's ideas (*History*, III, 18).

> Failing to obtain guidance from the President, Gallatin wrote a Report. . . . For clearness and calmness of statement this paper . . . has never been surpassed in the political literature of the United States (*History*, IV, 370-71).

Developed principally by the literary technique of accretion, the composite figure of Gallatin is impressive. As Adams touches upon familiar points—ability and character, balance and control, achievement and disappointment—"the Genevan" gradually acquires a special status as the appropriate measure for other outstanding men.

Even brief references to Gallatin call up by allusion the fuller description of the man as a nearly ideal standard: "Even Gallatin, who in 1809 had been most decided for war, was believed in 1812 to wish and to think that it might be avoided" (*History*, VI, 225). Finally, more than any other figure in the *History*—more than Jefferson or John or John Quincy Adams—it is Gallatin who provides the test case for human ability and intelligence. Thus, the ultimate denial to Gallatin of a place on the top rung of national leadership—the office of President—represents in the author's view yet another example, to be cataloged alongside the careers of the two Adamses, of outstanding human ability and character scorned by a nation of ingrates. For the failure of the nation to reward individual greatness is an important theme of the *History*.

> History showed the financial charlatan to be popular, not so much because he was dishonest as because he gratified an instinct for gambling as deep as the instinct of selfishness; and a common notion of a financier was that of a man whose merit lay in the discovery of new sources of wealth, or in inventing means of borrowing without repayment. Gallatin professed to do neither (*History*, VI, 127).

John Randolph, on the other hand, as Gallatin had recognized and as Henry Adams agreed, failed because of his own flawed character. The course of his individual actions traced a decline in usefulness and, finally, in sanity. The young man of ability entered the political scene in 1801, and soon accepted leadership of his party. By 1805, serious weaknesses in his character appeared; by 1816 his historical energies had been destroyed by "eccentricities, which amounted to insanity." These assertions constitute a bare outline of Randolph's career during the period covered by the *History*.

Again, by making this "Virginian" a representative of the weaknesses and errors of his party, and then by undercutting the man and his associates, Adams is able to suggest, from almost the first page of the *History*, that Randolph's role must finally be judged more pathetic than tragic, exactly the fate of the "State-rights school." One extended example will illustrate the power of Adams's attack:

> Speaker [of the House of Representatives Nathaniel] Macon, in appointing his standing committees, passed over both [William B. Giles and Samuel Smith] in order to bring forward a young favorite of his own,—a Virginian barely twenty-eight years old, whose natural quickness of mind and faculty for ready speaking gave him prominence in a body of men so little marked by ability as was the Seventh Congress. During several years the Federalist newspapers never wearied of gibing at the long lean figure, the shrill voice and beardless face of the boyish Republican leader, among whose peculiarities of mind and person common shrewishness seemed often to get the better of intense masculine pride. Besides his natural abilities and his superior education, the young man had the advantage of belonging to the most widely connected of all Virginia families; and this social distinction counted for everything in a party which, although reviled as democratic, would be led by no man without birth and training. Incomprehensible to New England Federalists, who looked on him as a freak of Nature; obnoxious to Northern democrats, who groaned in secret under his insane spur and curb; especially exasperating to those Southern Republicans whose political morality or whose manners did not suit him,—Randolph, by his independence, courage, wit, sarcasm, and extreme political orthodoxy, commanded strong influence among the best Virginians of the State-rights school. More than half the Virginia delegation belonged to the same social and political caste; but none of them could express so well as Randolph the mixture of contradictory theories, the breadth and narrowness, the aspirations and ignorance, the genius and prejudices of Virginia (*History*, I, 267–68).

Adams adds to this forceful beginning with stroke after stroke, which together compose a progressively less attractive human figure and a growing danger in national politics. Indeed, this passage actually seems subdued alongside later additions, which depart as far as anything in the *History* from the author's announced ideal of unprejudiced "facts" arranged in sequence.

Apart from his vitriolic energy, Adams's general treatment of the Virginian derives most of its impact from an oblique insistence upon Randolph's eccentricity. For this purpose the literature of the Adams family supplied contemporary documentation and a useful second voice to add to the historian's own. Randolph's performance during the session of 1804-1805, for example, is described in words taken directly from John Quincy Adams's diary:

> Randolph's closing speech was overcharged with vituperation and with misstatements of fact and law, but was chiefly remarkable on account of the strange and almost irrational behavior of the speaker. Randolph's tall, thin figure, his penetrating eyes and shrill voice, were familiar to the society of Washington, and his violence of manner in the House only a short time before, in denouncing [Gideon] Granger and the Yazoo men, had prepared his audience for some eccentric outburst; but no one expected to see him, "with much distortion of face and contortion of body, tears, groans, and sobs," break down in the middle of his self-appointed task, and congratulate the Senate that this was "the last day of my sufferings and of yours" (*History*, II, 236-37).

As if these two portraits were not enough, Henry Adams adds a third, one which could not be directly linked to Adams family prejudice (although it was also recorded in John Quincy Adams's diary): "Senator Giles said in private that Randolph's report was 'a perfect transcript of Randolph's own character; it began by setting the claims of the Louisianians at defiance, and concluded with a proposal to give them more than they asked'" (*History*, II, 400-401). Three generations of Adamses had shared a laugh at Randolph's expense, thanks to the family tradition of careful record keeping.

The more serious significance of John Randolph emerges from Adams's treatment of the period between 1805 and 1810, in particular; Randolph becomes a generic representative of human failure, the unsound man placed in a position that requires qualities of mentality and leadership that he simply does not possess. Randolph, in short, is made into a polar opposite for Albert Gallatin. The Virginian displays a foolish inconsistency, an inability to gain the confidence of his fellow representatives, and a dangerously unsound mind. Most interesting of all, perhaps, Randolph becomes the standard by which extreme mental obtuseness (so great as to suggest a national danger) and savage incivility are measured: "The treasonable plans of Burr and Wilkinson were a matter of common notoriety, and roused anxious comment *even* in the mind of John Randolph. . . . *Even* John Randolph had never gone so far as to charge his opponents with being the willing and conscious tools of a foreign despot."[15]

On the other hand, Adams freely admitted that Randolph, when he exerted the necessary self-control, could make effective use of his natural abilities and talents, as he did in the Congress of 1808, when "he alone shone among this mass of mediocrities, and like the water-snakes in Coleridge's silent ocean his every track was a flash of golden fire" (*History*, IV, 379). And after 1809, when "discord had become his single object in public life," there were still brief moments of brilliance and effectiveness (*History*, IV, 438). All this, of course, made the destruction of Randolph at his own hands the more pathetic, Adams shows, because, even in the role of obstructionist Randolph sometimes exhibited signs of a greatness that, except for the flaws in his character, might have changed his fate: "With all Randolph's faults, he had more of the qualities, training, and insight of a statesman than were to be found elsewhere among the representatives in the Eleventh Congress; . . ." (*History*, V, 209). In John Randolph, then, Adams saw a man with great human potential destroyed by the failure to achieve firm personal discipline, which New England training had produced in the famous Adamses: "Randolph became almost statesmanlike, and for a brief moment showed how valuable he might have been had his balance equalled his intelligence" (*History*, V, 362–63).

In portraying John Randolph, Adams was concerned not only with a single man but also with a region, a class, and a political faction: "The Southern gentry could not learn patience. John Randolph, in many respects the most gifted man produced by the South in his generation, and certainly the one who most exaggerated the peculiar qualities and faults of his class, flung away the advantages of every success by attempting to punish his opponents,—as though the hare had stopped in his race to beat the tortoise with a whip" (*History*, III, 367). Randolph "spoke the voice of Virginia with autocratic distinctness," and with unfortunate effects: "the influence of Randolph and of popular prejudices peculiar to Southern society held the House stiffly to an impracticable creed" (*History*, II, 97; III, 355). Adams's sentiment would later be echoed in his treatment of another symbolic representative of Southern character, the figure of "Roony" Lee in the *Education*. In the *History*, the author begins by equating Randolph with the South and then lays bare the deficiencies of both:

> The disasters of the Southern, or what was afterward known as the State-rights, party were largely due to temper. The habit of command, giving self-confidence and vigor of will, opened a boundless field for extravagances. The strength of men like Randolph and Early was their chief weakness; they had every sense except the sense of proportion (*History*, III, 366).

The historian attempts to prove that the political disasters of 1800–1816 derived from the failure of Southern leadership to carry out the Jeffersonian program. Using his familiar method of historical shorthand, Adams maintains that this larger failure can conveniently be measured in miniature by studying the career of John Randolph.

One additional detail makes Randolph especially useful for Adams's purpose: reentering the House in 1816, Randolph reappears upon the scene at the moment near the end of the *History* when the historian is ready to summarize: "Randolph's eccentricities, which amounted to insanity," had long before limited his influence among his colleagues; these "eccentricities," however, "did not prevent him from reflecting the opinions of a large part of the nation, particularly in the South" (*History*, IX, 111). Randolph's historical value then, finally must be measured not within the House, or even within the South, but in a larger context—one that includes consideration of the whole American nation and her history:

> Although his early career had ended in the most conspicuous failure yet known in American politics, he returned to the House, with intelligence morbidly sharpened, to begin a second epoch of his life with powers and materials that gave him the position of equal among men like Calhoun, Pinkney, and Webster. Randolph held a decisive advantage in wishing only to obstruct. . . . In every growing people two or more distinct characters were likely to rise, else the people would not grow; but the primal character, which Randolph meant to represent, enjoyed the political advantage of passive resistance to impulse from every direction (*History*, IX, 109–10).

Adams's identification of Randolph as a "primal" character type ties him to Ratcliffe in *Democracy* and to President Grant in the *Education*. Each figure came to symbolize, in the mind of the writer, an example of the barriers human nature had placed in the path of any real progress.

A Study of Men and Issues

Henry Adams's portrait of Jefferson in the *History* has already received generous attention from critics.[16] They generally agree that, while finding much to fault in Jefferson's character, especially in manners, dress, and conduct while in office, Adams still displays great sympathy for the leader of the Virginia school. This conclusion should not be surprising: for the magnitude of his task; the wide range of opinions available (much of it in sources never before introduced into American history); and the interplay of contrast and contradiction, keen perception and obvious misunderstanding, contribute to the writing of a history that must challenge many older assumptions, including some previously held by the historian himself.

One such assumption about history, inherited as a part of the family philosophy, concerned the whole value of the historical study of men. The role of the individual man in making and writing history had impressed Henry Adams as early as the time of his "Captain John Smith." And, at particular places in the *History*, the writer does acknowledge that, especially in the circumstances of "diplomacy and generalship"—for example at Ghent and during the War of 1812—individual leaders actually determined the course of events. At less dramatic moments, Adams's descriptions still reveal an acceptance of the underlying analogy between men and nations. "Nations like individuals, when driven to choose between desperate courses, might at times be compelled to take the chances of destruction, often destroying themselves, or suffering irreparable harm" (*History*, VI, 113-14).

Of course, the Adams family history was rich with examples of human destruction (the most recent being the suicide of Mrs. Henry Adams); and, among the figures in the *History*, John Randolph showed a comparable tendency toward self-destruction. But Adams's choice of words carried him further: "driven," "compelled" (by what?) hint at undefined forces that limit individual will and action. In his *History*, Adams touches upon these forces, if not finally to describe or analyze them, at least to acknowledge, in the fact of their existence, the uncertain boundaries of human responsibility and the historical inadequacy of any study concentrating exclusively upon individual men.

Some of the evidence that convinced Adams that studying men alone would not explain the workings of history derived from family sources. John Adams, in the heat of his feud with Timothy Pickering, had claimed to recognize motives of personal ambition in Pickering which he could not see in himself. Pickering, "under the simple appearance of a bald head and straight hair . . . and under professions of profound republicanism, . . . conceals an ardent ambition, envious of every superior, and impatient of obscurity" (*History*, IV, 402). Henry Adams reprinted these words from John Adams's diary, but he also qualified the original author's judgment by presenting new evidence to refute it. Letters sent to Pickering by George Henry Rose, an English politician, proved that John Adams had been wrong in his judgment because he took too narrow a view. Once again, Henry Adams used the advantage of a larger historical perspective to correct the historical record, remarking that Pickering was less a case of ambition than of human vanity; "and man, almost in the full degree of his antipathy to demagogy, yearns for the popular regard he will not seek" (*History*, IV, 402). Better information and a larger understanding led the great-grandson to a literary act of forgiveness, a response that had been quite impossible for John Adams himself. Henry Adams showed his greater objectivity by stating an historical generalization that applied as much to kinsman John Adams as to Pickering, the old family enemy.

For the same John Adams who had often denied his own ambition, or at least kept it hidden beneath his plea of "public service," had been all too quick to recognize ambition in the men around him. George Ticknor once recorded a remark of the second President which later found its way into the *History*: "Thank God! thank God! George Cabot's close-buttoned ambition has broke out at last: he wants to be President of New England, sir!" (*History*, VIII, 308). Now, having benefited from Lodge's research into George Cabot's affairs, Henry Adams could gauge the distance in time and knowledge which separated him from John Adams's remark, and then use the advantage of perspective, to summarize the general human role in the larger play of history: "Whether George Cabot wanted it or not, he was in danger of becoming what John Adams predicted. He was far from being the first man who had unwillingly allowed himself to be drawn into a position from which escape was impossible. After going so far, neither leaders nor people could retreat" (*History*, VIII, 308). Here as elsewhere Henry Adams wrote with a clear awareness that, when the historian traced only individual human figures, his search for historic explanations all too often met with defeat. The study of men was simply insufficient: "Even after Napoleon's character has been the favorite study of biographers and historians for nearly a hundred years, the shrewdest criticism might fail in the effort to conjecture what shape the Emperor's resentment took" (*History*, V, 40).

But, for Adams, the task of systematic explanation had not yet become, as it would in the late essays, the chief appeal of history. Rather, his *History* shows that fascination with human character remained a compelling motive. It was still strong, perhaps too strong, an intellectual survival of the Adams family quest to understand human nature. The old interest had been reinforced by family papers and strengthened and refined as Henry wrote his biographies and novels. In short, the habit of character analysis still had a firm grip on the historian's mind, even though Adams had reached a critical point in his own development, at which he could recognize the limitations of his method even while he savored the results. Of all the figures in the *History*, Thomas Jefferson provided the most severe test:

> The contradictions in Jefferson's character have always rendered it a fascinating study. Excepting his rival Alexander Hamilton, no American has been the object of estimates so widely differing and so difficult to reconcile. Almost every other American statesman might be described in a parenthesis. A few broad strokes of the brush would paint the portraits of all the early Presidents with this exception, and a few more strokes would answer for any member of their many cabinets; but Jefferson could be painted only touch by touch, with a fine pencil, and the perfection of the likeness depended upon the shifting and uncertain flicker of its semitransparent shadows (*History*, I, 277).

Certainly Adams's explanation owes more to the light and dark of Hawthorne's "Custom House" than to any plan for the sequential ordering of "facts." Any "perfection of the likeness," in such a light, must always remain beyond the grasp of the writer, and a history based upon such likenesses could not possibly take a shape firm enough to provide the didactic tool which Adams was searching for.

Because the study of men, by itself, proved unsuited to the purposes of the *History*, Adams went on to consider carefully the main political and social issues of the period. He especially sought to reaffirm the value of old principles, some of which had remained characteristic of family thought for four generations.

With John Randolph, as we have seen, any recourse to the larger context of "principles" was patently unnecessary. The irrational forces of his personality had determined his actions; and the part that Randolph played in the *History* could be delimited simply by tracing his relations with other men. Jefferson, on the other hand, required analysis at a higher level of abstraction. His mind demanded a far more complex historical method, one that found room to consider issues and ideas:

> The essence and genius of Jefferson's statesmanship lay in peace. Through difficulties, trials, and temptations of every kind he held fast to this idea, which was the clew to whatever seemed inconsistent, feeble, or deceptive in his administration. Yielding often, with the suppleness of his nature, to the violence of party, he allowed himself to use language which at first sight seemed inconsistent, and even untruthful; but such concessions were momentary: the unswerving intent could always be detected under every superficial disguise; the consistency of the career became more remarkable on account of the seeming inconsistencies of the moment. He was pliant and yielding in manner, but steady as the magnet itself in aim (*History*, I, 445).

What Adams had learned from his studies of individual men now led him to search further and to seek a better historical method, one that went beyond simplistic, man-centered explanations. Considered solely along lines of character, and ignoring other varieties of force, history offered no greater value than gossip or spectacle. Only a reader who loved paradox and irony for the sake of entertainment would be satisfied with such history, which made a mockery of didactic education. The War of 1812 provided a case in point: ". . . only with difficulty could history offer a better example of its processes than when it showed Madison, Gallatin, Macon, Monroe, and Jefferson joining to create a mercenary army and a great national debt, for no other attainable object than that which had guided Alexander Hamilton and the Federalists toward the establishment of a strong government fifteen years before" (*History*, VI, 418). Beneath this surface paradox, another moral was clear to Henry

Adams: his investigations had served to expose the limitations of his own method. The study of men had led him to identify new causes of failure and tragedy and thus to arrive at a larger understanding of human behavior, sometimes among members of his own family. The results, on balance, supported a philosophical belief in unchanging and unchanged human nature, the same philosophy that had long formed a basic part of the Adams tradition. Nowhere did the study of individual character give evidence to support the contradictory argument for evolutionary progress, an alternative case in which the fourth-generation Adams wished fervently to believe, both because of his family position and because he considered himself a disciple of Darwin.

Yet a significant evolution had taken place in Henry Adams's mind. As the context of his study was broadened to include a consideration of historical forces outside the human personality, and as his point of view shifted away from the actors themselves, Adams managed to increase his own objectivity; but he also became more ambitious. A limited explanation of historical causes, like the portraits in the biographies, no longer satisfied the author who had learned to demand more comprehensive answers from history—answers that applied to many men and that explained the complicated events in which they took part. Finally in the *History*, the achievements of key individuals and of men in such combinations as political parties had to be weighed alongside the largest interests of the nation. A profoundly skeptical historian summarized his view in 1883, when he wrote of Jefferson, Madison, and Monroe: "I am at times almost sorry that I ever undertook to write their history, for they appear like mere grasshoppers kicking and gesticulating on the middle of the Mississippi River. . . . They were carried along on a stream which floated them, after a fashion, without much regard to themselves."[17]

In discussing Randolph, Pickering, and the other personalities of the *History*, Adams clearly intended to warn his readers against the real dangers of sectionalism and ultimately, disunion. Perhaps the exact relationship between character and abstract political principle remains even now too complicated for easy comprehension; but it is important to recall that Adams associated his forebears with a very different set of political values, the chief of which was the cause of national union. Ten years before the *History*, in Henry Adams's "Preface" to *Documents*, he insisted that John Quincy Adams withheld his "Reply" to Mr. Otis because Union meant more to John Quincy than did his personal vanity. Thus, the "Preface" complimented John Quincy's elevation of political ideals—at the cost of personal satisfaction—without once admitting that his motives when he drafted the "Reply" might be open to serious question. In this way, Henry Adams saved himself from having to answer the charges in *George Cabot*. He also avoided opening a painful chapter of family history by turning one historical question aside in favor of another, less embarrassing one, and by subtly claiming for his own efforts as historian the same balance and judicial temperament he so often praised in others.

Nevertheless, John Quincy Adams's action in composing his "Reply" did mark a departure (however short-lived) from the highest personal ideals, including emotional balance, under the stress of disappointment, despair, and a powerful sense of failure. In his example, Henry read a general lesson, which surpassed the limits of any merely regional (New England) interpretation. It also reinforced the parallel lesson taught by John Randolph, who showed what might result if the famous Adams temper became permanently undisciplined or uncontrolled (rather than only occasionally, as in John and John Quincy Adams). For Henry Adams, the old family problem— keeping tight rein upon oneself—existed still, but now in rather different circumstances. As the writer wavered between the high ideal of "scientific" or objective history and the subjectivity of personal irritation or emotional involvement that would distort sound judgment, he was continuing the old family battle for balance and self-control—but now as a writer, rather than as a maker, of history.

The Union and the Constitution

Measured alongside the principle of Union, all other abstract issues are made to seem merely practical and almost evanescent in the *History*. This view on Adams's part should come as no surprise. His own historical position imposed the perspective of a post–Civil War observer; and thus, as an historian, he could be expected to gauge every event in the 1800–1817 period in relation to the terrible consequences of the recent war. Adams begins by acknowledging that Jefferson's inauguration brought to an end the dominance of one set of political principles; the Virginia school sought to replace them with a new set, built around a reformed fiscal policy and a devotion to the ideal of peace. Jefferson's party soon destroyed the accepted interpretation of the Constitution by concluding the Louisiana Purchase; and Jefferson himself led the way by advocating political pragmatism. As a result, there existed no systematic exposition of the Virginia or Southern position to compare with the carefully articulated political philosophy of the Federalist North. The single attempt to set forth the thinking of the Southern school— the writings of John Taylor of Carolina—Adams marked down as hopelessly incomplete. For Adams, then, no analysis of Southern politics in terms of principles seems possible. For, after taking power, Jefferson and the Republicans acted against every belief they had previously expressed, until they appeared to be endorsing the very program they had pledged to overthrow. Finally, Adams argues from his summit position above parties and factions, political principles simply will not serve to explain history. Like the study of men, a concentration upon principles must lead the historian only to contradiction and confusion.

More particularly, the paramount national ideal, preservation of the Union, could not be reconciled with Jefferson's policies, because the most obvious threat to the Union came from foreign nations, who simply made a mockery of Jefferson's often expressed desire for peace. These foreign dangers Henry Adams (unlike Jefferson) could not entirely ignore. To him, they seemed sufficient evidence of a nearly fatal lack of vision among the Republican leaders, who had focused their attention too narrowly on domestic development. Yet Adams takes his lead from Jefferson and makes the theme of domestic development— the near-doubling of the nation during Jefferson's administration—a narrative key to the entire *History*. In the constitutional question of the Louisiana Purchase, Adams finds the most important clues to Jefferson's character and to American national fortunes. He treats the Louisiana transaction with a complicated and subtle historical analysis, which the problems of international relations (excepting the working of diplomacy) never receive. But if the vision of Jefferson seems too narrow with respect to defense of the Union against threats from abroad, his exercise of power proves to be more than visionary in other ways. The peculiarities of Jefferson's mind, as Adams defines them, help to explain his expansive application of presidential powers. They tell us why Jefferson traded the restraint of a principled political philosophy for a sweeping demonstration of his executive abilities: "His instincts led him to widen rather than to narrow the bounds of every intellectual exercise; and if vested with political authority, he could no more resist the temptation to stretch his powers than he could abstain from using his mind on any subject merely because he might be drawn upon ground supposed to be dangerous" (*History*, I, 145). No other passage in the *History* shows so clearly the basis for Henry Adams's sympathy with the mind of Jefferson, or the personal danger that Adams recognized in his own "instincts." For the historian, the old political arguments which had appeared in the papers of Gallatin, Jefferson, and the Adamses, and in the speeches of Randolph—as well as the principles of the political parties and of the geographical sections of pre–Civil War America—seemed now in the 1880s to be merely irrelevant. Even the question of slavery had long been decided. All of the old issues, in short, seemed as dead as the men of the past.

Even so, where he could point to a "right" position or action, he took some trouble to do so. For example, John Quincy Adams and Albert Gallatin both had held views that reflected their independence of political parties, although Gallatin, a loyal member of Jefferson's cabinet, often acted to support his chief against his personal convictions. Conversely, John Quincy Adams, at the crucial moment of the Louisiana Purchase, objected to the unconstitutionality of using treaty powers to admit new territories into the Union. The evidence of his rational, principled behavior, taken from his diary and from papers included in *Documents*, supported Henry Adams's contention that an Adams, even at a time of national frenzy, would not allow himself to be swept along into any precipitous action. But, going further, the historian makes of the incident not simply a justification of his grandfather, according to the precepts of family thought, but also an example of independent political action at the price of political martyrdom. John Quincy's morally right conduct has been lost in the pragmatic operation of national self-interest:

> The only man in Congress who showed a sincere wish to save what could be preserved of the old constitutional theory was Senator Adams of Massachusetts, who called upon Madison October 28, before the debate, to ask whether the Executive intended . . . to propose an amendment of the Constitution to carry the treaty into effect. . . .
>
> At length, November 25, Senator Adams, becoming impatient, called again on the Secretary of State, with the draft of an amendment which he meant to propose. Madison thought it too comprehensive, and suggested a simple declaration to meet the special case: "Louisiana is hereby admitted into this Union." On the same day Adams accordingly moved for a committee, but could not obtain a seconder. The Senate unanimously refused even the usual civility of a reference. No more was ever heard of amending the Constitution (*History*, II, 117–18).

Beneath the apparent matter-of-factness of this account lies the germ of Adams's argument about the most significant difference between John Quincy Adams and Thomas Jefferson. John Quincy stands as a lonely champion of the "old constitutional theory," on grounds of political principle. Jefferson (and later Madison) represents the pragmatic opposition, determined to deal with political matters such as Louisiana without appeal to principle, simply by making of each a "special case." The alignment of 1803—Adamsian principles against Jeffersonian pragmatism—both explains what had become of the Adamses in American history and ominously foreshadows the obsolescence that Henry Adams would later claim for family politics in the *Education*.

Elsewhere in the *History* Adams makes clear that John Quincy Adams was not alone among government leaders (only among congressmen) in holding strong reservations concerning

the propriety of treaty action without constitutional change.
Albert Gallatin had written to Jefferson in January 1803: "If the
acquisition of territory is not warranted by the Constitution . . .
it is not more legal to acquire for one State than for the United
States," adding that "the United States as a nation" had an
inherent right to do whatever the States in union cared to do
(*History*, II, 79). Such thinking, Adams contends, raised Gallatin above the clash of constitutional positions; it is true that he
acted in the Louisiana affair in a manner that "advanced Federal
doctrine," but he did so without actually understanding the
issues in the controversy. For these were American party issues:
the lines of opposition were drawn by Federalists and State-
rights Republicans, and only a native American could fully
understand the political complexities.

In a curious departure from the usual emphasis upon
Gallatin's superiority, Henry Adams simply exempts him from
all responsibility because of his foreign birth:

> No foreigner, not even Gallatin, could master the theory of
> Virginia and New England, or distinguish between the
> nation of States in union which granted certain powers, and
> the creature [federal government] at Washington to which
> these powers were granted, and which might be strength-
> ened, weakened, or abolished without necessarily affecting
> the nation. Whether the inability to grasp this distinction
> was the result of clearer insight or of coarser intelligence,
> the fact was the same; and on this point . . . Gallatin
> belonged to the school of Hamilton . . . (*History*, II, 80).

In 1803, party issues such as State-rights, which were firmly
rooted in American geography, simply did not exist in the
"scientific" mind of Gallatin. And by 1883, when Henry Adams
was writing, these differences no longer seemed important or
relevant (except by way of explanation) to the purposes of an
objective historian.

No political "points" or principles had troubled Gallatin in
a political matter that John Quincy Adams understood to be
entirely a question of constitutional principle. Thus, without
holding Adams's scruples, Gallatin was left free to act upon his

loyalty to Jefferson, to move with the spirit of the times, and, in so doing, to avoid the personal isolation that was John Quincy Adams's only reward. In his own view Gallatin faced a more important task than that of preserving the Constitution; he had set himself the job "of reducing to a system the theories with which he had indoctrinated his party," and among such theories, constitutional interpretation of the treaty clause did not figure (*History*, I, 238). In fact no single issue was important enough to stand as a test of principle in Gallatin's career; rather, his political success, as Henry Adams remarks early in the *History*, depended upon the creation of a whole new political system in America. However, "By an unlucky chance the system never became fully established" (*History*, I, 243).

The chief advantage of Gallatin's system lay in its dynamic qualities—the opportunities for national leaders to change their policies with the changing times. A reliance upon static principles (or upon outdated, static interpretations of principles and issues) on the other hand, made possible only an artificial separation of opinion from adaptive action. In the *History*, Henry Adams attempts to define and make use of, at least in a limited way, this dynamic view of events. With it, he hoped to replace the simpler yardsticks of unchanging political and social values, which he had inherited from John Adams and the other eighteenth-century influences on family thought.

Of course this attempt at dynamic history created its own special problems, because no historical scale could be clearly calibrated or easily located and described. But even with these difficulties, the dynamic interpretation of history proved to be a pragmatic tool. It allowed Henry Adams to avoid most of the clichés and tired generalities, the already well-marked historical positions—based upon political parties, sectional loyalties, cults of personality—as he composed instead something comparable to the literary "flank attack" in his essay "Captain John Smith." This time, however, Adams attacked the accepted versions of history. Jefferson's complex character, for example, had to be explained in terms of an enigmatic division between his commitment to democratic ideals, which were complemented by the larger forces of change at work in the country, and another side to his "character"—an anachronistic loyalty to the politics of

State-rights (proved even more anachronistic by the recent Civil War). The latter attachment, in Adams's view, produced a partial failure of the man because it was simply not congruent with the larger movements of history. Yet only both parts together could satisfactorily explain Jefferson. By 1803,

> Federalism was already an old-fashioned thing; a subject of ridicule to people who had no faith in forms; a half-way house between the European past and the American future. The mass of Americans had become democratic in thought as well as act; not even another political revolution could undo what had been done. As a democrat, Jefferson's social success was sweeping and final; but he was more than a democrat,—and in his other character, as a Virginia republican of the State-rights school, he was not equally successful (*History*, II, 76–77).

The historian leaves unwritten an equally interesting truth about his family's adherence to the Federalist view of the Constitution: the Adams principle had become as outdated and obsolete as Jefferson's State-rights position of 1803. Perhaps an ideal actor on the stage of political history (or better, an ideal mind in the actor) might adjust effortlessly to new forces and changed conditions—without any loss of personal integrity and without giving way to personal ambition. But, instead of finding such an ideal, Adams knew and sought to show that real men always have failed to understand fully enough their own places in time. The period 1800–1817, for example, had been characterized by sectional (rather than national) experience; and in the arena of the human mind, sectional differences had prevented the easy and effective solution of basic political problems, such as the Louisiana Purchase. The limitations and dangers in Northern and Southern thinking were different, but the resulting handicap proved to be the same—a common form of mental inertia that fooled the actors and distorted the real movements of history: "If the spirit of New England Calvinism contained an element of self-deceit, Virginia metaphysics occasionally ran into slippery evasion ..." (*History*, II, 112). By skillfully developing his multiple interests in men, geography, and abstract principles, Adams is able to make several lines of attention (or force) converge at a single point. Here, the historian explains, sectionalism provides the necessary key to a satisfactory understanding of American history (especially for unlocking meaning in documentary sources). But national Union, both as fact and as an intellectual premise, must also be considered.

This use of comparative technique recalls Adams's method of inviting his reader to balance particular passages of the *History* against the larger frame organization, a balance that neatly parallels this development of dramatic tension between the necessity of sectionalism and the priority of Union. In describing America, 1800–1817, Adams creates a need for the reader to accept intellectually both parts of this bi-focal view of history, and at the same time makes him feel the tension caused by being drawn toward both the sectional and national positions simultaneously. Of course, in the *History*, the "slippery evasion" and anachronistic irrelevancies of State-rights—in short, those dangers most typical of Southern experience—receive greater attention than do the New England disabilities arising from "self-deceit" and from the lack of broadly democratic sympathies. But Adams does present the Essex Junto and the ambitions of New England Federalism as threats to American national unity, especially during the crisis of 1812. Throughout the *History* the theme of Union pays a special compliment to the Adams family, all of the members of which emerge as nationalists first and New Englanders after. And, despite the ample evidence available in the diaries of John and John Quincy Adams, not much "self-deceit" can be found in Henry Adams's account of his family. The historian's doubts about the quality of mind produced by New England and its attendant benefits and damages to his forebears and to himself were largely left aside, later to become part of the *Education of Henry Adams*.

Political Philosophy

In a more oblique fashion, the *History* actually invites the reader's consideration of Adams family ideals by attempting to measure their value on a grand scale of historical change. The historian begins by discussing John Taylor, the acknowledged philosophical leader of the State-rights school, and by making clear what must inevitably happen to all principles inherited from the past:

> His first large volume, "An Inquiry into the Principles and Policy of the Government of the United States," published in 1814, during the war, was in form an answer to John Adams's "Defense of the Constitutions" published in London twenty-five years before. In 1787 John Adams, like Jefferson, Hamilton, Madison, Jay, and other constitution makers, might, without losing the interest of readers, indulge in speculations more or less visionary in regard to the future character of a nation yet in its cradle; but in 1814 the character of people and government was formed; the lines of their activity were fixed. A people which had in 1787 been indifferent or hostile to roads, banks, funded debt, and nationality, had become in 1815 habituated to ideas and machinery of the sort on a great scale. Monarchy or aristocracy no longer entered into the public mind as factors in future development. Yet Taylor resumed the discussions of 1787 as though the interval were a blank; and his only conclusion from the experience of thirty years was that both political parties were equally moving in a wrong direction. . . .
>
> The principle to which Taylor so strenuously objected was nevertheless the chief political result of national experience. Somewhere or another a point was always reached where opposition [to the federal government] became treasonable,—as Virginia, like Massachusetts, had learned both when in power and when out. Taylor's speculations ended only in an admission of their own practical sterility, and his suggestions for restraining the growth of authority assumed the possibility of returning to the conditions of 1787 (*History*, IX, 195–97).

History and the *History* both vindicated the progressive views of John and John Quincy Adams. Their ideas had triumphed in practice, whereas critics like Taylor had been refuted by the passage of time.

Still, the historian could not end his lesson with so small a victory. For principles, like men and parties, had proved to be merely the captives of great and mysterious forces, which dwarfed all traditional categories of analysis. More than anything else, the *History* attempted to study the use of political power—presidential power—as seen primarily in Jefferson but in the Adams ancestors as well. Finally, in sum, the effects of such power were awesome. Treated as a force, it made history almost enigmatic by enlarging the historian's concern with character and principle beyond all possible limits of rational analysis.

Adams uses a double example to illustrate this point: on one single day in history, October 16,1814, Jefferson and his chief disciple, Monroe, both reversed their positions on the important issue of a standing army, each adopting the other's previous stance. Faced with such a coincidental "fact," Adams confesses himself helpless to explain history on any grounds of rational motive, character, party, or regional influence. His final resort is to the undefined nature of power itself: "As Jefferson lost the habits of power and became once more a Virginia planter, he reverted to the opinions and prejudices of his earlier life and of the society in which he lived. As Monroe grew accustomed to the exercise and the necessities of power, he threw aside Virginian ideas and accepted the responsibilities of government" (*History*, VIII, 263-64). Later, in the *Education*, Adams would make this lesson from history much more personal: "A friend in power is a friend lost." But, for the moment, he was left in his *History* with a largely unworkable alternative to the older views of historical force that he had inherited from traditional historiography. As a category of historical explanation, power remained vague and imprecise.

On the other hand, the act of attaching political labels to men and actions could also be, as Adams well knew, difficult, tentative, and not very useful, even when a slight advantage could be claimed for one's grandfather. By the winter of 1816-17, the historian noted:

> Old Republicans, like Macon and John Randolph, were at a loss to know whether James Monroe or J. Q. Adams had departed farthest from their original starting points. At times they charged one, at times the other, with desertion of principle; but on the whole their acts tended to betray a conviction that J. Q. Adams was still a Federalist in essentials, while Monroe had ceased to be an old Republican (*History*, IX, 140).

Where politics could be separated from personalities, the historian had clearly moved away from fixed family principles, except in the matter of slavery, which no longer was an issue in the 1880s. If, as Henry Adams suggests, John Quincy Adams could still be called a Federalist at the close of the 1800–1817 period, despite changes in his thinking, he represented both an important individual response to his times and a convenient standard of measure for the Jeffersonian Republicans. In fact, grandson Henry uses John Quincy to underscore the irony of a Jeffersonian school that ended its first sixteen years in power having accepted the very (Federalist) propositions that it had begun by deploring.

In this argument, the historian is not simply defending his family's political philosophy or the position of John Quincy Adams, who had always proved willing to make necessary changes. Henry Adams goes further, showing his great sympathy for Jefferson and for that part of Republican policy that aided in the development of the American nation. Thus, the historian who seemed at first, in the essays and biographies, to be concerned only with political history, here broadens his focus to include the nonpolitical influences that also helped to shape history—events that proved far more difficult to explain than did war or diplomacy, events that the historian often had to treat by means of hints and suggestions. Long before he had completed his book, of course, Adams realized that it was largely a traditional rather than a genuinely experimental or futuristic treatment. Yet, even with this heavy debt to the old historiography, the *History* still displayed a powerful undercurrent of its author's dissatisfaction with the older methods of writing history. Its real modernity lies in the author's commentary (sometimes carefully veiled) about the future implications of two presidential administrations, rather than about their philosophical inheritance from the American past.

Religion

In Jefferson, Adams confronted an obvious example of departure from traditional religious practice. Of course, the old charges of atheism were no longer worth repeating, and in any case the evidence of Jefferson's belief in the existence of some "higher power," drawn from the correspondence with John Adams, belied those more extreme accusations. Even so, the surprisingly small part that any consideration of religion plays in the whole of the *History* betrays the author's growing conviction (later to be amplified in *Chartres* and the *Education*) that religion had become almost impotent in modern American life.

In a summary chapter of the final volume, devoted to "Religious and Political Thought," Adams sought to repair what, in the *History* as a whole, must have seemed to him an obvious omission. From 1800 to 1817, religion remained outside the chief movement of history, he contends; its energies, "emotional rather than intellectual," pointed toward the past, rather than to the future. For that reason, religion deserved only a minor place in the *History*. What really mattered about religion was its "direction" rather than its power, for its power was pure emotion, as the *Education* would later insist. The two most important religious developments rooted in "the old intellectual pre-eminence" of New England were Unitarianism and Transcendentalism. Both require some consideration in Adams's view (even though their effects had been severely limited during the dominantly Southern administrations of Jefferson and Madison) because their intellectual influence could be measured in the cultural "Renaissance" of the later nineteenth century. Once again, his knowledge of what had happened *after* 1817, the nominal closing date of the *History*, imposed upon Adams an intellectual obligation to comment and explain.

As he viewed the situation, the older forms of New England

religion were as obsolete by 1815 as the political doctrines of Federalism. The religious consciousness of John Adams lay dormant, like his principles of personal conduct and political idealism. Conventional religion had become as much a victim of historical forces as the New England Puritan interpretation of history itself: "To men who believed that every calamity was a Divine judgment, politics and religion could not be made to accord. Practical politics, being commonly an affair of compromise and relative truth,—a human attempt to modify the severity of Nature's processes,—could not expect sympathy from the absolute and abstract behests of religion" (*History*, VIII, 20). How John Adams would have puzzled over his great-grandson's notion of "relative truth"! Such a pragmatic view, based upon "practical politics" and oriented toward the future, alienated the writer from the strength and comfort of his own religious heritage. Yet that heritage remained strong enough, finally, to lead him into a confession of failed purpose in the *Education*: "although he attempted the journey, he never could reach Concord." Overall, in the pages of the *History*, Henry Adams forced himself to write a painful epitaph for traditional family belief, an act which must have been all the more difficult because the writer knew that he could not claim to have found any adequate replacement.

Education and Science

The disappearance of conventional religion did not leave a complete vacuum, however. Henry Adams recognized both a personal and a national demand for new and more modern forms of education, especially in science and technology. The old family belief in learning, the historian found, had become a source of national pride by 1817, and the possibilities seemed even more promising by the time the *History* was written. In his book, Adams sought to include the most important landmarks on this glory road of intellectual (rather than military or political) progress. The reader learns, for example, that John Adams had served education "as a Yankee schoolmaster" and that John Quincy Adams left his mark upon American oratory when, in 1806, "J. Q. Adams was made Professor of Rhetoric [at Harvard], and delivered a course of lectures, which created the school of oratory to which Edward Everett's generation adhered" (*History*, IX, 205–206). Yet the author also takes some trouble to point out that the Adams family conception of science had never been conspicuously modern or advanced or as progressive as the historian might wish. By the rigorous and forward-looking standards of Henry Adams, at least, neither John nor John Quincy Adams emerges from the *History* as a representative of modernity. In fact, Henry could have gone much further in making a strong case for the scientific interests of his forebears— according to the terms in which they had conceived the "science" of their times.

When he turns to consider Jefferson, and to fix upon his chief scientific error (based, as we might expect, upon a misconception of regional difference) the result seems at most a mild demurrer: "Jefferson prided himself on his services to freethought," especially in "the scientific arena" where "he stood, or thought he stood, alone." His mistake, as Adams defined it, was rooted in deficient understanding:

> His knowledge of New England was so slight that he readily adopted a belief in the intolerance of Puritan society toward every form of learning; *he loved to contrast himself with his predecessor in the encouragement of science,* and he held that to break down the theory and practice of a state-church in New England was necessary not only to his own complete triumph, but to the introduction of scientific thought (*History*, I, 310; italics mine).

The historian goes on to show that all New England, including John Adams, was, contrary to Jefferson's belief, actively encouraging "scientific thought." Ironically, the real deficiency showed itself instead in Jefferson's thinking: "Had he known the people of New England better, he would have let them alone . . ." (*History*, I, 310).

It should be apparent that the tone of this defense of John Adams and New England does not match the stridency that Henry Adams achieves elsewhere in the *History*. The author's restraint in judgment, and especially his deference to vaguely scientific values which seem no clearer to the historian than the situation in New England was to Jefferson, point up Adams's dissatisfaction with both parties to the old controversy. He uses as well as he can an uncertain standard of progressive scientific measurement to find fault with the Adamses and with Jefferson, and also, by virtue of their representative values, with New England and Virginia. Briefly, both parties are found wanting because of the larger scientific truths revealed by the passage of time. Neither man nor section knew enough about science to use it properly, nor enough about the power of technology to claim a monopoly on progress. On this largest scale of scientific measurement, all human minds are simply judged inadequate.

The one seminal event in Henry Adams's *History* that clearly foreshadowed the future occurred on August 17, 1807. In it, anyone with enlightened understanding, North or South, should have been able to read the true course of national progress:

> . . . Fulton's success left room for little doubt or dispute, except in minds impervious to proof. The problem of steam navigation, so far as it applied to rivers and harbors was settled, and for the first time America could consider herself mistress of her vast resources. Compared with such a step in her progress, the mediaeval barbarisms of Napoleon and Spencer Perceval signified little more to her than the doings of Achilles and Agamemnon . . . but . . . Government took no notice of Fulton's achievement, and the public for some years continued, as a rule, to travel in sailing packets and on flat-boats. The reign of politics showed no sign of ending (*History*, IV, 135).

Progressive and scientific standards dwarfed men and politics, the public and the government. Adams here employs as his context a wide perspective on history, ancient and modern, to demonstrate the importance of his finding. The historian, like his chief hero Jefferson, has been led first to "widen" the "intellectual exercise" and then to measure the limits of men and their ideas. In this process, human failure may be expected but not so easily excused. For the practical application, if not the full scientific importance, of Fulton's work was clearly within the grasp of America in 1807: "Fulton's steamer, the 'Clermont,' with a single gun would have been more effective for harbor defense than all the gunboats in the service, and if supplemented by Fulton's torpedoes would have protected New York from any line-of-battle ship; but President Jefferson, lover of science and of paradox as he was, suggested no such experiment" (*History*, IV, 161).

The irony of Jefferson's criticism of John Adams on grounds of the latter's hostility toward science is underlined by these remarks. In Henry Adams's view, at least the national leader, if not the nation, should have been alert to change. Natural qualification for high position (in which both Jefferson and John Adams believed) required a receptive mind, ready to welcome progress. The American people as a whole could not have been expected to share this special awareness. Thus, not Fulton's steamboat but rather "the fast-sailing schooner with its pivot-gun—an invention that grew out of the common stock of nautical intelligence—best illustrated the character of the people" (*History*, IX, 236). Adams's metaphor appears near the end of the final volume, where he attempts to show that the identification of common democratic energies in the nation could serve the historian (as the study of individual men and individual principles did not) by helping him gain some measure of understanding and control over the raw materials of history.

Henry Adams himself was struggling to comprehend the values of scientific education in both a theoretical and a practical way, as the *Education* and late essays on scientific history would demonstrate. For the moment, however, his application of scientific principles aimed at providing a long-term value measure for the events described within the *History*:

Another significant result of the war was the sudden development of scientific engineering in the United States. This branch of the military service owed its efficiency and almost its existence to the military school at West Point, established in 1802. The school was at first much neglected by government. The number of graduates before the year

> 1812 was very small; but at the outbreak of the war the corps
> of engineers was already efficient (*History*, IX, 235).

Scientific education, as Adams conceived of it, was not finally
important as merely a quality of individual genius, found in a
man like Fulton. Rather, and particularly for the historian, this
new type of training affected mankind at large, and it played a
role in history too great to be ignored. By using "efficient"
(above), for example, Adams meant to suggest that the results of
scientific and practical training should be traced in history and
in historical conjecture. Not a single fortification constructed by
a West Point graduate, for example, "was captured by the
enemy," and furthermore, "had an engineer been employed at
Washington . . . the city would have been easily saved" (*History*,
IX, 236).

When he makes such far-reaching evaluations, Adams has
once again left far behind the simple notion of history as "facts
in their sequence." Science adds novelty to past "facts" and
nurtures a companion interest in the future. This futurism, in
turn, helps to establish a rhetorical balance between optimism
and pessimism, as Henry Adams recognizes that the old con-
troversies and principles of the Adams family are now obsolete.
He has documented page by page the ironic fact that science was
always the weakest and least understood part of the Adams
inheritance, even in himself; and yet science alone now seems
usable and useful to the historian and to modern man. The
History notes this discovery but only in passing; for Henry
Adams was not yet ready to remake history as a scientific
experiment. The future, he hints, can be expected, nonetheless,
to bring forth a very different interpretation of the past: "The
law of physics could easily be applied to politics; force could be
converted only into its equivalent force. If the embargo—an
exertion of force less violent than war—was to do the work of
war, it must extend over a longer time the development of an
equivalent energy" (*History*, IV, 289).

The seeds of Adams's own future as a writer are hidden in
the words of this aside, which he must have written with as
much regret as excitement. For in this analysis, the Adams
heritage appears hopelessly displaced. Yet the same historian

who, in his *History*, found himself only momentarily and obliquely concerned with science, when he came to consider his own history and especially his personal education, would feel the need to balance in his mind these new interests in "force" and "energy" against older, nonscientific habits of thought. That conflict of interests eventually gave shape to *The Education of Henry Adams*, his greatest single work.

5.

The Education of Henry Adams

The famous ancestor, still more immediate ancestors of the highest distinction in successive generations bring to their descendants with an unrelenting insistence, from which the average man is free, Carlyle's question, "What then have you done?" The effort, not unfamiliar, by which a man of independent spirit strives to show that he has merits of his own, stands on his own feet and refuses to be simply "the son of his father," is a severe one. How much more severe the ordeal when a man is forced to demonstrate that he is not only something more than the "son of his father," but also more and other than the "grandson of his grandfather," and the "great-grandson of his great-grandfather."

—Henry Cabot Lodge, "Memorial Address,"
Charles Francis Adams: An Autobiography.

The final period of Henry Adams's life, from 1886 until his death in 1918, is the story of a man in motion. From the moment of his wife's suicide in 1885, the quiet routine of research and writing, which had made the *History* possible, gave way to an extended round of intellectual and physical excursions into unfamiliar regions. Adams's physical journeys took him to Europe, Japan, Cuba, Hawaii, Samoa, Tahiti, Australia, and Mexico; his journeys of the mind were even more extensive, ranging backward and forward in time, from the medieval birth of his favorite cathedrals to the uncertain futurities of historical prediction, such as the probable death date of the universe. In all of this, the old family habit of writing played an impressive part.

144

Henry Adams's private correspondence, during the last thirty years, was simply voluminous; and today his popular reputation rests upon two titles of this "Major Phase": *Mont-Saint-Michel and Chartres*, privately printed in 1904 and first published in 1913; and *The Education of Henry Adams*, privately printed in 1907, published in 1918.

The distinctive character of Adams's late works may be found in the various uses the author was able to make of his own shifting concern for his subjects and in his retrospective point of view. Aside from the specialized essays devoted to scientific possibilities in history and the final section of the *Education*, the writings from 1886 to 1918 show the author's marked disposition to review the past. Adams also insisted upon expressing his own deep sense of inner division, the divided personality of Henry Adams acting as author and subject, which he had noted in his letters as early as the 1860s but which now began to stamp itself upon the materials of his life in new and surprising ways. Perhaps the best sampling of this personal conviction can be found in five lines of his poem "Buddha and Brahma," composed in 1891 but withheld from publication until 1915:

> But we, who cannot fly the world, must seek
> To live two separate lives; one, in the world
> Which we must ever seem to treat as real;
> The other in ourselves, behind a veil
> Not to be raised without disturbing both.[1]

In his final years, Adams returned again and again to this favorite notion of the divided self, and he was fascinated by the complexity of his own position: "The contrast between my actual life and my thoughts is fantastic. The double life is almost like one's idea of the next world," he remarked to Elizabeth Cameron.

Even though this favorite pose had become something of a game, the writer actually was learning to control the intellectual power of imagination and memory and to help himself escape at will from "actual life." *Mont-Saint-Michel and Chartres* details one such flight, backward in time and in pursuit of an alien culture, far distant from the family inheritance and from the author's present troubles. That book was an act of literary escapism, which Adams sought to justify only after he had begun the *Education,* by claiming *Chartres* as a part of the historical synthesis that would link the medieval past with the personal present. As other critics have noted, the truth is different. "The impression conveyed by the *Education* that *Mont-Saint-Michel* and the *Education* were conceived together as 'two points of relation' is quite erroneous." [2] And even more important for our purposes, *Chartres* represents just that part of its author's divided and complex mind which stands for resistance to—rather than the development of—his Adams inheritance. Thus, my consideration of *Chartres* in these pages is severely limited.

The more general notion of division in the author's personality and viewpoint, on the other hand, requires discussion. The idea already had found expression in the heroines of *Democracy* and *Esther,* in John Randolph, and in the enigmatic figure of Jefferson in the *History.* All of these expressions of divided personality are really preliminary developments, pointing toward the autobiographical treatment of Henry Adams, observer and actor, who dominates the *Education.* In fact, Adams's unique position as a complex, seemingly objective, and yet a captive observer marks the ostensible starting point in the investigations of himself and his surroundings which become the story of the *Education.* As a conscious experiment in narrative expression, the book brings together its author's interests in private and public literature, in confession and exposition—and it treats all of these within a context of family influence, as the author applies an experimental literary technique that combines introspective self-examination with a method of public instruction.

Intention and Method

The personal isolation of Henry Adams during the last thirty years of his life and his seeming lack of direction and purpose as a writer both have contributed to the mystery surrounding *The Education of Henry Adams.* Composition of the book was a more closely kept secret than the authorship of *Democracy*. Not even Adams's best friends knew much about the manuscript, although he sometimes dropped provocative hints of a literary experiment in progress: "There is nothing new to say—at least in our formulas. Everything has been said many-many-many times. The pleasure is in saying it over to ourselves, in a whisper, so that nobody will hear, and so that neither vanity nor money can get in so much as a lisp." [3] Few such traces of the embryonic *Education* exist, however, although Adams's indebtedness to two specific sources, both of which bear upon the question of family heritage, should be made clear. Henry knew about the existence of brother Charles's *Memorabilia*, an autobiographical memoir devoted primarily to justifying Charles's early career in business, before he became an historian and a man of letters. *Memorabilia*, like John Adams's *Autobiography*, was built directly upon the writer's personal diary, and Charles's book was well underway by 1900. A year earlier, in 1899, Henry had enjoyed reading another little volume that explored the general questions of family and of success in the world through the format of a dialogue between a student and teacher: Marivaux's *L'Éducation d'un Prince*.

Henry Adams found his own use for the key word in Marivaux's title when the American came to entitle his own volume in 1907. The *Education* was privately printed and distributed to fewer than one hundred people, with a request for imprimatur and return, in an effort to test the response of every "friend" whose name entered the narrative. As Adams explained in a letter of 1915, "In general, one may say that in America an author never gets profit from printed comments on his work. What help he gets is from private inquiry or conversation—and very little of that." [4]

This "private inquiry" yielded a staggering variety of reactions, which in their turn brought forth a stream of new responses from Adams. Thus, in its earliest, privately printed form, the *Education* succeeded in establishing a dialogue between author and reader; it was a successful experiment in two-way communication, unlike Adams's essays and novels. In fact, the surviving letters of those readers who replied, considered alongside the equally varied responses of the author—who alternately denied and affirmed all sorts of intentions in his work—constitute a remarkable early history of this literary experiment. Even today, Adams's own position remains far from clear. Aside from the difficult question of authorial intention, however, the record shows that the multiplicity of Henry Adams's voices in his private correspondence paralleled one of his favorite narrative techniques—the changing voices of a persona—which he had also employed in the *Education*. In letters written throughout the remainder of his life, Adams perpetuated and even added to the enigma of the book.[5]

Of course, the small number of readers who received copies of the *Education* in 1907, all of whom were well acquainted with the author, could be expected to know already the facts of history and inheritance in the Adams family. For such readers, an author needed merely to evoke, rather than to describe and explain, the distinctive hereditary interests that stamped the spokesman of the *Education* as an Adams. But not every reader could share the sense of family in equal degree, and Adams must have realized this fact while he was writing, or, at the latest, when the first acknowledgments of his gift began to appear. His brother, Charles Francis Adams II, set down his reactions to the opening section in words that underscore this point:

> I yesterday read the first chapter—Quincy—of the *Education*; it is charming, to me uniquely delightful! But, as I read it, I couldn't help thinking that it was written for me alone of the whole living world. I already could detect the full subtle flavor! Curious! that old Boston and Quincy and Medford atmosphere of the 40's; and you brought it all back out of that remote past![6]

Brother Charles, more than any other reader, could penetrate the depths and shadows in Henry's retrospective account. But to a lesser degree, every friend in the original, private audience was better prepared than the general reading public to understand the family heritage. Nonetheless, when the *Education* was released for the general publication of 1918, the author made no attempt to supply, by means of additions or substantial changes in the earlier text, any new information. In his usual independent way, Adams allowed his final intentions to remain inconclusively demonstrated, perhaps with the expectation of studying further an enlarged public response—which, since 1918, has proved to be as varied as the initial reactions from the narrow circle of the author's friends.

To these warnings about the enigmatic qualities of the *Education*, I should add one additional caveat: my attempt to consider the book from the perspective of Henry Adams's inheritance holds no magic key to overall meaning. The following discussion does not aim at an exhaustive explication of this complex literary work or even at a balanced evaluation of the many elements that together compose the book. This study of the *Education* seeks to demonstrate the importance of the Adams inheritance in the author's thought and to explain his use of family materials as matters of content, style, and form.

Like the *History*, the most important literary problem of the *Education* is one of overall form. At the time, it seemed so significant to the author that he often discussed the matter in his letters. And, in fact, Adams never really satisfied himself that he had solved that problem in his book: "Its shape is— provisional,—and its proportions intended to be shrunk at least one fourth." But no such revisions were made. As Adams went on to explain, "Every artist is fascinated by the temptation to try to do the undoable, and I am not exempt from this weakness."[7] As early as 1887, he playfully confessed:

> [Clarence] King says we [John Hay and Adams] ought to publish our joint works under the title of "The Impasse Series," because they all ask questions which have no answers; but nothing has any real answer, and when one walks deliberately into these blind alleys where Impasse is stuck up at every step, one cannot, without a certain ridicule, knock one's head very violently against the brick wall at the end.[8]

By the time he came to write the *Education*, Adams had given more thought to the matter, finding at least the possibility of a solution in a more sophisticated theory of literary technique:

The pen works for itself, and acts like a hand, modelling the plastic material over and over again to the form that suits it best. The form is never arbitrary, but is a sort of growth like crystallization, as any artist knows too well; for often the pencil or pen runs into side-paths and shapelessness, loses its relations, stops or is bogged. Then it has to return on its trail, and recover, if it can, its line of force. The result of a year's work depends more on what is struck out than on what is left in; on the sequence of the main lines of thought, than on their play or variety (*Education*, 389).

Appearing almost four-fifths of the way through the *Education*, this passage pays tribute to its author's ideal of organization, but with the same mixture of apology and failure that the reader so often encounters elsewhere in the book. Like "facts" placed "in their sequence," the objective form that Adams once had hoped to achieve in the *History*, his new goal once again described an example of what actually became "undoable" in the work itself. For, alongside this artistic formula, the reader must consider also the almost uncontrollable play of forces acting upon the author:

Science has proved that forces, sensible and occult, physical and metaphysical, simple and complex, surround, traverse, vibrate, rotate, repel, attract, without stop; that man's senses are conscious of few, and only in a partial degree; but that, from the beginning of organic existence his consciousness has been induced, expanded, trained in the lines of his sensitiveness; and that the rise of his faculties from a lower power to a higher, or from a narrower to a wider field, may be due to the function of assimilating and storing outside force or forces (*Education*, 487).

In Henry Adams's mind, the whole process was nothing less than human education—and the subject of his *Education*—viewed from the perspective of modern science. Science had simply expanded the meaning of "education" beyond anything the earlier Adamses ever dreamed of. In "force or forces" was hidden the vital power that Henry Adams's pen had to model "over and over again to the form that suits it best."

Once these two sides to Adams's literary problem in the *Education*—the ideal of form and the acknowledgment of force—are well understood, we are ready to study the author's quest for a usable solution. Perhaps that quest must be judged a failure at any level short of final synthesis, where Adams may have succeeded in making his book a unified demonstration of chaos, but only if the narrative and didactic elements remain satisfactorily fused. Such a judgment is highly subjective, and it should be based on the broadest possible understanding of what Henry Adams sought to accomplish with his innovative literary method. He knew much about problems of form, for example, since important documents among the Adams papers had put such difficulties on display for family readers (if not the larger world) to see. John Adams's *Autobiography* foundered when the author could no longer push the theme of his life through the other materials he had collected from memory and from his diary writings; and the diaries from the first two generations exhibited no dramatic unity or overall form, despite the dramatic qualities of individual passages. Henry Adams himself had once attempted a narrative life of his grandmother, Louisa Catherine Adams, only to have the biographical frame collapse into a mere collection of her letters, which the author put aside and left in manuscript. Henry also had been dissatisfied with his biographies of Randolph and Gallatin, in the first case because the life of his subject moved away from, rather than toward, any dramatic climax; and, in the second, because the author's concentration on politics did serious injustice to the possibly greater value of Gallatin's career in science. In both books, the writer had managed his task competently enough to satisfy the traditional requirements of history and biography only because he had sacrificed experimental narrative possibilities (like those used in his novels) by falling back on the old-fashioned method: chronological organization, centered on a single life.

In the *Education* the problem of overall form became even more complex because the book was personal. To combine thoughts with dramatic incidents from life, to decide what to include and omit, to achieve a consistent tone and narrative logic throughout—all would be required in a successfully unified work of art. As it was written, the book abounds with expressions of doubt about its author's success in finding any satisfactory solution. When Adams considers his position as an heir of an ordered intellectual system, he makes a case for his shortcomings by declaring that family thought had reached a point of unity with his father, and that by the fourth generation the Adams mind could not be expected to retain any ideal of order transferable to thought and writing: "The Minister's mind like his writings showed a correctness of form and line that his son would have been well pleased had he inherited" (*Education*, 213). But inherit, he did not.

Adams was most successful in defining his problem when he turned away from his own experience to write the last of his biographies, *The Life of George Cabot Lodge* (1911). Lodge had lived as an artist, whose poetry the biographer could not simply ignore, to concentrate instead on the matter-of-fact details of his life. The biographer met this challenge by offering a sympathetic criticism of the young poet's major work, "Herakles," a dramatization of the religious myth, written in a way that revealed Adams's own artistic concern with the seemingly irreconcilable differences between "dramatic" and "philosophic" existence, between life and thought:

> Critics object to the "Herakles" of Euripides that it consists of two separate dramas. The same objection applies to the myth itself. The Savior—whether Greek, or Christian, or Buddhist—always represents two distinct motives—the dramatic and the philosophic. The dramatic climax in the Christian version is reached in the Crucifixion; the philosophic climax, in the Resurrection and Ascension; but the same personal ties connect the whole action, and give it unity. This is not the case either with Herackles or Buddha.[9]

Nor was it the case with Henry Adams, the chief subject of the *Education*. If the poet Lodge should be forgiven because his materials failed to provide for unified "dramatic construction," the narrator in prose of a complex and divided set of actions and thoughts, belonging to a single individual, might also be excused for holding such a *donnée* only loosely together within the frame of a single life.

Once that overall form of the *Education* had been determined, it became the author's business to fill the outlines of Henry Adams's life with the multitude of individual lessons, which all together made up an education. The simplest sequence, following the theme of individual existence and appropriate to the author's training as an historian, had to be an ordering by time; and indeed Adams makes use of a time sequence in both usual and unusual ways. Thus, the book first appears to be a chronological history of the titular character from birth to old age (with a strong suggestion of impending death in the later pages). Also, the reader's historical sense is constantly evoked by reference to centuries and geological periods: "... one's earliest ancestor and nearest relative ... was *Pteraspis,* a cousin of the sturgeon, ... whose kingdom ... was called Siluria" (*Education,* 229). Simultaneously, however, Adams attempts to surprise or startle the reader who expects simple continuity by occasionally disregarding the time sequence entirely, by creating such interruptions as the twenty-year break between Chapters XX and XXI, "Twenty Years After." The hiatus in time parallels the omissions in geological evidence, and both refute the possibility of an orderly education. Adams tried to explain the meaning of the game he played with time in a letter of 1903: "Science has given up the whole fabric of cause and effect. Even time–sequence is beginning to be threatened. I should not at all wonder if some one should upset time."[10]

Adams did "upset time" in the *Education.* The violations of a linear time organization become an important part of the author's message, offered to the reader by demonstration as well as in the commentary. Adams underscores his objections to the old time conventions by drawing lessons from those parts of his past that seem most traditional and nonscientific:

> Historians undertake to arrange sequences,—called stories, or histories—assuming in silence a relation of cause and effect. These assumptions, hidden in the depths of dusty libraries, have been astounding, but commonly unconscious and childlike; so much so, that if any captious critic were to drag them to light, historians would probably reply,

with one voice, that they had never supposed themselves required to know what they were talking about. . . . Where he saw sequence, other men saw something quite different, and no one saw the same unit of measure. . . . Satisfied that the sequence of men led to nothing and that the sequence of their society could lead no further, while the mere sequence of time was artificial, and the sequence of thought was chaos, he turned at last to the sequence of force . . . (*Education*, 382).

As an Adams, the spokesman was declaring himself free of his inheritance in politics and religion; as a writer, he was by the same declaration freed from methods of expressing what he found in any literary mode that depended upon the very sequences he found fault with. History, whether considered as a succession of time units or of men, of individuals or of institutions, was valueless as an exhibition of sequence; and the notion of progress seemed hardly less of a sham. When Adams turned his back on the family tradition, as he did in the last two-fifths of the *Education* (beginning with "Chicago," Chapter XXII), his essays into science ranged farther and farther from man and toward those impersonal and nonhuman forms of force which alone appeared to provide some hope for measuring sequence.

Only after reading the final chapter, "Nunc Age," however, do we realize what has happened to the child who was born into the Adams household in Chapter I. As a center of attention in the volume and as a representative of the Adams family, that figure has been made the victim of "the new powers that had been created since 1840, and were obnoxious because of their vigorous and non-scrupulous energy." Henry Adams as the subject has been superseded and the "sequence of men" has been broken in the book, just as the Adamses as an institution were replaced in society by the new forces that the childless writer labors to make graphic for his audience:

They were revolutionary, troubling all the old conventions and values, as the screws of ocean steamers must trouble a school of herring. They tore society to pieces and trampled it under foot. As one of their earliest victims, a citizen of

Quincy, born in 1838, had learned submission and silence, for he knew that, under the laws of mechanics, any change, within the range of the forces, must make his situation only worse; but he was beyond measure curious to see whether the conflict of forces would produce the new man, since no other energies seemed left on earth to breed. The new man could be only a child born of contact between the new and the old energies (*Education*, 500).

While the instructive value of the family is emphasized in the early chapters of the *Education* (which we shall study in some detail) a sense of family is missing from the last sections of the book, where all traditional forms of education have been replaced by abstract speculations about force. The author uses this conjunction of ideas to represent a human process—maturation of the mind. Concomitantly, the rhetorical emphasis upon Adams's individual identity diminishes, as consciousness is "induced, expanded, trained." Thus, the literary setting becomes identifiable as a theater of thought and no longer one of human actions, as old-fashioned history had been.

The artistic creation of this effect relies upon a complex narrative point of view and a developing rather than a static persona, to act as subject. The device of third-person narration not only establishes a tone of scientific detachment but also serves in a larger way to keep the author separate from the subject figure. Adams is left free to comment as a retrospective observer, one who has already completed an education and now is teaching what he has himself learned. In fact, his commentary forms a sequence of its own, a sequence of lessons shaped to the purpose of his reader's education. It is not arranged to show the personal experience of the titular subject.

The result of this shift may be difficult to comprehend (especially while reading the book for the first time) or even to explain fully. It amounts to an expansion of the original narrative line, by means of which each incident described becomes a model lesson, fitted into a sequence in the education of the reader. For example, when the author discusses Charles Sumner's election to the Senate in 1851, he ties the event to a major political line of force being developed throughout the book, the issue of slavery:

The next day, when the boy went to school, he noticed numbers of boys and men in the streets wearing black crape on their arm [*sic*]. He knew few Free Soil boys in Boston; his acquaintances were what he called pro-slavery; so he thought proper to tie a bit of white silk ribbon round his own arm by way of showing that his friend Mr. Sumner was not wholly alone. This little piece of bravado passed unnoticed; no one even cuffed his ears; but in later life he was a little puzzled to decide which symbol was the more correct. No one then dreamed of four years' war, but everyone dreamed of secession. The symbol for either might well be matter of doubt (*Education*, 51).

This paragraph begins as a simple narration, stressing first the perception and then the limits of comprehension in "the boy." A retrospective point of view allows the author to focus on the education of the subject rather than upon the action described. The narrative persona plays both actor and observer, and the author's description of what has been learned is directed to his readers as much as to the implicit question of cause. Finally, the problem of symbolic value—white and black—remains unsolved, a public as well as personal puzzle, which readers are invited to consider. Their experience (as well as his) is brought into play, and the narrative method of the lesson prevents them from finding in the book merely what they might have expected from Henry Adams—an attack on the evils of slavery.

By the time he came to write the *Education*, Adams had studied his audience fully enough to understand that the reception of his writing might be affected as much by the predispositions of his readers as by the set of experiences which had conditioned his attitudes as a writer. In short, he knew that he had to use all of the literary devices he could command in order to prevent his readers from finding in his book only what they were looking for to begin with. In particular, his apprenticeship in working with the family papers had alerted him to the problems created by the special biases and prejudices of the public:

I am always interested to see how, in spite of themselves, our extra-New-England writers are driven back on J.

Q. Adams's Diary. That the Diary is far from pleasant, one must own; but the real want of sympathy touches all New England. You are the only person I have ever heard speak of John Adams as a letter-writer and humorist. If he had lived in Pennsylvania or Virginia, he would have been a classic.[11]

His historical research led Adams to understand that regionalism was not only a dangerous bias in historical judgment—one that had to be overcome if he was to write objective history or to evaluate fairly the historical records of the past—but also a particular form of prejudice from which the Adams family could not easily escape. All New England writing must encounter, within the nation, a critical reception based upon regional bias—in brief, a regional criticism. Adams knew that as a New England writer he could expect to be judged not simply on the merits of his work but also by his position in a distinguished New England family, and, what amounted to much the same thing, his association with New England, the ancestral home of the Adamses.[12] As Henry reminded his brother Brooks,

No man that ever lived can talk or write incessantly without wearying or annoying his hearers if they have to take it in a lump. Thanks entirely to our family-habit of writing, we exist in the public mind only as a typical expression of disagreeable qualities. Our dogmatism is certainly odious, but it was not extravagant till we made it a record.[13]

And what a massive record it was, no one but an Adams knew!

Henry prepared the *Education* as a kind of literary defense against the tacit indictment contained in family papers. He avoided "dogmatism," and, by experimenting with organization (especially to avoid any simple unity of subject or chronology), he fashioned a book that could hardly be taken "in a lump." Moreover, because of the author's special treatment of the subject, through the medium of a persona, the reader is constantly warned that he should not understand the book as merely another installment of Adams family writings, regardless of the author's name. In fact, the introduction of a "manikin" figure called "Henry Adams" actually serves to protect the author from excessive self-revelation by offering the disguise of personal experience as a covering for didactic art.

In almost the first words of the *Education*, the reader is told that he must not expect another confessional, in the manner of Rousseau. Adams's "Preface" declares that the *Confessions*, although written like the *Education* "in the manner of the eighteenth century," can be instructive in the twentieth century only when correctly viewed. Timely interpretation emphasizes limitations and not accomplishments, and makes the *Confessions* useful as a warning rather than a model.

> As educator, Jean Jacques was, in one respect, easily first; he erected a monument of warning against the Ego. Since his time, and largely thanks to him, the Ego has steadily tended to efface itself, and, for purposes of model, to become a manikin on which the toilet of education is to be draped in order to show the fit or misfit of the clothes. The object of study is the garment, not the figure. The tailor adapts the manikin as well as the clothes to his patron's wants. The tailor's object, in this volume, is to fit young men, in universities or elsewhere, to be men of the world, equipped for any emergency; and the garment offered to them is meant to show the faults of the patchwork fitted on their fathers. . . .
>
> The manikin, therefore, has the same value as any other geometrical figure of three or more dimensions, which is used for the study of relation. For that purpose it cannot be spared; it is the only measure of motion, of proportion, of human condition; it must have the air of reality; must be taken for real; must be treated as though it had life. Who knows? Possibly it had! (*Education*, X).

Adams's broader claims for the didactic value of his book will be considered below. Here, it is important to note that, as a literary technique, the use of the manikin figure serves to make more distinct the author's break with the Adams past. In short, he disclaims any special authority as a spokesman for representatives of an earlier age of success, writing in a later time that, as he hoped to make clear, denied the standard of values by which that success had been judged. In the case of the Adams forebears, readers had been able all too often to locate the Adams ego, on display in the family writings, and to mark it as a "unitary, indestructible and unchanging self." Henry objected and, as a fourth-generation author, sought to prevent this mistake by employing the sophisticated literary persona called "Henry Adams" in the *Education*.

His "Henry Adams" grows from a boy to an old man, showing himself meanwhile in a sequence of different poses: the diplomat-secretary, studying conditions in England; the young newspaperman who "is, more than most men, a double personality . . . writing in one sense and thinking in another"; the historian who sits "with Gibbon on the steps of Ara Coeli" and reviews the past until he realizes that, "No honest historian can take part with—or against—the forces he has to study"; and finally, "the man of science" who stands "bewildered and helpless" in 1900 before "the new class of supersensual forces."[14] Once again, like the use of retrospective narration, the rejection of a static figure as subject offered Adams a special freedom to investigate the alternative lines of education that present themselves when one pose after another ends with the author's judgment of failure.

That failure most often takes narrative shape as an inability to find unity in thought and instinct or to apply what has been learned to the business of living—two important parts of "education" as the word defines itself in the book as a whole. The overall lesson of failure is taught to the reader through the simple device of repetition; from beginning to end the manikin's ideas are misfit:

> Thus, at the outset, he was condemned to failure more or less complete in the life awaiting him, but not more so than his companions (*Education*, 38). . . . He had never been able to acquire knowledge, still less to impart it . . . (*Education*, 496).

Placed between these two characteristic statements of failure are at least a dozen reminders, including an entire chapter (XX) entitled "Failure," which purports to summarize the progress of the persona up to 1871, the point at which the time sequence of his life is broken by the twenty-year hiatus.

In another way, repetition also helps to overcome those special difficulties created by the absence of a conventional unity and organization. Certain points of reference are established, to which the writer returns again and again from "side-paths and shapelessness," in order to "recover its [the pen's] line of force." But old lessons are not merely repeated: rather, the reader finds himself on familiar ground only long enough to reestablish his understanding; then he is quickly moved away in the direction of a new idea. Alongside the theme of failure, for example, Adams develops a companion theme, the notion of a quest or lifelong search, which, after once being fully identified with Gibbon and Ara Coeli, is evoked by frequent references to those names, repeated throughout the book.[15] Of course the parallel suggested to the reader is the fall of America: Gibbon had studied the fall of Rome in historical accounts of action already past; Adams studies decline as it is in the process of occurring. Thus the later, shorthand references to Gibbon or Ara Coeli bring into intellectual play a larger-scale comparison of political and social forces, as well as the contrast of time sequences. Again, in a more modest way, every brief mention of "Quincy" and "Boston," after the values of those two places have been fully treated in the opening two chapters of the *Education*, serves to evoke the rich possibilities presented in those lengthy descriptions, as much as an earlier time in the personal history of the persona.

As in the case of these two sets of paired ideas, "Quincy" and "Boston," "Gibbon" and "Adams," the author often uses a relationship of contradiction or paradox to demonstrate the lack of simplicity or unity in what passes as education for the persona. Such inconclusiveness will hardly be surprising to an experienced reader of Adams's novels. But in the *Education* the effect is much stronger than in any earlier work, because this familiar device combines with the discontinuity in time organization, a changing awareness of the subject figure, and an intrusive use of a retrospective point of view, to disrupt any set pattern of expectation that may be present in the reader's mind.

Henry Adams's Debt to Family

Having touched upon these general matters, we are now ready to look more closely at the debt that the *Education* owes to Henry Adams's view of the Adams family and his place in it. Even in the final years of his life, Adams was a man badly divided by conflicts between alienation and responsibility, ambition and disappointment. He knew that the problem of ambition had pervaded the writings of earlier Adams diarists, as each generation acknowledged the struggle between inherited ideals and ambitious self-interest, and he realized that all his actions and his writings were subject to misinterpretation just because he was an Adams. With wry humor, he explained to Henry Cabot Lodge in 1876, "The tendency to blackguard the Adamses generally is, however, irresistible to the average American politician and as we shall catch it equally whether we vote for Hayes or Tilden or not at all, we can afford to grin at it." [16] In the *Education* too, humor found a place as only one of many masks the author needed to describe his curious situation.

Meanwhile, in the years between the letter and the book, Adams developed his appreciation of the family as an institution and of genealogy as a subject for serious study. In 1886 he noted: "genealogy has a curious, personal interest, which history wants"; and in *The Life of George Cabot Lodge* and the *Memoirs of Marau Taaroa Last Queen of Tahiti* (1893), Adams made it clear that he believed in the importance of the family as a determining influence in the life of the individual.[17] The latter book, enlarged and revised to become *Memoirs of Arii Taimai E Marama of Eimeo Teriierere of Tooarai of Tahiti* (1901), displayed both the author's long-standing respect for the institution of the family and his new-found excitement at having discovered what he thought to be a vital force of primitive natural energy, not as yet entirely corrupted by Western civilization. The result was high praise for Tahitian efforts in genealogy, which seemed to represent the most highly intellectualized form of such energy on display in Tahitian culture, as Adams made clear: ". . . genealogy grew into a science, and was the only science in the islands which could fairly claim rank with the intellectual work of Europe and Asia. Genealogy swallowed up history and made law a field of its own."[18] Such a unity and simplicity in science Adams must have envied almost as much as a social order in which human value and rank could be determined simply by genealogy.

The world described in the *Education*, however, was far removed from the island of Tahiti. Still, the author realized that his manikin subject had to be placed securely within the framework created by name and by place of birth. The opening two chapters, in particular, display the author's sense of family duty. The second paragraph of the first chapter, "Quincy," tells the burdens and benefits of his origins:

> Had he been born in Jerusalem under the shadow of the Temple and circumcised in the Synagogue by his uncle the high priest, under the name of Israel Cohen, he would scarcely have been more distinctly branded, and not much more heavily handicapped in the races of the coming century, in running for such stakes as the century was to offer; but, on the other hand, the ordinary traveller, who does not enter the field of racing, finds advantage in being, so to speak, ticketed through life, with the safeguards of an old, established traffic (*Education*, 3).

From this paragraph—the earliest development of the family theme—to the end of the book, the reader learns much about the sense of personal division and contradiction that the author perceives as a key to the meaning of the Adams experience.

The early chapters make clear that only origins can explain, in a fundamental way, who Henry Adams is and what he expects to learn from life. But another and an even larger thematic demonstration—the failure of all personal experience—also begins in this treatment of family inheritance: "Whatever was peculiar about him was education, not character, and came to him, directly and indirectly, as the result of that eighteenth-century inheritance which he took with his name" (*Education*, 7). Adams characterizes this legacy as a handicap and not an advantage, a fundamental source of contradictory experience rather than a unified interpretation of life. For the child born in

1838, he claims, contradiction was already in the blood; because of the marriage two generations earlier between John Quincy Adams and Louisa Catherine Johnson, the boy began his life (and thus his education) as a "half-exotic" New Englander. "As a child of Quincy he was not a true Bostonian, but even as a child of Quincy he inherited a quarter taint of Maryland blood" (*Education*, 19).

After introducing this hereditary accident as explanation, Adams fashions a political sequence leading from facts about his family to feeling and thought about the South and slavery. The conclusion, however, appears only at a much later stage of consciousness, one which will admit contradiction in place of singularity of impression, to confound the grown man. But the reader must be prepared in advance; so the author first labors to dispel preconceptions of unity and then to replace them with a preliminary understanding of the divided consciousness that the persona will later illustrate. The titles of the opening chapters, "Quincy" and "Boston," are set side by side, suggesting close association; yet the two places are treated as polar opposites in the mind of the child, each of which, in turn, is provided with its complementary set of contrasting influences. "Town [Boston] was restraint, law, unity. Country [Quincy], only seven miles away, was liberty, diversity, outlawry . . . " (*Education*, 8). As the *Education* unfolds, the two lists of opposing qualities grow longer. Quincy comes to represent the Adams side of the family and political idealism; Boston, the Brooks side and mercantilism. "Life was a double thing. . . . From earliest childhood the boy was accustomed to feel that, for him, life was double" (*Education*, 9).

These chapters echo a familiar theme of John Adams's diaries, in which he endlessly debated the choice of a political career in terms of the symbolic alternatives of Braintree (later renamed Quincy) and Boston. Now, the great-grandson characteristically turns attention away from the problem of personal ambition by making the Quincy-Boston pattern only the first of many sets of contradictions which—taken all together— convincingly document the absence of any unified consciousness in the persona. In the early pages of the book, the virtual impossibility of either a unitary summary of experience—any simple meaning in life—or a unified form of expression is not explicit. But these ideas are organically present in Adams's words; the remainder of the book develops their implications. The author begins by anticipating the contradictions of the adult mind and the absence of any unifying system, and ends his book having demonstrated both.

In the process, Adams's artistic method allows him freedom to expand the limits of his own experience, to criticize as well as narrate, and finally to encourage further speculation from his readers. Finding himself "an eighteenth-century child" who could "never compel himself to care for nineteenth-century style," the author purposely obscures his own position; first, by developing the contradiction and then by making judgments of the moment accord with either set of values, whichever suits his purpose. The pose of detachment forestalls any charge of dogmatism or familial piety and also opens the way for the reader to form a judgment of his own—sympathetic or antithetic to Adams's. Education within the family becomes the first in a series of insufficient modes of training for twentieth-century life. Once family education has been proved inadequate, the alert reader need only follow out other paths of intellectual interest, in order to test for himself each of the author's further conclusions.

Even before he began writing the *Education*, its author had revealed that he felt himself to be in an historically retrospective position, considering the Adamses from his post at the end of the family line. Worldly events simply had forced him to make some final accounting of what the whole Adams family signified or represented, and to note the dislocation of the fourth generation from traditional Adams positions. Quincy, for example, could no longer be associated in Henry's mind simply with the Adams branch of the family after the death of his mother, as his report of the event to a close friend made clear:

> Apparently I am to be the last of the family to occupy this house which has been our retreat in all times of trouble for just one hundred years. I suppose if two Presidents could come back here to eat out their hearts in disappointment and disgust, one of their unknown descendants can bore

himself for a single season to close up the family den. None of us want it, or will take it. We have too many houses already, and no love for this. . . .[19]

The Quincy described in this private letter clashes with the picture of Quincy that emerges from the *Education*, an image sifted through the memory of an aged author, who sets down his impressions for a larger public than the single friendly reader of his letter, and who attempts to re-create a consciousness of Quincy as it existed in the mind of a young boy rather than an old man.

Nowhere in the *Education* is Adams's mature evaluation of the fate of his family expressed with the simple directness of the same author's private letter. Rather, the writer treats his family with a calculated reticence, which serves to protect him from any obvious exhibition of pride in his forebears, even while he takes note of the special values of his distinctive inheritance. In the chapter "Indian Summer," Adams looks back over his past and admits:

> He thought himself perhaps the only person living who could get full enjoyment of the drama. He carried every scene of it, in a century and a half since the Stamp Act, quite alive in his mind—all the interminable disputes of his disputatious ancestors as far back as the year 1750—as well as his own insignificance in the Civil War, every step in which had the object of bringing England into an American system. For this they had written libraries of argument and remonstrance, and had piled war on war, losing their tempers for life, and souring the gentle and patient Puritan nature of their descendants, until even their private secretaries at times used language almost intemperate . . . (*Education*, 362).

Of course, "intemperate" does not fairly describe the Civil War letters of the real Henry Adams, who is here so well hidden behind the third-person pronoun and the simple label "private secretaries," any more than "disputatious" does justice to the violent reports, public and private, of temper in John and John

Quincy Adams. Instead of candid treatment, the affairs of family
are deftly handled by means of the authorial devices that
contribute to indirect narration. Thus, the obvious opportunity
for a sincere acknowledgment of family influence is quietly
passed over.

Elsewhere, the *Education* does provide a graphic demonstration of the manikin's indebtedness to Adams family members
for certain important parts of his training for life. The earliest
and one of the most notable incidents, in which John Quincy
Adams leads the reluctant boy by the hand to school, teaches a
first lesson in what Henry can expect from the world and how he
must respond to it. When the boy rebelled, his grandfather "had
shown no temper, no irritation, no personal feeling, and had
made no display of force. Above all, he had held his tongue"
(*Education*, 13). And the boy, like other generations of Adamses
before him, began to learn an important lesson from the family
model:

> For this forbearance he felt instinctive respect. He admitted
> force as a form of right; he admitted even temper, under
> protest; but the seeds of a moral education would at that
> moment have fallen on the stoniest soil in Quincy, which is,
> as everyone knows, the stoniest glacial and tidal drift known
> in any Puritan land (*Education*, 14).

By making full use of his narrative freedom as a retrospective
commentator in this passage, Adams tells us why this lesson
holds a permanent place in education: it was a lesson in force;
and, as such, it belonged to the most meaningful sequence in
nineteenth-century history and in the *Education* itself. It was not
a lesson in the old-fashioned moral rightness of family actions,
however, nor an exercise in the kind of moral didacticism that
seemed obsolete in a later time.

As the persona changes and the boy grows into a young
man, he is educated in turn by other Adamses. Henry's father,
Charles Francis Adams, in particular, assumes a symbolic
position as chief tutor to his son. What he teaches Henry
represents not merely the wisdom born of his own individual
sagacity but knowledge drawn from the collective experience of

the Adams forebears as well. To make this point, the author describes his manikin-subject as a mere "cabin-boy" who is sent along with his father to England to do the diplomatic work of a man:

> ... he was the most fortunate person in the party, having for master only his father who never fretted, never dictated, never disciplined, and whose idea of American diplomacy was that of the eighteenth century. Minister Adams remembered how his grandfather had sailed from Mount Wollaston in midwinter, 1778, on the little frigate Boston, taking his eleven-year-old son John Quincy with him, for secretary, on a diplomacy of adventure that had hardly a parallel for success. He remembered how John Quincy, in 1809, had sailed for Russia, with himself, a baby of two years old, to cope with Napoleon and the Czar Alexander single-handed, almost as much of an adventurer as John Adams before him, and almost as successful. He thought it natural that the Government should send him out as an adventurer also, with a twenty-three-year-old son, and he did not even notice that he left not a friend behind him. . . . He thought it right to play the adventurer as his father and grandfather had done before him, without a murmur. This was a lofty view, and for him answered his objects, but it bore hard on cabin-boys, and when, in time, the young man realized what had happened, he felt it as a betrayal. He modestly thought himself unfit for the career of adventurer, and judged his father to be less fit than himself (*Education*, 112–113).

In these lines a nearly complete merger of individual knowledge into collective family experience is accomplished: After opening with a faint echo of the earlier lesson in "discipline" taught by grandfather John Quincy Adams (discussed above), the writer goes on to describe in personal terms the essential problems caused by being an Adams. Taken as education, the family inheritance balances independence against discipline; the disposition to follow the track laid down by previous generations against the instinct to rebel against the duties owed to the family, even as the boy at Quincy had earlier rebelled against the

whole idea of education. Also, by mentioning the different ages
of the Adams sons who participated in parallel experiences of
"adventure," the narrator once again makes his case for Henry
Adams's inability to learn things at the proper time, an important theme in the book as a whole.

The final "betrayal" by the family is, conversely, also the
manikin's rejection of an eighteenth-century family inheritance—a rejection or a failure (depending on the point of view
at a given moment) which is repeated, as we have noted, in other
incidents and emphasized in the overall organization of the
volume. Even the judgment, "modestly felt" and retrospectively
delivered, serves to undercut the reader's respect for the narrator's position and to call his ideas into question once again; for
the father judged by the persona "less fit than himself" later
turns the "adventure" into a family success greater than those
ascribed to John and John Quincy Adams. He does it, moreover,
by exercising the same family talents that the son recognizes only
as causes of his own failure. In fact, the value of each idea as
education is double; and the sum is contradiction, although
from either point of view—eighteenth or nineteenth century, for
or against the usefulness of family—the importance of the
Adamses as an influence has been clearly demonstrated.

Another part of this demonstration takes the form of
Adams's tribute to the figure and educative value of the eternal
woman. In such writings as *Chartres* and *Esther*, as much as in
the *Education*, Henry attempted to pay homage to the extraordinary women of the Adams family—Abigail, Louisa Catherine,
Marian Hooper, among others. In his own generation, Henry
claims to have learned most from the distaff side. His sister, Mrs.
Kuhn, once again teaches a double lesson: how to live and how
to die. In the chapter "Rome," she shows her "double superiority" as she demonstrates the value of the sensuous, as against the
rationalistic, approach to life; her natural warmth triumphs
over the coldly intellectual existence of "Berlin" as it had been
described in the chapter preceding. The manikin finds her mode
of instruction warm and charming; he begins to be educated in a
way never possible under the tutelage of Charles Francis Adams
or under the influence of the traditional, rationalistic, male-
centered thought of the family:

It was his first experiment in giving the reins to a woman, and he was so much pleased with the results that he never wanted to take them back. In after life he made a general law of experience—no woman had ever driven him wrong; no man had ever driven him right (*Education*, 85).

Two hundred pages later, this "experiment" in family education ends in a disastrous final demonstration: "The last lesson—the sum and term of education"—quite properly, the lesson of death. As Mrs. Kuhn lay dying of lockjaw, "the muscles grew rigid, while the mind remained bright, until after ten days of fiendish torture she died in convulsions." Meanwhile, nature and the principle of sensuousness, which Henry's sister had taught him to appreciate during her life, combined with the grim horror of death to point up (at least as the author recalled) one final lesson for the manikin about the paradox of human existence.

Death took features altogether new to him, in these rich and sensuous surroundings. Nature enjoyed it, played with it, the horror added to her charm, she liked the torture, and smothered her victim with caresses. Never had one seen her so winning (*Education*, 288).

This experience leads the narrator to denounce family religious beliefs, as we shall later see. Another result is that the continuing line of education within the family has been broken in Henry's generation, because after his sister's death he must attempt to reorganize "Chaos" (the title of the chapter that includes the account of Mrs. Kuhn's death) independently, using only his own processes of thought, to arrive at the speculations of the following chapters. His sister had provided a different and a nontraditional type of family education, and with her death even that exotic mode of family influence has ended. The family as a direct force of education has been left behind forever in the manikin's quest for learning.

In treating grandfather, father, and sister, Adams exercised the same freedom with biographical facts that he used in the story of his own life. In 1908, Henry Adams explained his intentions in the *Education*, as he sent along a copy to Henry James, who had often surveyed the border between fact and fiction himself: "The volume is a mere shield of protection in the grave. I advise you to take your own life in the same way, in order to prevent biographers from taking it in theirs."[20] *Randolph* and *Gallatin* had helped to make Adams aware of the power of the writer, who could paint any single character from an absolutely consistent—and therefore persuasive—point of view, and then give his portrait the permanence of art. When brother Charles in 1900 published a life of their father, moreover, Henry realized what close scrutiny of one family member by another might mean.[21] He shared these feelings about the book with his younger brother, Brooks:

> . . . I am making myself a martyr trying to read it. . . . I should prefer not to dissipate the atmospheric effects of time and distance, and not to bring our figures too near for perspective. Our father would stand out better, larger and even truer, without definition. I do not like the microscope, or even the telescope, as a family ornament, and I loathe the photograph and Sargent's analysis of character.
>
> At any rate, I have, at awful cost, learned to hold my tongue, except in letters, and am getting nervous even about them.[22]

His reticence did not prevent Adams from using family members as figures in the changing patterns of the *Education*, but it did seriously limit the historical veracity of his portraits and the fullness of their development. Most often the Adamses represent a standard of evaluation similar to that employed in the biographies, and one especially useful for judging the character and actions of men like William Seward or for charting the progress of their fourth-generation descendant:

> Probably he knew more than his father, or his grandfather, or his great-grandfather had known at sixteen years old. Only on looking back, fifty years later, at his own figure in 1854, and pondering on the needs of the twentieth century, he wondered whether, on the whole, the boy of 1854 stood

nearer to the thought of 1904, or to that of the year 1. He found himself unable to give a sure answer (*Education*, 53).

Nowhere more clearly than in these three sentences is the narrative pattern for Adams's treatment of family education displayed. The manikin is first measured; the standards of measurement are questioned, using the benefits gained from retrospective wisdom. And finally, the results are proved to be inconclusive.

In his "Preface" to the *Education* the author warns: " . . . the twentieth century finds few recent guides to avoid, or to follow. American literature offers scarcely one working model for high education" (*Education*, ix). "American literature," for an Adams, included the public and private records of the family, which Henry had studied as a child and a man. By providing a summary statement of what he found, the *Education* documents his experience in learning whether "to avoid, or to follow" the models bequeathed him as an Adams. While the final value of that inheritance remains undetermined, even to the last lines of the book, Henry's own sense of personal isolation is never left in doubt. He recognizes that the family and all it represented as a "force" in the American past has now been lost, and with it much of the historical rationale for his life. Even worse, no alternative modern explanation offered itself as a replacement for what was left behind.

Using another of his polemical contradictions, Henry confronts the manikin with the symbolic alternatives of Concord and Boston—illustrating in this choice between contradictory values the painful dilemma of being an Adams:

As practical a New Englander as any, he leaned towards the Concord faith rather than towards Boston where he properly belonged; for Concord, in the dark days of 1856, glowed with pure light. Adams approached it in much the same spirit as he would have entered a Gothic Cathedral, for he well knew that the priests regarded him as only a worm. To the Concord Church all Adamses were minds of dust and emptiness, devoid of feeling, poetry or imagination; little higher than the common scourings of State Street; politicians of doubtful honesty; natures of narrow scope; and already, at eighteen years old, Henry had begun to feel uncertainty about so many matters more important than Adamses that his mind rebelled against no discipline merely personal, and he was ready to admit his unworthiness if only he might penetrate the shrine. The influence of Harvard College was beginning to have its effect. He was slipping away from fixed principles; from Mount Vernon Street; from Quincy; from the eighteenth century; and his first steps led toward Concord.

He never reached Concord, and to Concord Church he, like the rest of mankind who accepted a material universe, remained always an insect, or something much lower—a man (*Education*, 62-63).

As he contemplated "matters more important than Adamses," the author was being led away (just as he leads his reader away, in turn) from any real evaluation of the family. New paths open in many directions, but before the manikin takes another step, it is clear that the influence of the Adamses has already played out its special role in shaping the materials of consciousness—whether political, religious, scientific or other— into lessons that had to be learned on the way to some larger education.

Politics

The chief lesson that Henry Adams had to bring alive for the evolving consciousness that served as persona of the *Education* was a lesson in politics. No other subject had become so deeply rooted in the family past or so closely associated with the reputation of the Adamses; and none provided a more obvious demonstration of failure in the fourth generation. As soon as the author has placed his manikin subject in the contradictory family environment described by the first two chapters, the third chapter, "Washington," brings to the manikin figure (and to the reader) an evolving awareness of the larger political world which the child must enter automatically as an Adams: "This first step

in national politics was a little like the walk before breakfast; . . .
The second step was like the first, except that it led to . . . the
White House [and] . . . all the boy's family had lived there" . . .
(*Education*, 46). So far the path of education has been easy to
follow, but almost immediately the boy is confronted with
paradox, the technique by means of which the author structures
this new lesson in politics. The third step leads to Mount
Vernon, and it impresses upon Henry's youthful consciousness
the conflict of elements which formed his heritage, as he goes
there with his father:

> Mr. Adams took the boy there in a carriage and pair, over a
> road that gave him a complete Virginia education for use
> ten years afterward. To the New England mind, roads,
> schools, clothes and a clear face were connected as part of
> the law of order or divine system. Bad roads meant bad
> morals. The moral of this Virginia road was clear, and the
> boy fully learned it. Slavery was wicked, and slavery was the
> cause of this road's badness which amounted to social
> crime—and yet, at the end of the road and product of the
> crime stood Mount Vernon and George Washington. . . .
>   George Washington was a primary, or, if Virginians
> like it better, an ultimate relation, like the Pole Star, and
> amid the endless restless motion of every other visible point
> in space, he alone remained steady, in the mind of Henry
> Adams, to the end (*Education*, 47).

The incontestable value of George Washington as an honorific
symbol provides the lesson with its shock effect; at the end of the
political road, Mount Vernon and George Washington contradict the otherwise clear moral of Virginia and slavery. The result
is impasse. Education can go no further and still remain within
the limits of Adams's experience and control.

As we have noted, these sets of contradictory regional values
are only some of the polarities useful to the author as a means of
expressing the complications of a personal experience—
complications that finally resist all attempts at unification in a
single pattern or form. Finding himself, for example, "an
eighteenth-century child" who can "never compel himself to

care for nineteenth-century style," Adams adopts for his purpose
either set of values from one of the pairs in contradiction. He
tips the scales momentarily, in order to express an opinion or
render a judgment. At the same time (and in the same manner
which the writer had used in the *History* to suggest limitations
in his sources) the suggestion is made to the reader of a possible
further contradiction, yet to be introduced; and this anticipation
helps (along with such devices as third person narration) to keep
the writer from appearing dogmatic or excessively prejudiced,
whatever he writes about.

Where political traditions are strongest and absolutes ru-
mored to exist, Virginia values have been accepted by New
England, and no difference of opinion is left to create contradiction. Thus (in the passage above) Adams pays compliments to
George Washington and to the principle of unity he represented
for South and North alike. Already Washington and Mount
Vernon had been used by Adams in *Democracy* as historical and
geographic representations of an accepted ideal. In the *Education*, this unifying function is reintroduced, but with an important change: as abstract symbols, the two have become remote
or "ultimate" (the word choice of "Virginians"), until they can
no longer be reached by means of a pleasant ride on horseback or
in a carriage. The trip takes on new proportions that supersede
geographical regionalism: a physically impossible journey to
"the Pole Star."

For his mind, if not for the whole man, however, such a
voyage must still be possible. Failure in the attempt to reach and
then hold to the ideals of the past seems now to be a failure in
Adams's own individual experience, more often labeled simply
"education." For such failure the author blames only the
manikin; he never questions the values that enjoy general
historical sanction as ideals. Yet these values appear to alter,
under changing conditions of observation and experience, and
to become, as the observer approaches (or studies) more closely,
something less impressive than the originals. Still, the similarity
of Mount Vernon to Quincy and of George Washington to John
Adams is not left open to question:

> . . . Mount Vernon always remained where it was, with no
> practicable road to reach it; and yet, when he got there,

Mount Vernon was only Quincy in a Southern setting. No doubt it was much more charming, but it was the same eighteenth-century, the same old furniture, the same old patriot, and the same old President (*Education*, 48).

Here, contradiction finds expression in the paradox of "ultimate" relations opposed to relations first in space (distance) and afterward in time. John Adams, unlike Washington, represented one of the "points" which "shifted their bearings" as the manikin studied them closely.

The journey itself was at fault. The boy (earlier in the *Education*) had been forced, in the act of visiting Mount Vernon, to exchange his simplistic notions about the South and slavery for a more sophisticated mental stance, which allowed for complication and contradiction. Later, the teller of the boy's story, having by now assumed an alternative, retrospective narrative position, can identify not only what has been gained but also what has been lost in personal terms by the youthful voyager through life: "He was slipping away from fixed principles; from Mount Vernon Street; from Quincy; from the eighteenth century" (*Education*, 63). In the same way, the usefulness of every traditional Adams ideal becomes a matter of doubt in the course of the book.

In order to understand how far the author has traveled to reach this point, the thoughtful reader need only recall Adams's observation of 1873. "America or Europe, our own century or prehistoric time, are all alike to the historian if he can only find out what men are and have been driving at, consciously or unconsciously." Now, twenty-five years later, in the *Education*, the author traces out this old formula but only to disprove its value in a new and more scientific age. For Henry Adams, the sequence of men led nowhere: Charles Sumner had turned from friend to foe and back to friend; Charles Francis Adams had achieved success in diplomacy in spite of his serious misjudgments of both Gladstone and Palmerston, and not because of any inherited ability to analyze motives or men; and Henry Adams himself had failed to recognize the special power or character of Lincoln, who already seemed to require some acknowledgment as the most potent human force of Henry's lifetime.[23]

In brief, the old family study of men, whether of individuals or types, now leads the manikin to no form of useful knowledge. So the narrator intrudes upon the life story to express a moral which, in the later sections of the book, replaces the traditional Adams concern for men with a new and much more impersonal hypothesis, as the basis of political study:

> Modern politics is, at bottom, a struggle not of men but of forces. The men become every year more and more creatures of force, massed about central power-houses. The conflict is no longer between the men, but between the motors that drive the men, and the men tend to succumb to their own motive forces (*Education*, 421–22).

Ratcliffe, in *Democracy*, had provided a frightening example of what one might usually expect from modern politicians. On the other hand, the diplomatic successes of Adams's friend, Secretary of State John Hay, who died "wielding his power to the last" (*Education*, 504), served as contradictory human evidence, a cause for reopening the whole question at the very end of the *Education*. But Hay, like Thurlow Weed, "was one of the exceptions" (*Education*, 147). The old family standards might still be adequate for the study of exceptions; yet they could not explain behavior in the mass, where modern political power was centered.

In fact the modern situation excluded from politics the familiar principle of independent conduct which John Adams had worked to establish and then passed on to his heirs. Henry already had warned against the dangers to be found in the process of replacing the individual with a political party in both "Civil Service Reform" and *Democracy*. The latter, as we have seen, developed an extended contrast of eighteenth-and nineteenth-century politicians, using the characters of Carrington and Ratcliffe, to the distinct disadvantage of "the Prairie Giant." Now, in the *Education*, Adams employs the same literary device, this time pairing the real name and career of a modern politician with the figure of the manikin-subject, and then stating his own conclusions from a third point of view, that of the observer-narrator. The relationship between Senator "Don" Cameron of Pennsylvania and Henry Adams,[24]

led to an intimacy which had the singular effect of educat-
ing him in knowledge of the very class of American politician who had done most to block his intended path in
life. . . .

Months of close contact teach character, if character has
interest; and to Adams the Cameron type had keen interest,
ever since it had shipwrecked his career in the person of
President Grant (*Education*, 332–33).

Once the parallel has been established and the motive for his
interest disclosed, the author undertakes to weigh his two
specimen figures. His earlier chapters have already demonstrated
the moral value of Adams and New England; now he begins by
making a case for the Pennsylvanian as a type, with special
attention to the past.

Time present and future are the usual settings of consciousness in those sections of the *Education* that emphasize complexity, just as time past (especially in the passages about childhood)
is related to simplicity. The famous Pennsylvanians of an earlier
type, Benjamin Franklin and "Albert Gallatin of Geneva,"
belong not to the Pennsylvania of Henry Adams's age but to an
historical past which the *Education* and its author are attempting to supersede. Franklin is briefly treated as an exotic, a mere
exception to regional type; Gallatin is acknowledged to have
been the subject of an earlier "voluminous study and an elabor-
ate picture," which, the writer now claims (in contradiction to
the *History*), served "only to show that he [Gallatin] was, if
American at all, a New Yorker, with a Calvinistic strain—rather
Connecticut than Pennsylvanian" (*Education*, 333). The
Gallatin of the biography simply cannot be recognized in the
representative portrait of a modern Pennsylvanian that Adams
provides: "The Pennsylvania mind, as minds go, was not
complex; it reasoned little and never talked; but in practical
matters it was the steadiest of all American types; perhaps the
most efficient; certainly the safest" (*Education*, 333).

This, like a rule of law, is the rule of history, to which only
Franklin had proved an exception; and of course Franklin was a
Bostonian by birth. Both the rule and the identification of
Cameron as a representative obstruction in the "path" of politi-
cal life show the generalizing attitude of the author, who once

again enlarges upon his subject's personal experience in order to give greater meaning to the lesson.

For Adams's "Cameron type" refers to both Senator "Don" and his father, Simon Cameron. Together they represent the family political machine, and their combined example teaches not merely the obsolescence of the manikin Henry Adams but also of New England and the Adams family. Those types—the New Englander and the Adams—have become the historical victims not of the South or the Southerner, but of largely undefined forces and movements that have operated to replace the old family principles with modern values of individual mediocrity and mechanical utility:

> Never in the range of human possibilities had a Cameron believed in an Adams—or an Adams in a Cameron—but they had, curiously enough, almost always worked together. The Camerons had what the Adamses thought the political vice of reaching their objects without much regard to their methods. The loftiest virtue of the Pennsylvania machine had never been its scrupulous purity or sparkling professions. The machine worked by coarse means on coarse interests; but its practical success had been the most curious subject of study in American history. When one summed up the results of Pennsylvanian influence, one inclined to think that Pennsylvania set up the Government in 1789; saved it in 1861; created the American system; developed its iron and coal power; and invented its great railways. Following up the same line, in his studies of American character, Adams reached the result—to him altogether paradoxical—that Cameron's qualities and defects united in equal share to make him the most useful member of the Senate (*Education*, 334).

Adams's "paradoxical" review of the past sets Pennsylvania history against the traditional New England view, which for the author meant a family perspective on history, shaped by his father and brothers and informed by contributions of the Adamses in every generation. But once more, certain important questions are left unasked. From the original dual lines of consideration, the Cameron and the Adams, which carry the symbolic values of the two different character types and of the historical achievements in two opposed regions of the country, the passage turns neatly to focus the point of view of narrator and reader on only one. The logical remainder must be supplied: if the modern Pennsylvanian is "most useful," the modern New Englander—Henry Adams—must then be obsolete. In fact, the aura of obsolescence surrounds the portrayal of New England experience at every point in the manikin's education: as an eighteenth-century child, he finds himself unalterably displaced in the nineteenth and twentieth; old lessons amount to "Failure" in a "Nunc Age." Using characteristic indirection, as well as selective omission, the author of the *Education* manages to protect his family and himself against every charge of unwarranted pride, even while he preaches the familiar moral of the *Gallatin*, this time as a lesson for the present age: "There are moments in politics when great results can be reached only by small men" (*Gallatin*, 432).

Elsewhere in the *Education*, when the author turns his attention away from the family interest in men and to the great issues in which he had an inherited concern, the lessons taught to the manikin also end in paradox. On one side, the family traditionally stood opposed to slavery: "They were anti-slavery by birth, as their name was Adams and their home was Quincy" (*Education*, 25). On the other side of the family was the Southern charm of Louisa Catherine Johnson, and of Washington and the associated set of political principles centered in the proslavery South, at Mount Vernon. Again, the lesson equals contradiction; and the narrative voice adds a final note of impenetrable self-mockery: "In practice, such trifles as contradictions in principle are easily set aside; the faculty of ignoring them makes the practical man; but any attempt to deal with them seriously as education is fatal" (*Education*, 48). The manikin's search for unified knowledge is doomed to failure from the moment he begins seriously to test the political heritage of his family and of New England by the standard of usefulness.

Without being put to a pragmatic test, the heritage of Henry Adams appeared to guarantee his success: "Viewed from Mount Vernon Street, the problem of life was as simple as it was classic.

Politics offered no difficulties, for there the moral law was a sure guide" (*Education*, 33). Carried through an experimental education by the manikin, however, the same family principles meet with contradiction and their bearer with defeat: "The moral law had expired—like the Constitution" (*Education*, 280). Of course, any real conclusion to this political line of thought must be identified by means of the reader's familiarity with Adams's usual methods of narration. Judging from the repetition of the theme and its predominance in the later sections of the *Education*, for example, the chief political lesson for Adams's reader is the same one he had so often expressed to his favorite student-politician, Henry Cabot Lodge—a warning against corruption. The unqualified simplicity of Henry Adams's declarations on that subject outweighs every possible exception—like Hay or Weed or Hugh McCulloch—at the same time that it overbalances every possible paradox:[25]

> Every friend in power is a friend lost. This rule is so nearly absolute that it may be taken in practice as admitting no exception (*Education*, 248).

> No one in his experience had ever passed unscathed through that malarious marsh. In his fancy, office was poison; it killed—body and soul—physically and socially. Office was more poisonous than priestcraft or pedagogy in proportion as it held more power . . . (*Education*, 365).

> Power is poison. Its effect on Presidents had always been tragic. . . . The effect of unlimited power on limited mind is worth noting in Presidents because it must represent the same process in society, and the power of self-control must have limit somewhere in face of the control of the infinite (*Education*, 418).

By placing these fragments together, I have done some injustice to the complex organization of the *Education*, but with the hope that the force of Adams's thought will emerge more clearly. Here, the lesson, rather than being learned piecemeal, is unified and concentrated in exactly the way that Adams avoided.

Once the skillful indirectness of Adams's method begins to work on the reader's mind, the unusual strength of the author's denunciation of politics as the source of inevitable corruption—a sweeping denunciation excepting not even the Adams forebears who filled the office of President—helps to establish a special kind of irony in the manikin's situation. The fourth-generation heir, who never for a moment wielded political power, concludes his political education by decrying the effects of power upon those who did, including his Adams forebears. In all, this ironic treatment, regardless of inherent exaggeration, proves that politics and family pride remain, in the late moments of the fourth generation, basic parts of the Adams heritage, even when they are partially hidden beneath a sophisticated literary technique.

Religion and Philosophy

As we might expect, the lessons in politics make greater use of Henry Adams's family heritage than does any other didactic theme of the *Education*. The typical narrative pattern of investigation leading to contradiction and paradox, once established as the model lesson for any education the manikin may receive, is then applied with almost overly insistent regularity to religion, philosophy, and science. These lines of thought in the *Education* actually lead beyond the limits of the book (and beyond the scope of this study) to other writings of the late period in Adams's life. His commentary about religious faith, for example, depends upon *Mont-Saint-Michel and Chartres* for full development, and the chapters of scientific speculation in the *Education* should be read in conjunction with Adams's late essays, "The Rule of Phase Applied to History" (written 1908; published 1919) and *A Letter to American Teachers of History* (1910). Considering the *Education* alone, however, we can quickly establish that the burden of Adams's discussion of both religion and science rests upon his repeated insistence that he has been seriously handicapped by his family inheritance.

As early as the second chapter, the narrator warns about the content of the religious and philosophical lesson to follow:

> Of all the conditions of his youth which afterwards puzzled the grown-up man, this disappearance of religion puzzled him most. The boy went to church twice every Sunday; he was taught to read his Bible, and he learned religious poetry by heart; he believed in a mild deism; he prayed; he went through all the forms; but neither to him nor his brothers or sisters was religion real. . . . The religious instinct had vanished, and could not be revived, although one made in later life many efforts to recover it. . . . In religion and philosophy no one protested (*Education*, 34–35).

In this statement, the boy-man division of the narrative point of view, the retrospective freedom to comment, and the enigmatic result are all combined. But the simple narrative expression still lacks the "scientific" force of a compelling proof, which Adams hopes to supply by filling in the details a few at a time.

In fact, the final demonstration used to educate the manikin is a family affair. The refutation of three generations of Adams faith in a personal God takes place at the deathbed of Henry's sister: the passage begins to make its point with a description of her horrible suffering and painful death in the agonies of lockjaw. The scene is surely the most moving in the whole of the *Education*; yet Adams refused to let it stand alone as a sufficient "show of proof," partly because the story of this personal loss cannot be told by means of commonly shared symbols, like the White House or George Washington. The author's distrust of emotion goes beyond any possible effort to protect himself against embarrassment. He shows a larger unwillingness to rely upon emotional communication between himself and his audience as, to his graphic description, he appends a specific moral meant to intensify the lesson:

> . . . the idea that any personal deity could find pleasure or profit in torturing a poor woman, by accident, with a fiendish cruelty known to man only in perverted and insane

temperaments, could not be held for a moment. For pure blasphemy, it made pure atheism a comfort. God might be, as the Church said, a Substance, but He could not be a Person (*Education*, 289).

In an age of science the distance between "blasphemy" and "atheism" and between "Substance" and "Person" must be measured in thought rather than feeling. By refusing to make his own position clear and by providing evidence, instead of assertion, to show why "this disappearance of religion puzzled him most," Adams involves the reader's judgment at the same time that he hides his own feelings. In place of an answer, the author poses a new question, in terms intellectual rather than spiritual, general and no longer personal. The *Education* has become a quest-in-being, and one that denies its own importance as an exercise in history. For, once the family belief is put behind him, the manikin's plight parallels that of Esther. No part of modern education enables him to recapture lost instincts.

Yet the power of family principles was not entirely lost to the fourth generation. Charles Francis Adams, "the only perfectly balanced mind that ever existed in the name," still served as a model for his manikin son, whose "artificial balance was acquired habit" (*Education*, 434). The general usefulness of ideals, however, had become doubtful and their value inconclusively demonstrated in an age of forces rather than men: "The generation that lived from 1840 to 1870 could do very well with the old forms of education; that which had its work to do between 1870 and 1900 needed something quite new" (*Education*, 26). That "something" might well combine the old family interest in human nature with what was modern in human knowledge; for the problem faced by the manikin was still the problem of John Adams, who had studied the character of Colonel Quincy in order to learn what he could about human nature. The Adams descendant found his task to be less simple, however: ". . . the practical difficulty in education which a mere student could never overcome; a difficulty not in theory, or knowledge, or even want of experience, but in the sheer chaos of human nature" (*Education*, 153). Nevertheless, the study of human nature remains important. The results have simply become more confusing: "Under a very strong light human nature will always appear complex and full of contradictions . . ." (*Education*, 163). The "very strong light" is the lamp of modern psychology, but even the best of "psychological study" had yielded chaos rather than unitary understanding, ever since "Henry James . . . taught the world to read a volume for the pleasure of seeing the lights of his burning-glass turned on alternate sides of the same figure" (*Education*, 163).

The only alternatives to the anarchy of this modern human science, according to Adams, are philosophy and religion, which finally offer us the same definition of unity—one that brings us full circle, back again to the study of science:

> Metaphysics insisted on treating the universe as one thought or treating thought as one universe; and philosophers agreed, like kinetic gas, that the universe could be known only as motion of mind, and therefore as unity. One could know it only as one's self; it was psychology (*Education*, 432).

As the author noted elsewhere, the lesson of religion was merely the obverse:

> The church had said the same thing from the beginning; and the Greek, or Oriental, or German philosophy changed the idea only in order to merge the universe in man instead of merging man in the universe. The Man attained, not by absorption of himself in the infinite, but by absorbing the infinite and finite together, in himself, as his own Thought,—his will . . . (*Life of George Cabot Lodge*, 179).

Each line of thought turns back to introspection. Moreover, the investigation of the self, as both an extension of the old family study of human nature and as an apparent (but mistaken) alternative to modern science, helps to explain the literary strategy of divided characterization—Henry Adams as narrator and manikin—and also the value of the *Education* as an exercise in self-analysis. To any reader familiar with the writings of the earlier Adams diarists, it is abundantly clear that no nineteenth-century author was better prepared than Henry Adams to apply the methods of self-interrogation as a means of reaching larger verities about New England or the universe.

If, as Adams suggests, the disappearance of every convenient explanation constituted a distinct professional loss to the historian, a far more serious personal injury was done to the man— who knew that he could not escape the influence of a past he had defined in terms of mordant skepticism. His only reward was a double view of personal experience that actually eroded self-confidence and led to an indictment of his own "education." What Adams termed "the self-esteem of the Yankee, which tended naturally to self-distrust," had shown him in the course of his study that even the most appealing lines of thought could be followed to painful and self-destructive conclusions. His private doubts were raised in a letter to Henry James, after the latter's biography of William Wetmore Story appeared in 1903:

> The painful truth is that all of my New England generation, counting the half-century, 1820–1870, were in actual fact only one mind and nature; the individual was a facet of Boston . . . *Type bourgeois-bostonien* [*sic*]! A type quite as good as another, but more uniform. . . . God knows that we knew our want of knowledge! the [*sic*] self-distrust became introspection—nervous self-consciousness—irritable dislike of America, and antipathy to Boston. . . . So you have written not Story's life, but your own and mine— pure autobiography. . . .[26]

As Adams pondered the value of habitual introspection, the "painful truth" became even more personal. His *Education* emerged as a special kind of autobiography, one which turned on itself by adding the weight of protest to the writer's respect for narrative form and introspective technique. Even while he acknowledged the positive values of the family habit of introspection, Adams also insisted that the exercise had proved harmful to his manikin subject and to his authorial self.

The *Education*, that carefully veiled testament of personal dissatisfaction, captures all the anguish of Adams's novelistic heroines, the frustrations of his historical and biographical heroes, plus the painful sense of duty that had driven three generations of family statesmen to record their most intimate thoughts. His are the confessions of a fourth-generation author, caught in the act of transcribing his own diary of mind:

> Of all studies, the one he would rather have avoided was that of his own mind. He knew no tragedy so heartrending as introspection, and the more, because—as Mephistophcles said of Marguerite—he was not the first. Nearly all the highest intelligence known to history had drowned itself in the reflection of its own thought, and the bovine survivors had rudely told the truth about it, without affecting the intelligent (*Education*, 432).

Certainly Henry "was not the first." If mental chaos threatened to swamp individual intelligence in Henry Adams's time, family habit and the Adams philosophy might well be at fault. But a family member, nevertheless, could not easily escape. Instead, the *Education* attempted to turn a family habit and a personal way of looking at the world not merely into a protest against the ideas of earlier Adamses but also into better and sounder philosophy and a more meaningful expression of human experience, based upon using the materials of inheritance as method rather than conclusion. To Adams, that method must be modern and scientific, for science alone seemed to offer a way for the mind to move beyond its impasse: "If a time must come when complexity reaches irreconcileable [*sic*] contradiction—I believe the philosophers call them antinomies,—we want to fix it."[27]

Science

In Adams's view, the chief alternative line of intellectual interest, running beyond religion and metaphysics into the American future, had been laid down by the practice of modern science, which taught a series of lessons for the manikin's edification. The chapters following "Chicago" (XXII) in the *Education* lead toward the scientific possibilities of Adams's later essays; they preview the optimistic hope that science will learn to organize and control force: "Thus far, since five or ten thousand years, the mind had successfully reacted, and nothing yet proved that it would fail to react—but it would need to jump" (*Education*, 498). These final chapters are concerned with plotting those paths along which the mind might be trained to "jump." But considered as serious explorations of science, they are patently amateurish, and the target of much criticism—which is exactly the form of active response that Adams intended.

Aside from the usual critique of Henry Adams's faulty science, only a few additional points need be made in this study of family influence. By 1900, Adams was able to borrow ideas from Karl Pearson's *Grammar of Science*, just as, earlier, Adams had adapted the positions of Lyell and Agassiz to the essay form and used those of the geologist Clarence King in *Esther*. At the same time, Adams believed that he had correctly gauged the limitations of Pearson's usefulness, which depended upon a narrow—perhaps too narrow—selection of materials for experiment. Writing to Brooks, Henry explained, "The scientific . . . thinker . . . stretches out his hand to catch a stray energy, and tries to fit it into a machine. If it won't fit he throws it away."[28] What would not "fit" into the "machine" of science continued to bother Henry until he reworked Pearson's ideas and derived a new scientific moral for the manikin's benefit: "Chaos was the law of nature; Order was the dream of man" (*Education*, 451).

The inadequacy of Adams's own scientific training—everywhere decried in the book—thus becomes a general excuse for his failure to find any usable alternative to chaos, even in modern science, which had appeared to offer much more hope than politics or religion. Still, science must be tried pragmatically. Just as he had once used the scientific method to study modern geology in "Lyell," so Adams demonstrates his new thesis by a similar experiment: he tests the hypotheses of Darwinism with the materials available for his personal education. The manikin finds that "the progress of evolution from President Washington to President Grant, was alone evidence enough to upset Darwin" (*Education*, 266). The reader familiar with the Adams family is at the same time implicitly invited to consider the manikin itself, to see if evolution from John Adams to Henry Adams can provide evidence for a less pessimistic conclusion.

Again, the uncertain value of science applies not simply to specific studies such as Darwinism or geology, which end in contradiction and chaos, but also to the usefulness of all scientific study as a mode of training for life. The narrator's ambivalent attitude at one time makes science seem the best hope for the future and at another serves to destroy that very hope by pointing to a lack of progress displayed in both the product and the method. Early in the book, the author makes an observation which sums up the lesson he had written into *Gallatin*: "In theory one might say, with some show of proof, that a pure, scientific education was alone correct; yet many of his friends who took it, found reason to complain that it was anything but a pure, scientific world in which they lived" (*Education*, 88). At this point in the *Education*, the qualifying doubts about a scientific education are still tentative, the objection to scientific methods vague; final judgment by the manikin has been suspended, pending further investigation. Next, the demonstration begins, and the characters are made into tools for measurement. Just as Senator Cameron was used as the modern politician who showed by contrast what had become of the Adams line of statesmen, so the geologist, Clarence King, becomes the representative of modern science. For the benefit of the manikin and the reader alike, Adams tells King's story, dividing it as usual into separate installments.

The first meeting between King and Adams—significantly late in the manikin's education, long after its beginnings in Quincy and Washington—occurs in the chapter "Failure" (XX), which is set in the 1870s, just after the spectacle of Grant has shut off all hopes for a strictly political training:

> King had everything to interest and delight Adams. . . . As a companion, King's charm was great, but this was not the quality that so much attracted Adams. . . . King had moulded and directed his life logically, scientifically, as Adams thought American life should be directed. He had given himself education all of a piece, yet broad. Standing in the middle of his career, where their paths at last came together, he could look back and look forward on a straight line, with scientific knowledge for its base (*Education*, 311–12).

By giving himself a scientific education, King had managed to avoid the chief human problem imposed by the Adams heritage; moreover, King's example should have provided an ideal model for the manikin's self-education, the only possibility after the influence of family has been left behind. King's position makes him both backward-looking and forward-looking, able to apply his scientific training to problems of past or future, and to use what he knows in some straight-line sequence of thought and action, cause and effect. The close resemblance to the expressed ideal of the *Education* is unmistakable; in fact, the fortunes of the book itself appear to rest with King as much as with the persona Henry Adams. Only the ominous cloud created by the chapter title ("Failure") dims the optimistic expectation of King's achieving complete success, both as a man and as a usable example of unified, meaningful education for the modern world.

Twenty years afterward in time but only thirty-five pages later in the narrative, King and scientific education receive a more pragmatic evaluation. Now, despite the best efforts of all scientists, the world resembles chaos, after the financial "convulsion of 1893":

> Much that had made life pleasant between 1870 and 1890 perished in the ruin, and among the earliest wreckage had been the fortunes of Clarence King. The lesson taught whatever the bystander chose to read in it; but to Adams it seemed singularly full of moral, if he could but understand it. In 1871 he had thought King's education ideal, and his personal fitness unrivalled. No other young American approached him for the combination of chances—physical energy, social standing, mental scope and training, wit, geniality, and science, that seemed superlatively American and irresistibly strong. . . . The result of twenty years' effort proved that the theory of scientific education failed where most theory fails—for want of money (*Education*, 346).

The apparent reticence of the untrained, nonscientific narrator does not prevent Adams from mounting a convincing demonstration of scientific failure, described in the old family terms of failed men, and explained by the power of the old family enemy—the money forces of State Street. And, even as he modeled a lesson from the materials of science, the author disclaimed any responsibility to treat them in a scientific manner or to find that they led to any result except chaos:

> A student of history had no need to understand these scientific ideas of very great men; he sought only the relation with the ideas of their grandfathers, and their common direction towards the ideas of their grandsons. He had long ago reached, with Hegel, the limits of contradiction; and Ernst Mach scarcely added a shade of variety to the identity of opposites; but both of them seemed to be in agreement with Karl Pearson on the facts of the supersensual universe which could be known only as unknowable (*Education*, 453–54).

This lesson in scientific education is fitted into an overall pattern of failure, which both King and the manikin Adams exemplify in their attempts to get hold of some unified body of useful knowledge. Yet, in spite of the loud disclaimers, Henry Adams—while remaining like his ancestors essentially an amateur in science—performed in the *Education* a timely service for his readers. Almost alone among his generation, he pointed to the deficiencies in the "religion of progress which had swept his age." Characteristically, "His own way of taking action was to ask, more cogently than any of his countrymen then or since, the leading questions about science—in what spirit to cultivate it, in what ways to use it, how to relate it to other kinds of knowledge."[29]

The old divisions between pessimistic and optimistic philosophy, and between the traditional family values in politics and religion and the newer values of science, provide the materials for another case of education by contradiction. No other thematic line of thought in the *Education* has received so much critical attention; and, possibly because the author was able to employ the full range of past, present, and future times in his narrative exploration of science, in no other theme is his didactic intention more clearly exhibited. Yet the lesson of science was meant to be, in so far as possible, timeless and provocative rather than conclusive. Henry aimed at the same goal that John Quincy Adams's famous "light-houses of the sky" address had failed to achieve. By skillful use of the experimental method in the *Education*, the writer hoped to evoke enlightened responses from his readers, especially from those men who might offer in return better answers to the questions raised by Adams's life.

Education

As a demonstration of the continuing family interest in education, the *Education* requires little additional commentary. Its didactic purpose, as we have noted, is first spelled out in the author's "Preface": "The tailor's object, in this volume, is to fit young men, in universities or elsewhere, to be men of the world, equipped for any emergency. . . ." That goal remains clear throughout; lesson after lesson is shaped for the special benefit of "young men," wherever they may be. Of course, as writer, editor, and professor, Adams devoted much of his life to helping young men, and yet for the first time in his line of the family, there was no young son to benefit from his example; as the *Education* leaves no doubt, he had learned from the example of his father. During his own literary apprenticeship, Henry reviewed the lessons taught by John and John Quincy Adams, often within sight of the third-generation son, Charles Francis, who, in turn, corrected young Henry's ideas of what the earlier forebears had represented. Once he passed beyond this apprenticeship, Henry was left free to formulate his own critical understanding of the earlier Adamses—much of which found a place in his book. John Quincy Adams enters the pages of the *Education* as a lesson in force; Charles Francis illustrates another important value:

> Charles Francis Adams was singular for mental poise—absence of self-assertion or self-consciousness—the faculty of standing apart without seeming aware that he was alone—a balance of mind and temper that neither challenged nor avoided notice, nor admitted question of superiority or inferiority, of jealousy, of personal motives, from

any source, even under great pressure. This unusual poise of judgment and temper, ripened by age, became the more striking to his son Henry as he learned to measure the mental faculties themselves, which were in no way exceptional either for depth or range. Charles Francis Adams's memory was hardly above the average; his mind was not bold like his grandfather's or restless like his father's, or imaginative or oratorical—still less mathematical; but it worked with singular perfection, admirable self-restraint, and instinctive mastery of form. Within its range it was a model (*Education*, 27).

"Instinctive mastery of form"—in art and life—survived as a goal for the son. But, unlike his father, this Adams could not entirely escape questions "of superiority or inferiority" and "personal motives." In a new generation the family mind was turning upon itself, and "instinctive mastery" became almost impossible. Education by example, at least human example, was obsolete. Yet to learn about form remained the proper business of education, and more than anything else Henry Adams made education the business of his life.

Education must henceforth rely upon sound methods, rather than attempt to guarantee results, especially since the old methods had been proved ineffective as outward conditions changed. In short, education must depend upon technique and not upon men. Science had shown the representative man "that the rise of his faculties from a lower power to a higher, or from a narrower to a wider field, may be due to the function of assimilating and storing outside force or forces" (*Education*, 487). Now, only the process—not the product—of education could be certain to retain its usefulness, no matter how the forces altered.

Henry Adams had begun long before he wrote the *Education* to experiment with various methods of instruction. The essays, biographies, and novels had all been designed to convey their lessons to the reading public. In a more formal manner, as a professor of history, his seminar teaching had avoided pedagogical dogmatism and aimed at stimulating the individual research of his students. In 1873, Adams explained: "I propose no more to the fellows who are kind enough to think my teaching worth their listening to—those of them I mean who take the thing in the spirit I offer it in—than to teach them how to do their work. . . . it makes little difference what one teaches; the great thing is to train scholars for work. . . ."[30] Twenty-five years later, Adams recalled the power of that ideal and went on to recognize that, as a sequence of thought or a line of force, education connected the past and the present and even projected into the unknown future: "A teacher affects eternity; he can never tell where his influence stops" (*Education*, 300).

The real problem remained one of identifying those students who could learn and of finding the best methods for instructing them or, better, for helping them to learn by themselves.

> Barred from philosophy and bored by facts, he wanted to teach his students something not wholly useless. The number of students whose minds were of an order above the average was, in his experience, barely one in ten; the rest could not be much stimulated by any inducements a teacher could suggest. All were respectable, and in seven years of contact, Adams never had cause to complain of one; but nine minds in ten take polish passively, like a hard surface; only the tenth sensibly reacts (*Education*, 302).

That tenth mind had always been the target for Adams's teaching; to it the *Education* was directed. And, just as in his classes at Harvard, "Adams found himself obliged to force his material into some shape to which a method could be applied" (*Education*, 302-3). Only the reacting mind, Adams believed, could benefit fully from his lessons, which otherwise became surface polish for the merely passive manikin:

> The object of education for that mind should be the teaching itself how to react with vigor and economy. No doubt the world at large will always lag so far behind the active mind as to make a soft cushion of inertia to drop upon, as it did for Henry Adams; but education should try to lessen the obstacles, diminish the friction, invigorate the

energy, and should train minds to react, not at haphazard, but by choice, on the lines of force that attract their world. What one knows is, in youth, of little moment; they know enough who know how to learn (*Education*, 314).

Like page after page of the Adams diaries, the *Education* takes shape, from the didactic point of view, as an exercise book for mental training. Instead of copying maxims or letters and learning by imitation for example, however, the exceptional student is expected to trace the lines of thought, to the point where the manikin reaches an impasse. For that figure, "contradictions" mark the end of every effort at education; and "any attempt to deal with them seriously as education is fatal" (*Education*, 48). But the rare tenth mind follows the path only to react against the example of the manikin. For that mind, Adams holds out the hope of being prepared "by choice" to "jump" and stay ahead of expanding force. Such a mind might succeed where Adams knew himself to have failed, might complete the patterning of life and experience with a mastery that would replace chaos with design—whether religious, historical, scientific, or artistic. Through the medium of his text, the last of a line of Adams educators attempted to assure continuity in the sequence of human thought by using his own example as a warning against the results of miseducation.

Literature and Art

Of all the lines of investigation that the author traces to a conclusion of "failure" in his book, perhaps the most important is that concerned with education in literature and art. Here, the narrator warns early that little could be expected of the manikin: "all Adamses were minds of dust and emptiness, devoid of feeling, poetry or imagination." Of course, the exaggeration is patent. The poetry of John Quincy Adams or of Henry himself or the pages of *Mont-Saint-Michel and Chartres* belie the assertion. This authorial distortion, which seems indefensible in an historian, is necessary in the *Education* if the materials and the manikin are to fit the overall pattern of failure. In part,

Adams's sensitivity to criticism, dating back at least to the "roasting" he received in the English press, may explain the denigrating review of his own literary career. But that is only a partial explanation; his rhetorical insistence on the overall theme is more important. As Adams erroneously says of his earlier work:

> No one cared enough to criticise, except himself who soon began to suffer from reaching his own limits. . . . He had not wit or scope or force. . . . His work seemed to him thin, commonplace, feeble. . . . At best it showed only a feeling for form; an instinct of exclusion (*Education*, 66).

Elsewhere, the retrospective author is no less unfair to his youthful ambitions in journalism, characterizing the press as "the last resource of the educated poor who could not be artists and would not be tutors" (*Education*, 211).

Adams reckons the writing of his middle years a nearly total loss. The *Randolph* he entirely ignores, along with the fiction. (His authorship of both novels still remained a secret when the *Education* was written). The *Gallatin*, as we noted earlier, is reduced in importance to a minor character study of an atypical Pennsylvanian. And the *History* becomes, in the materialistic idiom of the later time, a simple financial mistake:

> Adams had given ten or a dozen years to Jefferson and Madison, with expenses which, in any mercantile business, could hardly have been reckoned at less than a hundred thousand dollars, on a salary of five thousand a year; and when he asked what return he got from this expenditure, rather more extravagant in proportion to his means than a racing-stable, he could see none whatever. . . . As far as Adams knew, he had but three serious readers . . . (*Education*, 327).

Of all his earlier work, only the "Lyell" retained its value for the author of the *Education*, because that essay still held the power to redirect his mind (and his pen) toward the most hopeful line of thought, which leads toward new science and thus toward the future:

> Maundering among the magnets he bethought himself that once, a full generation earlier, he had begun active life by writing a confession of geological faith at the bidding of Sir Charles Lyell, and that it might be worth looking at if only to steady his vision. He read it again, and thought it better than he could do at sixty-three, but elderly minds always work loose (*Education*, 398).

The irony of the manikin's having lost "geological faith" and of Adams's repeating the fact of that old loss rather than describing some new faith, in a later "confession," undercuts every possibility of progress in the sequence of the writings authored by Henry Adams.

Rather, the *Education* itself offers no literary solution, no metaphor of mastery, because the radiating lines of force and thought lead away from and not toward a center. Unlike the controlling comparisons in *Walden*, the seasonal cycle or the pond itself, the central figure in the *Education* seems to represent life already near its end, with little hope of continuation or renewal. The young writer, in fact, may have been more useful; his vision was most unified. For the aged manikin, experience had led away from instinct, and time had played him false, even while it pretended to educate:

> Truly the animal that is to be trained to unity must be caught young. Unity is vision; it must have been part of the process of learning to see. The older the mind, the older its complexities, and the further it looks, the more it sees, until even the stars resolve themselves into multiples; yet the child will always see but one (*Education*, 398–99).

As the philosophical conclusion of this passage and the last chapters in the *Education* demonstrate, Henry Adams knew that his mature vision had led him to distinguish complexity rather than unity, and to fix upon contradictions rather than upon simple explanations. A late member of the Adams family, he had

been left with an habitual need to express what he saw and felt—
the story of his personal dilemma—in an appropriate literary
form, one that did not exist among earlier examples of family
writing. Thus, Henry had to turn his back once again on the
family tradition and to try out some new solution of his own
making, since "American Literature offers scarcely one working
model for high education." Lacking a model, then, Henry
fashioned his own complex variant of the earlier public and
private Adams literature, which still made use of introspective
self-analysis. The misleading subtitle of the *Education*, "An
Autobiography," added to the 1918 version without Adams's
authorization, has induced many critics to view the book as
simply another example in the traditional autobiographical
form. But the volume, insofar as it is built around family
themes, represents instead an experimental extension of all that
had been accomplished by earlier Adams writers, and also of
what Henry had been able to achieve in the more conventional
forms of biography and novel. His dissatisfaction with inherited
Adams ideals in politics, religion, education, and literature
combined with the more particular flaws he had found in his
earlier writings, especially *Gallatin* and the *History*, to form one
important part of an even larger theme.

Against this accretion of negative criticism, Adams sought
to balance his appreciative demonstration of all the positive
values in the family heritage, representing them not in his
manikin so much as in the figure of Secretary of State John Hay,
whom the author selected to carry the Adams values into the new
age. Elsewhere, Henry alluded to the special nature of Hay's
relationship with the Adams family in an explanatory letter
about the *Education*: ". . . the volume is wholly due to piety on
account of my father and John Hay (the rest being thrown in to
make mass). . . ."[31] Henry's false modesty aside, the *Education*
treats the Adams family as a complex of human experiences
which yielded both gains and losses to the son and heir. From
that son as author, complexity exacted the same kind of rhetorical balance which he already had displayed in "Lyell" and,
along with it, the artistic requirement that the course of dramatic action should end inconclusively in the narrative, as it had
in *Democracy* and *Esther*.

Yet Adams's specific debts to all earlier works, both those of other family members and his own, are greatly reduced in significance by the novelty of his experiment. His family had always stressed the importance of literature as an aid to clear thought and expression, and also as a practical training for every ambitious Adams: "To a political man, a powerful controversial style is worth its weight in gold," Charles Francis Adams once observed. But his son looked back upon the family efforts with the pen and chiefly saw public misunderstanding and rejection, personal loss in place of gain. Literature like politics had led to no apparent progress in the family or in Henry's own career; indeed, because of a lack of proper artistic education, the Adamses had failed even to understand—much less to control— the real energies of art. And no one more than Henry: "Adams's instinct was blighted from babyhood" (*Education*, 387). His last years were spent in an attempt to recapture that sense of instinctive mastery that had been taken from him, because Adams felt himself to have been victimized by his own education.

As an experiment in literature, the *Education* actually goes further than any of the announced failures in literary art. It aims at stimulation, rather than control, of its readers, and the author's most useful artistic model exists outside the family tradition but in close association with his most personal family loss. That model is St. Gaudens's figure at the grave of Mrs. Henry Adams—the wife who never appears in the *Education*. Adams knew that one day the statue would mark his gravesite too, and thus the end of his earthly journey. Before that timeless figure, the manikin stands fascinated but without questions—his rational pursuit of knowledge held finally in check, as instinct overwhelms all thought:

> Naturally every detail interested him; every line; every touch of the artist; every change of light and shade; every point of relation; every possible doubt of St. Gaudens's correctness of taste or feeling; so that, as the spring approached, he was apt to stop there often to see what the figure had to tell him that was new; but, in all that it had to say, he never once thought of questioning what it meant. He supposed its

meaning to be the one commonplace about it—the oldest idea known to human thought. . . . The interest of the figure was not in its meaning, but in the response of the observer (*Education*, 329).

Art alone could transcend the impasse and reawaken the latent and instinctive mastery over chaos. But the act of responding, the direct personal involvement necessary for understanding and for education, was finally and individually the business of the audience.

This ideal, applied to literature, moved Henry to complete a work that went far beyond anything the earlier Adamses had achieved, while relieving the author from sole responsibility for communicating any single, specific meaning in his writing. Communication and instruction depended upon a balanced relationship between author and reader, teacher and pupil. In fact, Adams had relied on the principle of balance to give meaning and value to every important segment of his life—as an apprentice-son of a master-father; teacher to a whole series of pupils and nieces (including the audience for his essays and books); and husband to a now-dead wife. Finally, and more significant than any of these, it was only as art that the account of his life could achieve a permanent balance and meaning, and realize a practical alternative to failure. His message must have an audience.

As an independent observer of public response, Henry Adams had already experimented in the novels, testing his own opinions against a wider range of readers than he could expect among his friends. Now, lacking a satisfactory model for didactic autobiography, if Adams could not avoid making the materials of his life into the primary form of his book, he could at least use a sophisticated artistry to protect himself against painfully candid revelations. His rhetorical cry of "failure" drowned out the small inner voice and thus forestalled the curious probings of potential biographers. For his own experience as biographer had left Adams with a deep understanding of history. He knew that what he wrote in the *Education* would ultimately be balanced against what others thought and wrote about him. By "taking his own life," the author sought not to reveal but to protect himself for all time. He attempted to make himself a creation of art rather than life.

As an artistic experiment with words, the *Education* would fail only when its readers refused to respond at all. This argument for art was in Adams's thoughts when the book took shape. A letter written in 1904, once again on the subject of St. Gaudens's monument, explains: "All considerable artists make a point of compelling the public to think for itself, and their rule is to require each observer to see what he can, and this will be what the artist meant. To the artist the meaning is indifferent. Every man is his own artist before a work of art."[32]

Adams knew that the best possible refutation of his otherwise persuasive case for failure of the manikin Henry Adams existed in a demonstration of artistic unity, the aesthetic success of the *Education*. Experimental and didactic on its surface, the book remains foremost a "work of art." Its lines of organization stretch from past to future, from writer to reader, from personal confession to individual application. As a total experience, the narrative depends most upon what the audience can do with it. For the text itself is only one part of the *Education*; its statement remains unfinished. Only the reader can complete the lesson that Henry Adams began and thus determine its success as art.

Epilogue

The virtues and talents of ancestors should be considered as examples and solemn trusts, and produce meekness, modesty and humility, lest they should not be imitated and equalled. Mortification and humiliation can be the only legitimate feelings of a mind conscious that it falls short of its ancestors in merit.

—John Adams's *Diary.*

In 1907, Henry Adams wrote:

As my experience leads me to think that no one any longer cares or even knows what is said or printed, and that one's audience in history and literature has shrunk to a mere band of survivors, not exceeding a thousand people in the entire world, I am in hopes a kind of esoteric literary art may survive, the freer and happier for the sense of privacy and *abandon.* Therefore I stop at no apparent *naïveté.*[1]

Adams's letter accompanied a copy of the *Education,* that product of an "esoteric literary art" built upon "privacy," "*abandon,*" and "apparent naïveté." In this final book, more than in any earlier work, the author made literary use of his strong sense of a divided self, treating the possibilities it offered in terms of structure and style as well as content. Briefly, the *Education* was designed to study the collection of experiences, within and without the family, which all together made the titular figure what he seems to be. Adams approaches that evaluation from two points of view: what family means to an expanding consciousness, presented as the changing persona called "Henry Adams"; and what it means to the already mature narrative commentator, who consistently views the process of definition from a retrospective position, at the end of family history and, possibly, near the end of all human history.

Similarly, the modern religious paradox offered yet another demonstration of family impotence in the new time, and one which pointed up the contradictions that had long existed within the Adams tradition but without family members realizing that they were present. The old Adams faith in a personal God, which Henry Adams regarded as having disappeared, could never be regained by any powers of rational thought—the very instruments that the Adams heritage in education seemed committed to developing—for an authentic act of faith was beyond the limits of mind as the Adamses conceived those limits. "That the most powerful emotion of man, next to the sexual, should disappear, might be a personal defect of his own;" except that Adams saw the same defect mirrored in all of the society he knew (*Education*, 34). The family record, however, did offer a uniquely personal increment of meaning, a special proof of loss in his own generation. For the Adamses showed not only failure in politics and religion but sexual failure as well. Henry Adams studied it in the fictional characters of his heroines, in the meaning of the Virgin of *Chartres*, and in the *Education*. He confronted it also in his own life—his wife's childlessness added sexual failure to religious failure, and denied him the satisfaction of developing a better private education for a new generation of Adamses, which might allow them to deal more successfully with the problems that still baffled his own.

Like the habit of introspection, however, the inherent urge to educate had built its own inertia, regardless of the handicaps. Living without the reality of biological fatherhood, Henry Adams nevertheless determined to play the part of a father to the race, exploring every possibility for transmitting the value of his knowledge to his descendants, even while he questioned the inheritance itself. But the traditional dogmas of the Adamses no longer could justify the earlier forms of faith, as Henry sought to show in the "Preface" to *Mont-Saint-Michel and Chartres*:

The relationship, between reader and writer, of son and father, may have existed in Queen Elizabeth's time, but is much too close to be true for ours. The most that any writer could hope of his readers now is that they should consent to regard themselves as nephews, and even then he would expect only a civil refusal from most of them.[2]

Whatever education Adams was able to pass on to sons or nephews "in wishes" became an education that improved upon his own by making use of every optimistic possibility, and by closing off from futile investigation the paths which had led only to an impasse for all the Adamses, such as politics and religion.

Science, on the other hand, had been largely untried in family history, because the development of this study emerged as a nineteenth-century phenomenon, something too modern to belong to the Adamses of the past. Here, Henry's role as a writer-tutor was left open for him to define; and he chose to explore attractive possibilities, excite new interest, and most of all to stimulate other men so that they would work to surpass him. But, perhaps because he knew that he could never become a scientific man and that his only meaningful role must be in American letters, the family failures in literature seemed to confound Henry Adams most. For, the Adams heritage and an old fashioned eighteenth-century education together bound the fourth-generation author of novels, biographies, and letters to obsolete literary models, as much as to obsolete patterns of nonliterary thought. Again, chaos threatened the writer no less than the politician or scientist. "No one means all he says, and yet very few say all they mean, for words are slippery and thought is viscous; . . . (Education, 451). Small wonder, then, that the Adams writers had so often been misinterpreted and maligned, even when they produced genuinely useful guides for later generations.

For himself, Henry Adams sought protection against historical misunderstanding by destroying most of his personal journal and some of his letters, and by concealing his authorship. But he could no more stop putting words on paper than he could stop thinking. He could only keep searching for new forms and techniques that might demonstrate some kind of literary progress, at least within the history of the family, but possibly as a part of world literature as well. First, Henry Adams wrote history, biographies, and novels that made use of Adams standards and Adams records—to help him understand and judge men like Gallatin and Randolph, and to create characters like Carrington and Esther. The process of employing family materials in such limited ways drew him, in turn, to examine closely the larger inheritance they provided, and to recognize other possibilities for their greater usefulness in literature—just as John Adams had forged the beginnings of a modern autobiography from his diary, and Charles Francis had shaped new public images of both John and John Quincy through carefully edited selections from their writings. Henry's investigations, conducted in the light of a broad historical perspective and a developing scientific interest in the best psychology of his time, revealed the limitations of the family and also of its literature. In his attempt to reach a compromise with history, Henry Adams as a writer made skillful use of both.

As an Adams author, Henry's most important contribution to family literature was his carefully documented denial of the old grounds for public criticism—aristocratic pride in family and familial piety. He achieved this refutation by the literary act of making the meaning of "Adams" henceforth an inseparable part of something larger and more unified, thus democratizing his origins. Where in the *Education* Henry Adams closed off the family past from further consideration, as in politics and religion, the Adams heritage became merely another kind of recorded history, a collection of "facts" placed "in sequence" and left lying inert. But along other lines of thought, where the author used his discussion to keep open a channel to the future—as in science, education, and literature—he managed to make of the Adams heritage something more than a contemporary lesson drawn from history. As an artist in words, he hoped to produce a work of timeless value, which would continue to stimulate further progress in the sequential thought of men who, regardless of their names, would automatically incur an obligation to the Adams past.

Henceforth, these men would owe a debt to the family for that portion of the Adamses' thought that had been carried forward as a gain, rather than discarded as a loss—in short, for a useful rather than an obsolete part of the family tradition. In this way his heritage, Henry Adams believed, might operate forcefully in the future to help effect an intellectual, spiritual, physical, and aesthetic unity, a unity beyond his own conscious vision. Yet even in moments of doubt, Adams recognized that his family had provided him with a unique intellectual heritage. As Henry explained to Brooks Adams: "The family mind approaches unity more than is given to most of the works of God." [3]

A Guide to Editorial Apparatus

Adams family names: Following the practice of the editors of the printed *Adams Papers*, (hereafter, *A P*) I have shortened proper names of family members frequently mentioned in the "Notes." My own table of shortened forms is highly selective and includes only the members of each generation whose writings are often cited.

First Generation
JA   John Adams (1735–1826)
AA   Abigail Smith Adams (1744–1818)

Second Generation
JQA   John Quincy Adams (1767–1848)

Third Generation
CFA   Charles Francis Adams (1807–1886)

Fourth Generation
JQA II   John Quincy Adams II (1833–1894)
CFA II   Charles Francis Adams II (1835–1915)
HA   Henry Adams (1838–1918)
MHA   Marian Hooper Adams (1842–1885), wife of HA
BA   Brooks Adams (1848–1927)

A Note on Sources

This study of the Adams family could not have been written without access to the treasures contained in the Adams Papers, the collection of manuscript materials written over five generations and housed at the Massachusetts Historical Society in Boston. Most of these papers are available in microfilm form (608 reels) at several research libraries, including the Wisconsin Historical Society and the Howard-Tilton Library of Tulane University, where I used them. Other manuscript materials, especially the Adams Papers—Fourth Generation and the unpublished letters of Henry Adams, were made available for me to use by persmission of the Massachusetts Historical Society and the Harvard College Library.

Believing that at least some documents in the microfilm edition, as well as important manuscript materials, remain beyond the reach of many readers, I have endeavored, whenever possible, to document my remarks with citations to printed volumes and to editions that have achieved wide distribution. Also, I have attempted to limit the number of citations to sources of all kinds, so that the main lines of argument will be accessible to those readers who do not share my more specialized interest in the source materials.

Since I began the final version of this study, a new authoritative edition of *The Education of Henry Adams*, edited by

Ernest Samuels (Boston 1973), has appeared. For the first time, this edition makes use of the corrections in Adams's personal copies of his most famous book. Its text and editorial apparatus are invaluable, and each of my quotations from the *Education* has been verified in the Samuels edition.

Notes

Introduction

1. The subject of American family history has grown too large to summarize easily. Without attempting to be exhaustive, I am pleased to acknowledge a special indebtedness to: James Truslow Adams, *The Adams Family* (New York, 1930); Karl Schriftgiesser, *Families* (New York, 1940); Stephen Hess, *American Political Dynasties: From Adams to Kennedy* (Garden City, N.Y., 1966); Nathaniel Burt, *First Families: The Making of an American Aristocracy* (Boston, Toronto, 1970); and Paul Goodman, "Ethics and Enterprise: The Values of a Boston Elite, 1800–1860," *American Quarterly* 18 (Fall 1966): 437–51.
   In addition, I have gleaned valuable suggestions from many other sources, such as "The Family in History" (a special number of *The Journal of Interdisciplinary History*, 2, (Autumn 1971) and *The Family in Historical Perspective: An International Newsletter* (Newberry Library, Chicago, Ill.), first published in the spring of 1972.
2. N. G. Annan, "The Intellectual Aristocracy," *Studies in Social History*, ed. J. H. Plumb (London, New York, 1955), pp. 284–85.
3. James Truslow Adams, *The Adams Family*, p. v.
4. The most illuminating short accounts of the Adams women may be found in *Notable American Women 1607–1950: A Biographical Dictionary*, Vol. 1, ed. Edward T. James et al. (Cambridge, Mass., 1971).
5. Ltr., JA to AA, quoted in Page Smith, *John Adams*, Vol. 2 (Garden City, New York, 1962), p. 1015.
6. Martin B. Duberman, *Charles Francis Adams* (Cambridge, Mass., 1961), p. 12.
7. "Introduction," *Diary of Charles Francis Adams*, ed. Aïda Dipace Donald and David Donald (Cambridge, Mass., 1964), *A P*, Vol. 1, p. xxxi.

8. Timothy Paul Donovan, *Henry Adams and Brooks Adams: The Search for a Law* (Norman, 1961), p. 31.
9. John Adams, quoted in Smith, Vol. 1, p. 7.
10. Ltr., JA to AA, Roxbury, 14 March 1776, *A P* (microfilm).
11. *The Selected Writings of John and John Quincy Adams*, ed. Adrienne Koch and W. Peden (New York, 1946), p. 99.
12. *Selected Writings*, p. 66.
13. "Memoir," *Letters of Mrs. Adams, the Wife of John Adams*, 3rd ed., ed. C. F. Adams (Boston, 1841), p. xvi.
14. *Letters of Mrs. Adams*, p. xvii.
15. "Memoir," *Familiar Letters of John Adams and His Wife Abigail Adams, During the Revolution*, ed. C. F. Adams (Boston and New York, 1875), p. v.
16. Quoted in Hess, *American Political Dynasties*, p. 48.
17. Ltr., HA to Elizabeth Cameron, 29 December 1891, ms. in the Adams Papers.
18. *The Diary of John Quincy Adams, 1794–1845*, ed. Allan Nevins (New York, 1951), p. 406. Nevins reprints portions of: *Memoirs of John Quincy Adams*, 12 vols., ed. Charles Francis Adams (Philadelphia, 1874–77); hereafter, *Memoirs*.

Chapter 1

1. My general debt to published scholarship has been described in a review essay: "Henry Adams," in *Fifteen American Authors Before 1900: Bibliographic Essays on Research and Criticism*, ed. Robert A. Rees and Earl N. Harbert (Madison, Wisconsin, 1971, 1974), pp. 3–36. Only examples of more specific indebtedness are indicated in the notes that follow.
2. 21 May, *Letters of Henry Adams 1858–1918*, 2 vols., ed. Worthington C. Ford (Boston and New York; 1, 1930; 2, 1938), Vol. 1, p. 160; hereafter, *Letters*.
3. "Pandora," *The Novels and Tales of Henry James*, Vol. 18 (New York, 1909), p. 130.
4. *The Education of Henry Adams* (Boston, 1918), p. 34.
5. Ltr., HA to Daniel Coit Gilman, 3 November 1875, *Henry Adams and His Friends: A Collection of His Unpublished Letters*, ed. Harold Dean Cater (Boston, 1947), p. 73.
6. Ltr., HA to Simon Newcomb, 25 October, Cater, *Henry Adams*, pp. 71–72.
7. See "The Heritage of Henry Adams," *The Degradation of the Democratic Dogma* (New York, 1919), especially pp. 35, 45, 53.
8. *Education*, pp. 14–15.
9. Such late essays as *A Letter to American Teachers of History* (1910)

and "The Rule of Phase Applied to History" (1908) are obvious examples.

Chapter 2

1. Ernest Samuels, *The Young Henry Adams* (Cambridge, Mass., 1948) p. 8.
2. Ltr., HA to CFA II, 3 November 1858, Ford, *Letters*, Vol. 1, p. 5.
3. Ltr., HA to CFA II, 18 January, Ford, *Letters*, Vol. 1, p. 12.
4. Ltr., 12 February 1862, Cater, *Henry Adams*, p. 14.
5. Ltr. to CFA II, 9 December, Ford, *Letters*, Vol. 1, p. 62.
6. Ltr., HA to CFA II, 14 February 1862, *A Cycle of Adams Letters*, 2 vol., ed. Worthington C. Ford (Boston and New York, 1920) Vol. 1, pp. 112-13; hereafter, *Cycle*.
7. See Samuels, *Young HA*, p. 160.
8. Ltr., HA to CFA II, 21 November 1862, Ford, *Cycle*, Vol. 1, p. 196.
9. Vol. 104, 1-30; hereafter, *N A R*.
10. Ltr., HA to Palfrey, 23 October 1861, Cater, *Henry Adams*, p. 8.
11. Ltr. to Palfrey, 20 March 1862, Cater, *Henry Adams*, p. 15. See also HA to Palfrey, 27 March 1863, Cater, p. 16.
12. Ltr. to Palfrey, 23 October 1861, Cater, *Henry Adams*, p. 9.
13. Ltr. to Palfrey, 12 February 1862, Cater, *Henry Adams*, p. 13.
14. Ltr. to Palfrey, 20 March 1862, Cater, *Henry Adams*, p. 15.
15. See Samuels, *Young HA*, especially p. 128.
16. Ltr., 10 March 1868, Cater, *Henry Adams*, p. 42.
17. Ltr., HA to Elizabeth Cameron, 1 April 1901, Adams Papers— Fourth Generation.
18. HA to CFA II, 21 November 1862, Ford, *Cycle*, Vol. 1, p. 195.
19. First printed in *N A R* 109 (October 1869): 443-75. Page references in my text refer to the more available collection: *The Great Secession Winter of 1860-61 and Other Essays by Henry Adams*, ed. George Hochfield (New York, 1958), pp. 95-128, which reprints the *N A R* text; hereafter, *Essays*.
20. *Selected Writings*, pp. 173-74.
21. "The Session, 1869-1870," *Essays*, p. 195.
22. See *Essays*, pp. 107-108.

Chapter 3

1. Gallatin's letter is quoted in Ernest Samuels, *Henry Adams: The Middle Years* (Cambridge, Mass., 1958), p. 42.

2. See Smith, *John Adams*, Vol. 2 (New York, 1962), pp. 946, 959, 960, 1028.

3. JQA, *Memoirs*, 24 November 1823, Vol. 6, pp. 198–99.

4. CFA, *Diary*, 22 January 1824, *A P*, Vol. 1, p. 59.

5. Ltrs., JA to Jefferson, 30 June 1813 and 1 May 1812, *The Adams-Jefferson Letters*, ed. Lester J. Cappon (Chapel Hill, N.C., 1959), Vol. 2, pp. 348, 301.

6. JQA, *Memoirs*, 7 December 1804, Vol. 1, p. 320.

7. JQA, *Memoirs*, 6 December 1817, Vol. 4, p. 28.

8. JQA, *Memoirs*, 26 February 1820, Vol. 4, p. 532.

9. CFA, *Diary*, 24 and 30 January 1824, *A P*, Vol. 1, pp. 53, 73, 74.

10. Ltr., CFA to CFA II, 8 November 1861, Ford, *Cycle*, Vol. 1, pp. 67–68.

11. Ltr. to Henry Cabot Lodge; 2 January, Ford, *Letters*, Vol. 1, p. 237.

12. *John Randolph* (Greenwich, Conn., 1961), p. 110; hereafter, *Randolph*. This more available edition reprints the 1882 text; all quotations have been verified.

13. Quoted in HA's *The Life of Albert Gallatin* (Philadelphia, 1879), p. 598; hereafter, *Gallatin*.

14. Ltr., HA to Elizabeth Cameron, 17 April 1899 (?), Adams Papers—Fourth Generation.

15. See Henry B. Rule, "Henry Adams' Attack on Two Heroes of the Old South," *American Quarterly* 14 (Summer 1962): 174–84.

16. Quoted in *Gallatin*, p. 86.

17. HA's attitudes toward the constitutional issue are set down in "The Session: 1869–70," *Essays*, p. 219f.

18. "The Session: 1869–70," *Essays*, p. 222.

19. "The New York Gold Conspiracy," *Essays*, p. 189.

20. Gallatin to Badollet, 18 March 1825, quoted in *Gallatin*, p. 610.

21. Here and elsewhere in this chapter, I am indebted to J. C. Levenson for his invaluable study, *The Mind and Art of Henry Adams* (Boston, 1957). See also my "Henry Adams' New England View: A Regional Angle of Vision?" *Tulane Studies in English* 16 (1968): 107–134.

22. Ltr., HA to John Hay, 3 September 1882, Ford, *Letters*, Vol. 1, p. 338.

23. HA to Samuel Jones Tilden, 24 January 1883, Cater, *Henry Adams*, p. 125.

24. Ltr., HA to Henry Cabot Lodge, 6 October 1879, Ford, *Letters*, Vol. 1, p. 314.

25. For convenience, all citations in my text refer to the combined edition: *Democracy and Esther* (Garden City, 1961).

26. See, for example, Ltr., HA to Edwin Lawrence Godkin, 24 November 1880, Cater, *Henry Adams*, pp. 103–4. Adams was sometimes suggested as the author of *Democracy*, but his authorship was not generally accepted until the publisher, Henry Holt, issued his own

book, *Garrulities of An Octogenarian Editor*, in 1923, five years after Adams's death.

27. See Ltr., HA to Henry Holt, 21 September 1882, Cater, *Henry Adams*, pp. 122-23, and the Adams Papers—Fourth Generation.

28. Ltr. to Henry Holt, 6 January, Cater, *Henry Adams*, p. 136. See also pp. 130, 137.

29. Ltr. to John Hay, 23 August 1886, Ford, *Letters*, Vol. 1, p. 377.

30. A perceptive analysis of HA's attitudes toward the South, especially as they are displayed in Carrington, may be found in C. Vann Woodward, *The Burden of Southern History* (Baton Rouge, 1960), pp. 117-26, 134-40. Professor Woodward takes note of HA's interest in a "search" for "the antique valor and probity of the early Republic," but makes no connection with the Adams family.

31. Ltr., HA to Lodge, 15 November, Ford, *Letters*, Vol. 1, p. 331.

32. Ltr., HA to Elizabeth Cameron, 13 February 1891, Ford, *Letters*, Vol. 1, p. 468.

Chapter 4

1. New York: Charles Scribner's Sons, 1889-1891. HA had three draft volumes printed privately by John Wilson and Son: University Press, 1885-1888. Among recent estimates, Richard C. Vitzthum's *The American Compromise: Theme and Method in the Histories of Bancroft, Parkman, and Adams* (Norman, 1974) is especially useful.

2. See William R. Taylor, "Historical Bifocals on the Year 1800," *New England Quarterly* 23 (1950): 172-86.

3. JQA, *Memoirs*, 20 October 1821, Vol. 5, pp. 364-65. Without establishing a claim for completeness, the table below illustrates Henry Adams's acknowledged indebtedness to family sources. His inconsistent use of footnotes and the difficulties in identifying the specific source of quotations make an exhaustive listing impossible, even if one seemed necessary (as it does not) to establish the relationship.

Source	Number of References
JQA's *Memoirs*	53
"Adams Mss."	2
"Gallatin Mss."	3

Note: The Mss. designation refers to materials presumably not published in *Gallatin*, JA's *Diary*, or JQA's *Memoirs*.

Documents Relating to New-England Federalism (ed. *HA*)	23
Life and Writings of Albert Gallatin (Sometimes cited as "Works")	85
John Randolph	6

Henry Adams also refers to Henry Cabot Lodge, *Life and Letters of George Cabot*, at least a dozen times, and the portrayal of Aaron Burr depends upon Adams's manuscript biography, which was judged unacceptable for publication in the American Statesman Series.

4. "Introduction," *History of the United States During the Administrations of Jefferson and Madison*, Vol. 1 (New York, 1930), p. ix.

5. The six chapters are titled: "Physical and Economical Conditions," "Popular Characteristics," "Intellect of New England," "Intellect of the Middle States," "Intellect of the Southern States," "American Ideals." Together they compose the first part of a "frame" for the *History*, which is completed by the closing chapters of Volume 9. The opening and closing "frame" sections of the *History* together form an important example of the author's narrative technique. By skillful manipulation of point of view, employing sequential comparison and contrast and geographical organization, Adams is able to present two pictures of America at the beginning and ending of the 1800–1817 period, which balance the claims of all geographic sections to historical value and yet emphasize the overriding importance of national unity. Adams means to establish this national perspective as a context for the smaller-scale events of the *History*, treated in the chapters that fall between the two sections of the narrative frame. Thus, the reader must continually weigh the immediate context of Adams's remarks about a local or short-term political act alongside (in the reader's mind) more general and long-term principles, such as the need for national unity and national self-respect. General principles are intended to provide correctives for momentary eccentricities in conduct or thought, just as the moral principles or beliefs of a John Adams or a Charles Francis Adams provided them with the means for correcting mistakes caused by momentary aberration or surrender to temper. See my "Henry Adams' New England View: A Regional Angle of Vision?"

6. Ltr., HA to Martha Cameron, 22 August 1904; reprinted in Charles Vandersee, "Henry Adams' Education of Martha Cameron: Letters, 1888–1916," *Texas Studies in Literature and Language* (Summer 1968): 272.

7. *Documents Relating to New-England Federalism: 1800–1815*, ed. Henry Adams (Boston: 1877), p. v; hereafter, *Documents*.

8. *Life and Letters of George Cabot* (Boston, 1878), "Preface," pp. 198–200, 439.

9. *Documents*, pp. vii–viii.

10. *Documents*, p. vi.

11. For JA: *History*, Vol. 1, pp. 247, 274, 290, 389; Vol. 2, p. 130; for JQA: *History*, Vol. 2, p. 379; Vol. 3, pp. 127, 129.

12. Dallas to Gallatin, 30 July 1808, used in HA's *Gallatin*, p. 372; reprinted, *History*, Vol. 4, p. 455.

13. See "Historical Bifocals on the Year 1800," p. 178.
14. HA's analysis of Gallatin may be studied in the "Introduction" to *Albert Gallatin* and *History*, Vol. 4, p. 370.
15. Italics mine. *History*, Vol. 2, p. 408; Vol. 4, p. 203. For other uses of Randolph as a standard of measurement, introduced by "even" constructions, see: Vol. 1, p. 338; Vol. 4, p. 271; Vol. 9, p. 217.
16. See my discussion in "Henry Adams," *Fifteen American Authors Before 1900*. CFA II advised HA to excise many passages that displayed "compassionate feelings toward Jefferson" in the privately printed *History*; HA usually complied, as Samuels tells us in *Middle Years*, p. 390. On the other hand, HA's letter to George Bancroft, 25 April 1879, shows the author's willingness to delete language sharply critical of Jefferson as well (Cater, *Henry Adams*, pp. 89–90).
17. Ltr., HA to Samuel Jones Tilden, 24 January, Cater, *Henry Adams*, pp. 125–26.

Chapter 5

1. From "Buddha and Brahma," *The Yale Review* (October 1915): 82–89.
2. George Hochfield, *Henry Adams: An Introduction and Interpretation* (New York, 1962), p. 115. Ernest Samuels agrees, *Henry Adams: The Major Phase* (Cambridge, Mass., 1964), p. 312. The relationship between *Chartres* and the *Education* remains, however, a subject for lively debate among critics. See my "Henry Adams," *Fifteen American Authors Before 1900*, and Robert Mane's *Henry Adams on the Road to Chartres* (Cambridge, Mass., 1971), which appeared after my essay was completed.
3. Ltr., HA to Mabel Hooper LaFarge, 21 June 1895, Manuscript Collections, Houghton Library, Harvard University.
4. HA to William Roscoe Thayer, 17 December, Ford, *Letters*, Vol. 2, p. 635.
5. It is clear that HA was conscious of the various narrative voices that a letter-writer might employ. In *The Life of George Cabot Lodge* (Boston, 1911), for example, he noted of Lodge: "His letters to Langdon Mitchell expressed the same ideas, with such slight difference of form as one naturally uses in writing to a man rather than to a woman" (p. 189).
6. Ltr., CFA II to HA, 25 February 1907, Ford, *Letters*, Vol. 2, p. 472 nl.
7. Ltr., HA to James F. Rhodes, 10 February 1908, Adams Papers— Fourth Generation.
8. Ltr., HA to John Hay, 1 May, Ford, *Letters*, Vol. 1, p. 383.
9. *George Cabot Lodge*, p. 176.

10. HA to C. M. Gaskell, 14 June, Ford, *Letters*, Vol. 2, p. 409.
11. Ltr., HA to John Franklin Jameson, 2 February 1907, Cater, *Henry Adams*, p. 588.
12. For a more complete discussion of regional bias, see my "Henry Adams' New England View: A Regional Angle of Vision?"
13. Ltr., HA to BA, 4 March 1900, Cater, *Henry Adams*, p. 487.
14. For the full development of these poses, see *Education*, pp. 113–14, 262, 447, 486–87.
15. On the Gibbon-Ara Coeli theme, see *Education*, pp. 92, 209, 235, 282, 341, 342, 367, 471, 477, 497.
16. Ltr., 31 August, Ford, *Letters*, Vol. 1, p. 298.
17. Ltr., HA to Paul Leicester Ford, 22 March, Cater, *Henry Adams*, p. 159.
18. HA, *Travels: Tahiti* (New York and Ann Arbor, 1947), p. 17.
19. Ltr., HA to Elizabeth Cameron, 2 June 1889, Ford, *Letters*, Vol. 1, p. 399.
20. Ltr., 6 May 1908, Ford, *Letters*, Vol. 2, p. 495. In another letter (17 August 1891) HA showed that the germ of the *Education* had been present in his thought for many years: "The moral seems to be that every man should write his life, to prevent some other fellow from taking it. The moral is almost worse than the vicious alternative and, after all, the sacrifice would not ensure safety. I know no other escape except to be so obscure as not to need gibbeting at all; but who is safe even then?" (HA to Charles Milnes Gaskell, Adams Papers—Fourth Generation).
21. CFA II, *Charles Francis Adams* (Boston and New York, 1900).
22. Ltr., 4 March 1900, Cater, *Henry Adams*, p. 487.
23. See *Education*: Sumner, 31, 107–8, 251, 294–95; CFA, 128, 135, 149; Lincoln, 107; types, 57, 101–2.
24. James Donald Cameron (1833–1918) served as Secretary of War under President Grant and as U.S. Senator (1877–1897). The second generation head of a family political machine in Pennsylvania, Cameron has been described as "typical of the men of affairs who were beginning to dominate the life of the nation." Adams's selection of a representative political man of his own time is thus confirmed in the *Dictionary of American Biography* (Vol. 3, pp. 435–36) which continues: "On the whole his twenty years in the Senate were undistinguished. He made politics, not statesmanship, his principal public business."
25. Adams's attempts to deal with the human exceptions are interesting because he does not make them into a line of examples which contradict the main argument for corruption. In the case of Hay, Adams says of himself, "though he found his own position regular, he never quite understood that of John Hay." McColloch and Weed are simply treated as exceptions. See *Education*, pp. 146, 248, 323.

26. 18 November, Ford, *Letters*, Vol. 2, pp. 414-15.
27. Ltr., HA to BA, 11 January 1906, Adams Papers—Fourth Generation.
28. Ltr., HA to BA, 11 January 1906, Adams Papers—Fourth Generation.
29. J.C. Levenson, "Henry Adams and the Culture of Science," *Studies in American Culture*, ed. Joseph Kwait and Mary Turpie (Minneapolis, 1960), p. 123.
30. Ltr., HA to Henry Cabot Lodge, 2 January, Ford, *Letters*, Vol. 1, p. 236.
31. Ltr., HA to Charles Milnes Gaskell, 10 May 1907, Ford, *Letters*, Vol. 2, p. 476.
32. Ltr., HA to E. D. Shaw, 20 December, *The Letters of Mrs. Henry Adams, 1865-1883* (Boston, 1936), pp. 458-59.

Epilogue

1. Ltr., HA to Charles Milnes Gaskell, 10 May 1907, Adams Papers—Fourth Generation.
2. 1904 printing, p. v. Elsewhere HA played his literary role as the last of the Adamses with a sense of grim humor: "Here I am alone. Everyone is dead. Yesterday I was struck by seeing my own name in the columns of the *New York Times*, mentioned as *the late* H.A. *Tant mieux!*" Ltr., HA to Charles Milnes Gaskell, 23 April 1906, Ford, *Letters*, Vol. 2, p. 468.
3. Ltr., 5 June 1905, Adams Papers—Fourth Generation.

Index

Adams, Abigail Smith (wife of John Adams), 3, 7, 9, 13, 53, 72, 168

Adams, Brooks (brother of Henry Adams): quoted, 27; mentioned, 10, 20, 27, 31, 157, 170, 187, 205

Adams, Charles Francis (father of Henry Adams): archivist-editor, 13-14, 32, 204; minister to England, 24; 33, 167, 175; example to sons, 25, 31-32, 94, 152, 166-167, 183, 191-92; quoted, 13, 54, 55, 56, 78, 198; mentioned, 4, 7, 11, 12, 21, 22, 23, 36, 82, 94, 169, 175, 183, 197

Adams, Charles Francis II (brother of Henry Adams): works, *Charles Francis Adams: An Autobiography*, 18, 144; *Memorabilia*, 147; mentioned, 20, 31, 32, 33, 34, 35, 56, 144, 148

Adams family: heritage of, 15, 31-32, 44, 67, 75, 79; history of, 3-17, 18-30, 31-35, 36-39, 44-49, 51, 52-56, 62-64, 66-71, 72, 75-82, 84-87, 88-92, 94-95, 97-112, 117, 121-23, 125-26, 128-29, 132, 134-40, 142-43, 144-46, 148, 152, 154-55, 157, 158-59, 167, 169, 170, 186, 189, 191, 194, 201-05; John Adams's plan for, 9

Adams family papers, 3-5, 8, 11-17, 22-25, 31-35, 39, 44-48, 53-56, 58, 62, 67-70, 75, 77, 81, 88-95, 102, 109, 113, 117, 121-23, 128, 133, 147, 151, 152, 156-57, 159, 161, 163, 184, 187, 191, 194, 197, 198, 201, 204, 207, 213n3, 216n30

Adams, George Washington (son of John Quincy Adams), 4

Adams, Henry: mentioned, 3-5, 7, 8, 9, 10, 17, 31, 203, 204, 205 *passim;* and art, 82, 83, 84, 86, 194-200, 201, 205; and education, 24-26, 29-30, 35, 83, 95, 138-43, 150, 164, 166, 169, 172-75, 182, 189, 191-94, 199, 202-03; and family literature, 25, 30, 31-35; and genealogy, 161-62; and Germany, 24; and politics, 20-22, 26, 29, 32, 35, 43-51, 60, 61, 62, 64, 65, 66, 73-82, 83, 84, 92-93, 100-01, 110-12, 121-22, 123-26, 127-32, 133-37, 138, 140-41, 154-56, 167, 168, 172-81, 188, 202-03; and readers, 34, 40, 49, 57, 58, 72-73, 78, 86, 93, 96-97, 133, 147-49, 183, 193, 195, 199-200, 203-05; and religion, 22-24, 26, 29, 35, 39, 41, 82-87, 98, 103, 130, 138-43, 150, 175, 181, 183, 184, 186-94, 203-04; and "scientific" history, 26, 41, 89-90, 93, 94,